BUDDHIST-CHRISTIAN
DUAL BELONGING

Buddhist-Christian Dual Belonging

Affirmations, Objections, Explorations

Edited by

GAVIN D'COSTA
University of Bristol, UK

and

ROSS THOMPSON

ASHGATE

© Gavin D'Costa and Ross Thompson 2016

All rights reserved. No part of this publication may be reproduced, stored in a retrieval system or transmitted in any form or by any means, electronic, mechanical, photocopying, recording or otherwise without the prior permission of the publisher.

Gavin D'Costa and Ross Thompson have asserted their right under the Copyright, Designs and Patents Act, 1988, to be identified as the editors of this work.

Published by
Ashgate Publishing Limited
Wey Court East
Union Road
Farnham
Surrey, GU9 7PT
England

Ashgate Publishing Company
110 Cherry Street
Suite 3-1
Burlington, VT 05401-3818
USA

www.ashgate.com

British Library Cataloguing in Publication Data
A catalogue record for this book is available from the British Library

The Library of Congress Cataloging-in-Publication Data
Names: D'Costa, Gavin, 1958- editor. | Thompson, Ross, 1953- editor.
Title: Buddhist-Christian dual belonging : affirmations, objections, explorations / Edited by Gavin D'Costa and Ross Thompson.
Description: Burlington, VT : Ashgate Publishing Company, 2016. | Includes bibliographical references and index.
Identifiers: LCCN 2015021665 | ISBN 9781472460912 (hardcover) | ISBN 9781472460929 (ebook) | ISBN 9781472460936 (epub)
Subjects: LCSH: Christianity and other religions--Buddhism. | Buddhism--Relations--Christianity.
Classification: LCC BR128.B8 B819 2016 | DDC 261.2/43--dc23
LC record available at http://lccn.loc.gov/2015021665

ISBN 9781472460912 (hbk)
ISBN 9781472460929 (ebk – PDF)
ISBN 9781472460936 (ebk – ePUB)

Printed in the United Kingdom by Henry Ling Limited, at the Dorset Press, Dorchester, DT1 1HD

Contents

Notes on the Contributors   *vii*

Introduction   1
Ross Thompson and Gavin D'Costa

PART I   AFFIRMATIONS

1   Chasing Two Rabbits? Dual Belonging and the Question of
Salvation/Liberation   13
Rose Drew

2   The Question of Salvation/Liberation: A Double-Belonger's
Perspective   31
Paul F. Knitter

3   Creation, Dependent Arising and Dual Belonging   49
Ross Thompson

PART II   CHALLENGES

4   'There Can Be Only One': The Impossibility and Idolatry of
'Dual Belonging'   71
Daniel Strange

5   The Ultimate Buddhist Religious Goal, Nirvana and its
Implications for Buddhist-Christian Dual Belonging   89
Asanga Tilakaratne

6	A Roman Catholic Approach to Buddhist-Catholic 'Dual Belonging' *Gavin D'Costa*	107
7	Dual Belonging, Ritual and the Spiritual Revolution *Marianne Moyaert*	123
8	Strategies of Negotiation in Buddhist-Christian Dual Belonging *Catherine Cornille*	143

PART III   EXPLORATIONS

9	An Alternative Conception of Multiple Religious Belonging: A Buddhist-Catholic Perspective *Abraham Vélez de Cea*	161
10	The Buddhist Faith of Non-Buddhists: From Dual Belonging to Dual Attachment *Rupert Gethin*	179
11	Dual Belonging and Pure Land Buddhism *Caroline Brazier*	197
12	Going Beyond the Creator God: An Apophatic Approach to Buddhist-Christian Dual Religious Belonging *J.P. Williams*	217

Conclusion *Ross Thompson and Gavin D'Costa*	233

Index	*249*

Notes on Contributors

Caroline Brazier is a Pureland Buddhist, Buddhist psychotherapist and leader of the Tariki Training Programme in Other-Centred Psychotherapy. She is also actively involved in the development of Buddhist Healthcare Chaplaincy at a local and national level. Caroline is author of six books on Buddhism and psychology, her book *The Other Buddhism: Amida Comes West* (O-Books, 2007) provides an introduction to Pureland thought in a Western context. Daughter of a Methodist Minister, Caroline has an appreciation of the Christian paradigm, and, although she left the tradition many years ago, finds ground for dialogue through her Pureland affiliation.

Catherine Cornille is the Newton College Alumnae Chair of Western Culture and Professor of Comparative Theology at Boston College. Her teaching and research focus on methodological questions in Theology of Religions, Comparative Theology and Interreligious Dialogue. She has authored or edited 16 books in the area of interreligious dialogue, most recently *The Im-Possibility of Interreligious Dialogue* (Crossroad, 2008), *Criteria of Discernment in Interreligious Dialogue* (Cascade, 2009), *Interreligious Hermeneutics* (Cascade, 2010), *The World Market and Interreligious Dialogue* (Cascade, 2011) *Interreligious Dialogue and Cultural Change* (Cascade, 2012), *Women and Interreligious Dialogue* (Cascade, 2013) and *The Wiley-Blackwell Companion to Inter-Religious Dialogue* (Wiley-Blackwell, 2013). She is founding editor-in-chief of the book series 'Christian Commentaries on non-Christian Sacred Texts'.

Gavin D'Costa is Professor of Catholic Theology at the University of Bristol. He is author of seven books, most recently: *Christianity and the World Religions. Disputed Questions in the Theology of Religions* (Wiley-Blackwell, 2009); and *Vatican II and the World Religions* (OUP, 2014) He is an advisor to the Vatican, the Roman Catholic Bishops in England and Wales and to the Church of England, Board of Mission on matters related to other religions. His interests lie in systematic and dogmatic theology, gender and psychoanalysis and the Christian theology of interreligious dialogue.

Rose Drew, since completing her doctorate in 2008, has lectured in interfaith studies and Buddhism at the University of Glasgow and in 2011 held a research scholarship at Uppsala University, Sweden. Her research interests are predominantly in interreligious dialogue (especially Buddhist-Christian) and the theology of religions. Her monograph, *Buddhist and Christian? An Exploration of Dual Belonging* (Routledge, 2011), won the 2013 Frederick J. Streng Award for Excellence in Buddhist-Christian Studies. Rose has also been involved in practical interfaith work for a number of years and currently works full time for charity Interfaith Scotland, managing a new project to support and develop positive interfaith engagement in Glasgow.

Rupert Gethin is Professor of Buddhist Studies at the University of Bristol and President of the Pali Text Society. His books include *Sayings of the Buddha: A Selection of Suttas from the Pali Nikāyas* (Oxford University Press, 2008), *The Foundations of Buddhism* (Oxford University Press, 1998) and *The Buddhist Path to Awakening* (Leiden, 1992). He has a particular interest in early Indian Buddhist literature and Indian Buddhist systematic accounts of the mind and meditation. He is currently working on a book provisionally titled *Mapping the Buddha's Mind: A Study of Indian Buddhist Systematic Thought in the Abhidharma of the Theravāda, Sarvāstivāda, and Yogācāra Traditions*.

Paul Knitter is the Paul Tillich Emeritus Professor of Theology, Religions and Culture at Union Theological Seminary in New York City. After spending most of his career in trying to lay the foundations for Christian interreligious dialogue (especially in *No Other Name?* (1985) and *Introducing Theologies of Religions* (2002)) he has recently taken up his own comparative theological project in *Without Buddha I Could Not Be a Christian* (2009) and is presently co-authoring with Roger Haight, S.J. *Companions of Jesus and Buddha in Conversation: Toward a Mystical-Prophetic Spirituality*, to be published by Orbis Books.

Marianne Moyaert holds the Fenna Diemer Lindeboom Chair of Comparative Theology and Hermeneutics of Interreligious Dialogue at the Free University of Amsterdam. She also teaches at the KU Leuven, Belgium. She has authored three books, including *Fragile Identities: Towards a Theology of Interreligious Hospitality* (Rodopi, 2011), and co-edited *Ritual Participation and Interreligious Dialogue: Boundaries, Transgressions and Innovations* (Bloomsbury, 2015) (Peeters, 2010). She has published over 50 articles, treating a wide range of topics relating to interreligious dialogue, hermeneutics and comparative theology. Her book *In Response to the Religious Other: Ricoeur and the Fragility of Interreligious Encounters* was published in 2014 (Lexington Books).

Daniel Strange is Academic Vice-Principal and Tutor in Culture, Religion and Public Theology at Oak Hill Theological College, London. He is author *of The Possibility of Salvation Among the Unevangelised* (Paternoster, 2001) and *For Their Rock is Not as Our Rock: An Evangelical Theology of Religions* (Apollos, 2014). With Gavin D'Costa and Paul Knitter, he is co-author of *Only One Way? Three Christian Responses on the Uniqueness of Christ in a Pluralistic World* (SCM, 2011). He has also contributed to the SCM Core Text and Reader, *Christian Approaches to Other Faiths* (SCM, 2008).

Ross Thompson is a freelance writer living in Wiltshire. He served for 20 years as a parish priest in Bristol, and taught doctrine and ethics at St Michael's, Llandaff and Cardiff University. His recent works include *Buddhist Christianity: A Passionate Openness* (John Hunt, 2010) and *Wounded Wisdom: A Buddhist and Christian Response to Evil, Hurt and Harm* (John Hunt, 2011). He is currently contracted to write *The Interfaith Imperative: Dialogue and the Integrity of Theology* (Wipf and Stock, forthcoming 2016). His main current research interests are exploration of the interface between Christianity, Buddhism and science, and the development of a spirituality drawing on all three.

Asanga Tilakaratne graduated from Peradeniya University, Sri Lanka, specialising in Buddhist Philosophy, and has a Masters in Western philosophy and PhD in comparative philosophy from University of Hawaii at Manoa. Currently he is the Professor of Pali and Buddhist Studies, University of Colombo, Sri Lanka. He has published, both in Sinhala and English, more than 100 papers and authored and edited several books on Buddhist philosophy, philosophy of language, philosophy of religion, practical ethics, contemporary social and political issues, Buddhist epistemology and logic and interreligious understanding, including most recently *Theravada Buddhism: The View of Elders* (University of Hawaii Press, 2012).

J.P. (Janet) Williams lectures at Ripon College Cuddesdon, UK, and is Dean of the West of England Ministry Training Course. Her publications include *Denying Divinity: Apophasis in the Patristic Christian and the Soto Zen Buddhist Traditions* (OUP, 2000) *The Four Chalcedonian Adverbs: A Reflection on Buddhist-Christian Dual Belonging* (forthcoming, in *Currents of Encounter: The Typology of Religions*, Rodopi). Her research interests are Apophatic traditions in Christian and Zen thought; Interfaith; Christian Mystical and Spiritual Traditions.

Abraham Vélez de Cea is Associate Professor of Buddhism and Comparative Religion at Eastern Kentucky University. Before joining EKU in 2006, he taught Buddhism and Buddhist-Christian Mysticism at Georgetown University. His research interests include contemporary presentations of the historical Buddha, Raimon Panikkar, and Buddhist-Christian Studies (comparative theology of religions, comparative spirituality and contemplative practices in Buddhism and Catholicism). He has published *The Buddha and Religious Diversity* (Routledge, 2013). At present he is working on a book about discipleship and the question of whether it is possible to integrate ethical and spiritual practices from Buddhism and Christianity without contradiction.

Introduction

Ross Thompson and Gavin D'Costa

Traditionally the norm has been to profess just one religion. But by no means always. Allegiance to more than one religion has a long history. In East Asia many have claimed and still do claim allegiance, for example, to Daoism and Confucianism, or Buddhism and Shinto. The Abrahamic monotheisms have traditionally demanded a more exclusive allegiance, but today there are Christians in some parts of the world who claim dual belonging to Judaism (in, for example, Israel and the United States) to Islam (the Philippines and Indonesia) and to Hinduism (India). And there has arisen an increasing number of Christians (in Japan, China, Korea, India and growing numbers in Europe and the United States) who claim to be also Buddhists.

This last – the phenomenon of belonging to, owing allegiance to or believing in both the Buddhist and Christian faiths – is the one addressed in this book. We will call the phenomenon 'Buddhist-Christian dual belonging', or on occasion 'Buddhist-Christianity', without attempting a definition, a matter that is addressed in several of the chapters in the book. But to clarify, this is not a historical exploration of the question of where, when and why there have been people who claim to belong to both faiths. Rather it represents a kind of 'feasibility study' of whether it makes religious sense to do so. In that sense it represents a *theological*, *philosophical* and *intra-religious* investigation of the matter, understanding 'theological' in the broad sense that includes Buddhist as well as Christian attempts to formulate belief and practice.

Up until now there has been considerable sociological and cultural investigation of dual belonging but very little theological investigation. The impact of dual belonging on interreligious dialogue in particular is a matter that is under-researched. It is generally understood that interreligious dialogue has moved forward into a transformative phase in which partners are willing to allow their own faith to be transformed by encounter with the other. Dual belonging may be experienced as an intensification of this process, in which dialogue becomes internalised within the believer. As such, dual belonging in the long run may have a significant contribution to make to dialogue. On the

2   *Buddhist-Christian Dual Belonging*

other hand the question is often raised whether in this process dialogue begins to lose the clarity of commitment in which dialogue partners can truly claim to represent their faith tradition.

This book then represents an investigation – by a mixture of Buddhists, Christians and professed dual belongers – of whether being both Buddhist and Christian makes sense in terms of both Buddhist and Christian belief. If it does not make sense in terms of both, then Buddhist-Christian dual belonging, though it exists in the sense that some individuals do profess allegiance to both faiths, cannot be viewed as legitimate Buddhism or legitimate Christianity. It cannot then be viewed as a legitimate way in which either faith might grow. But conversely if Buddhist-Christian dual belonging does make both Buddhist and Christian sense, then it is a phenomenon both religions need to attend to, not only in terms of their dialogue, but in terms of their own development and self-understanding as religions.

The Symposium

The book represents the contributions made to a live act of Buddhist-Christian dialogue centred on the question of dual belonging, which took place at a two-day symposium held at Bristol University in June 2014. We are grateful to the generosity of the Spalding Trustees, the Bristol Institute for Research in the Humanities and Arts, the Arts Faculty Research Director's Fund and the Department of Religion and Theology, University of Bristol, who together sponsored our conference. [1] In 2009–11 Paul Knitter, Ross Thompson and Rose Drew had independently published books[2] exploring the phenomenon and its feasibility, and the time seemed ripe to gather a variety of thinkers, including these three, to interrogate the phenomenon critically. Ross Thompson and Gavin D'Costa invited 12 people, representing different parts of the world (Great Britain, Belgium, Spain the USA and Sri Lanka) and different faith commitments. Three were self-styled dual belongers. Five were definitely critical of dual belonging (three Catholics, one Reformed Evangelical and one Theravāda Buddhist). The five others were sympathetic to dual belonging from their own

---

[1]   Thanks also to Esra Akay Dag and Lindsay Carter who graciously helped with hospitality arrangements.

[2]   Paul Knitter, *Without Buddha I Could Not Be Christian* (New York: Oneworld, 2009); Ross Thompson, *Buddhist Christianity: A Passionate Openness* (Winchester: John Hunt Publishing, 2010); Rose Drew, *Buddhist and Christian? An Exploration of Dual Belonging* (London: Routledge, 2011).

Introduction 3

faith perspective: one Anglican, one Catholic, one Theravāda Buddhist and one Pure Land Buddhist. They also represented a balance of disciplines: confessional and systematic theologies along with Buddhist textual analysis, pastoral and psychotherapeutic approaches, philosophical theology and religious studies. Some had previous experience of Buddhist-Christian dialogue.

The discussion was organised in three sections around three questions. Firstly, can Christian and Buddhist understandings of the human situation and journey be reconciled without loss, or is the Buddhist-Christian a confused follower of two pathways leading in different directions? Secondly, is dual belonging possible when one faith is centred on a Creator God while the other rejects creation and regards belief in God as irrelevant or inimical? And thirdly, does dual belonging necessarily subordinate one religion to the framework of the other (or to a third, possibly liberal framework) or can it liberate both faiths from past cultural frameworks; and how separable is either religion from its cultural and material expressions? However, though these questions were addressed, many other issues also emerged, enriching the field of enquiry. Some of these are noted in the conclusion by the editors. The discussion over two days formed an intricate web of interlocking debates, proving how complex a matter it is to evaluate the theological feasibility of Buddhist-Christian dual belonging. In view of this it seemed best to adopt a simpler structure in the book, whereby three chapters introduce dual belonging and different strategies for defending it, followed by five chapters criticising it – three from a confessional and two from a more general point of view – and then four more carrying the discussion forward with a focus on the nature of faith.

Affirmations of Dual Belonging

The first three chapters, by Drew, Knitter and Thompson, the authors of the three volumes cited above, serve to introduce ways of understanding and advocating dual belonging. They show, in many respects, how differently Buddhist-Christianity can be understood and justified.

The opening chapter by Rose Drew serves as an excellent introduction to the subject. Though she describes herself as a Catholic deeply influenced by Buddhism rather than a dual belonger, her chapter draws on her interviews with six dual belongers. Drew is a strong advocate of what she terms 'authentic' dual belonging. What, she asks, are dual belongers aiming for? Is the Buddhist-Christian attempting, in vain, to follow two paths which lead in different directions, or 'chasing two rabbits?' She argues, on the contrary, there is enough convergence between Buddhist and Christian understandings of what the salvific/liberative transformation requires in the here and now to make possible the pursuit of a single salvific/liberative path informed by both traditions, even if one is uncertain about the precise nature of the trajectory and final destination of that path. She cites with approval John Hick's account of the 'transformation of human existence from self-centredness to Reality-centredness' as the goal of all religions'.

Paul Knitter's chapter represents the fully dual Buddhist-Christian position to which he has moved in the new edition of *Without Buddha I Could Not Be Christian*.[3] It argues for a 'dipolarity' or complementarity between his liberationist Christianity with its emphasis on social justice as complementing his Nyingma Tibetan Buddhism with its stress on spiritual transformation. The Buddha teaches that compassion must arise out of spiritual wisdom, while Jesus insists that compassion calls for social justice. Both poles are based on a shared diagnosis and general remedy: suffering (both for self and others) arises from a distorted sense of a separated, ego-clinging self and can be overcome by embodying the compassion/love that arises from enlightenment or conversion.

Ross Thompson's chapter is different again. Thompson remains Anglican in terms of most of his practice and community belonging, but locates his journey in a mainly Tibetan Vajrayana perspective. He argues that theist Christian and atheist Buddhist worldviews are neither opposed nor identical, but variants on a continuum, such that each faith is the 'subversive fulfilment'[4] of the other. His argument focuses on the seemingly intractable divide between the two faiths over the notion of creation and a creator God. He argues that creation cannot coherently be understood in terms of efficient causality, and proposes an alternative account in terms of emergent 'metacausality'. The sharp dichotomy between Christian creation and Buddhist co-arising then gives way to a continuum of possible understandings across which the dual belonger may freely roam.

Confessional Challenges

Three chapters follow arguing against dual belonging from diverse confessional standpoints: Theravāda Buddhist, Reformed Evangelical and Roman Catholic respectively. Firstly, from his Evangelical position Daniel Strange regards the

---

[3] Paul Knitter, *Without Buddha I Could Not Be Christian* (New York: Oneworld, 2009)
[4] Cf. the chapter by Dan Strange.

Introduction 5

goal of Christian life, God, to be by his very nature (as absolute transcendent truth, not because of any personal jealousy) exclusive of all others, such that the dual belonger is guilty of idolatry and unfaithfulness. Strange combines a constructivist approach such that the meaning of a religion's terms has to be determined from within its discourse, with a belief in an epistemologically authoritative biblical revelation. To deny not only this revelation of ultimate reality, but the exclusivity and particularity of this ultimate reality, is not only ontologically and epistemologically incoherent but ethically confused. Dual belonging is the claim that both the true and the counterfeit are equal. This is an idolatrous claim and should be rejected.

Like Strange, Asanga Tilakaratne starts from his scriptural text: in his case, the Pali Canon which is fundamental to Theravāda Buddhism. He uses two key concepts in these texts, purification (*visuddhi*) and liberation/release (*vimutti*), to highlight how suffering and its cessation have been understood in Buddhism as involving a process of individual practice characterised by such cognitive and behavioural aspects as understanding, removal, realisation and cultivation. In this process the path and the goal are ultimately one's own responsibility. The concept of a Saviour, transcendental or otherwise, is not found in the path. So there is a clear distinction between Buddhist liberation and Christian salvation. The 'shelterlessness' of the universe – its lack of a providential Creator – is integral to Buddhist belief and constitutive of its goal, nirvana, which should not be thought of as mystical or ineffable, or in any way compatible with Christian accounts of the goal.

In Chapter 6 Gavin D'Costa reflects on the phenomenon, asking whether a Roman Catholic who wished to follow the key magisterial documents of the Roman Catholic tradition could be a dual belonger. He acknowledges a range of dual belonging, some of which can be interior without commitment to actual communities. Some can be adherence to one community or, in the test case he focuses on, adherence to two actual communities with the wish to follow both those communities authoritative teachers without being over-selective. If dual belonging is possible in this type of case, then it could be a legitimate practice from a Catholic perspective. To his own surprise, D'Costa finds this is genuine possibility. However, to fulfil a Catholic understanding of what makes a Catholic, such a person would have to be a Catholic missionary seeking the conversion of the Buddhists. At the same time to be a genuine Buddhist, he or she would also have to be accepted by Buddhists as such. Such a sentient being is a theoretical possibility, but D'Costa knows of none that actually exist.

General Challenges

These preceding three chapters represent what we could call the theological critiques of dual belonging. They argue that dual belonging is incompatible with crucial parts of the *content* of Buddhism and Christianity (or if not strictly incompatible, as in D'Costa's argument, resulting in something unrecognisable as a genuinely balanced case of Buddhism and Christianity). In the following two, two Roman Catholics argue against dual belonging not on the basis of the specific content of their religious beliefs, but rather from the nature of religion as such – one from the religion-specific nature of ritual, the other from the all-demanding dynamic of faith commitment. The confessional arguments are specific to Buddhist-Christian dual belonging: different arguments would have to be mustered against say Islamic-Jewish or Confucian-Hindu dual belonging. But the arguments that follow are to the effect that any kind of dual belonging is bound to be, at best, requiring of awkward strategic somersaults, and at worst, schizophrenically divided or confused. (Strange too, of course, presents arguments on the basis of the nature of faith, but for him it is the specific demands of the Christian faith in the Christian God, rather than those of faith in general, that rules out dual belonging.)

The shift here from the content to the nature of belief marks a watershed in the book. In general the first six chapters focus mainly on the doctrinal content of Christian and Buddhist belief, while the remaining six focus mainly on the nature of Christian and Buddhist belief and practice.

Marianne Moyaert argues that the doctrinal issues that tend to dominate interreligious dialogue and the discussion of dual belonging are only part of the issue. Missing from this discussion is the understanding, more common amongst ritual scholars and liturgical theologians, that religion is not primarily a worldview, but should rather be understood as symbolic practice revolving around strongly incarnated meanings. The chapter therefore focuses on the ritual core of religion, and argues that dual belonging represents part of a more widespread movement, downplaying the objective material existence of religions in its rituals and practices, in favour of a detraditionalisation and spiritualisation in which the believer is a choosing consumer.

In Chapter 8 Catherine Cornille argues that dual belongers realise, implicitly or explicitly, that their position does not chime with the ideal conception of religious identity and belonging as defined by particular religious traditions. They develop various strategies to justify the possibility of dual belonging. The two religions may be seen as advocating the same ethical practice, relative to which doctrinal differences are seen as unimportant; they may be seen as converging

Introduction 7

on a common transcendent Ultimate; one religion may offer an interpretation of the other; or the religions may be regarded as distinct but complementary. The chapter points out many difficulties with each strategy, concluding that they 'provide meaning for those who inhabit them' but questioning 'whether they are meaningful or coherent for the religions to which they claim to belong'.[5]

Explorations: The Nature of Faith, Dual and Otherwise

The remaining chapters – by a dual belonger, a Theravāda Buddhist, a Pure Land Buddhist and an Anglican Christian – carry forward, in different directions, the question of the nature of faith, whether Christian or Buddhist. The chapters respectively question whether faith is necessarily exclusive as Cornille suggests; whether faith may be implicit in our actions and attitudes rather than explicitly confessed; whether faith in Pure Land Buddhism is close to Christian faith in phenomenological terms; and whether authentic faith needs an apophatic other, which another faith may represent.

Chapter 9, by Abraham Vélez de Cea, a Catholic-Buddhist dual belonger, represents a response to Cornville's, developing an alternative notion of 'interreligious belonging'. Instead of using the metaphor of monogamous marriage as the religious ideal, as both Cornille and Strange do, so rendering interreligious belonging as analogous to infidelity, the chapter proposes to use the metaphor of love for one's parents and one's children who are loved in their difference totally, not partially, but not exclusively of each other.[6] Vélez de Cea draws a distinction – worth comparing with D'Costa's distinction, above – between affiliative and incremental dimensions of belonging, which allows us to answer Cornille's critique. Adopting all the doctrines and practices of both faiths would indeed, as Cornille suggests, lead to self-contradiction and divided loyalty. But full belonging in a qualitative sense does not depend on the quantitative number of doctrines and practices embraced, but rather on a mixture of subjective personal identification on one's own part and objective acceptance as a belonger by the faith communities.

Rupert Gethin's chapter also develops, a radical step further, the notion of a quality of commitment that is independent of quantitative doctrinal adherence. According to Theravāda Buddhist principles, doing what is good can only

---

5   See 157 in this volume.
6   Thompson also uses the parental analogy for dual belonging, in *Buddhist Christianity*, op. cit. 16.

happen when the underlying state of mind is good. Buddhist systematic thought defines a 'good' state of mind as one that is characterised by among other states' 'faith' (*saddhā*) and 'knowledge' (*ñāṇa*). In early Buddhist texts these are commonly defined in terms of the core Buddhist doctrines. Nonetheless, Buddhist systematic thought resists the conclusion that good states of mind, and hence 'faith' and 'knowledge', are therefore restricted to pious Buddhists. In fact such states are a possibility for non-Buddhists (and even animals). This suggests an account of 'faith' and 'knowledge' ultimately without reference to specific Buddhist symbols and doctrines. Thus Gethin envisages a dual belonging that has a provisional status, quite different to the other types proposed in the book.

In Chapter 11 Caroline Brazier develops the notion of faith found in Pure Land Buddhism, where it is trust in Amida Buddha, not one's own efforts, that enables one to enter the Pure Land and thence nirvana. Comparisons have been drawn with a Lutheran emphasis on salvation by faith not works. Doctrinal differences are significant, but the faith experience may be similar. Pure Land is often viewed in the West as an eccentric variant of Buddhism, but Brazier locates it within the broader context of Buddhist doctrine as a whole, looking at teachings of non-self (*anattā*), and the three bodies teaching (*trikāya*) which provides an analogy for the three dimensions of all religions: spiritual, imaginative/devotional and embodied/practical. Brazier argues that the invocation of Amida Buddha can be understood as an encounter with the fundamental mystery of Otherness found also in theistic faiths like Christianity.

The emphasis on unknowing and otherness brings us finally to the chapter by J.P. Williams, which draws on the Christian apophatic tradition. That tradition both affirms and denies the existence and reality of a Creator God. From such an apophatic ground, the question arises whether the Buddhist 'no Creator God' might also need to be negated. Like several proponents of dual belonging, but contrary to Tilakaratne, Williams affirms the ineffable nature of the Ultimate. But she is less concerned than for example Drew and Thompson to create an intellectually coherent worldview; she regards antinomies and contradictions not as a challenge to be overcome intellectually but as a challenge to grow spiritually. Practitioners of dual belonging stand in the place where opposites coincide. Faith, of its nature, requires an apophatic process of affirmation, negation, and negation of negation. Buddhism and Christianity may therefore represent the apophatic other each other needs in order to be truly faithful.

The multidimensional complexity of the issues raised by Buddhist-Christian dual belonging should by now be apparent. But it is also clear that our discussions contained many interwoven themes, and gave rise at the end to a sense of 'unfinished business', some of which are noted in the final chapter of this

Introduction 9

book. There were no dramatic conversions, but there was a sense of movement. Dual belonging emerged as being no longer a marginal phenomenon worthy of sociological and historical study only, but something also provoking and demanding philosophical and theological reflection within both traditions, as well as further investigation by the dual belongers themselves.

PART I
Affirmations

Chapter 1

Chasing Two Rabbits? Dual Belonging and the Question of Salvation/Liberation

Rose Drew

My research on dual belonging has focused on Buddhist-Christian dual belongers living in the West who were raised in a Christian context and came to Buddhism later. When I speak of 'dual belonging', I do not have in mind the more common 'softer' forms of multireligious identity, in which, although individuals are influenced by more than one religious tradition, there is a clear primary identification with just one; or else no particular identification with any tradition despite the selection of ideas or practices from several. Rather, I understand 'dual belongers' as people who are firmly rooted in – and identify themselves as committed adherents of – two traditions. In the most unequivocal cases of Buddhist-Christian dual belonging, people practise within both traditions, belong to a Buddhist and a Christian community, identify themselves as fully Buddhist and fully Christian and have made a formal commitment to both traditions (usually through baptism and the taking of the three refuges).

How *justified* such people are in regarding themselves as both Buddhist and Christian has been a question central to my research. My monograph, *Buddhist and Christian? An Exploration of Dual Belonging*,[1] engages the theological issues from Buddhist and Christian perspectives, drawing on interviews with highly reflective individuals who have publicly identified themselves with both traditions: Sr Ruth Furneaux, an Anglican eremitic nun and Zen and *Satipatthāna* (mindfulnesss) practitioner; Sallie King, an American *Vippassana* (insight), formerly Zen, Buddhist practitioner and Quaker; Roger Corless, a Roman Catholic and Tibetan Buddhist in the Gelugpa tradition; Ruben Habito, a Roman Catholic (former priest) and Zen Master in the Sanbo Kyodan lineage; Maria Reis Habito, a Roman Catholic, Zen practitioner and disciple of a Taiwanese Buddhist Master; and John Keenan, an Episcopal, formerly Catholic, priest who sees himself as *philosophically* Buddhist and interprets the Gospels and Christian theology through the lens of Mahayana philosophy. My

---

[1]   London and New York: Routledge, 2011.

focus has been on how reflective individuals such as these combine the thought and practice of Buddhism and Christianity.

The challenge they face is twofold: on the one hand, reflective dual belongers must find satisfactory ways of integrating the Christian way of thinking and being and the Buddhist way of thinking and being. To achieve logical, psychological and spiritual coherence they must work out how the insights of these two traditions fit into a single coherent picture. On the other hand, they must at the same time ensure that their thought and practice is faithful to both Christianity and Buddhism, through demonstrable continuity with central strands of both. This latter requirement means the differences between these traditions cannot be ignored or eradicated.

In what follows, I will consider how this twofold challenge is grappled with when it comes to questions about the goal of the spiritual life and, relatedly, whether practising both traditions can be legitimately understood as the following of a single spiritual path.[2] By 'single path' here, I mean one which is recognisably Christian and Buddhist and not some third thing. On the face of it, it would seem that Buddhists and Christians have different spiritual goals: Buddhists aiming for the bliss of nirvana, and Christians for communion with God and the saints in heaven. If this is the case, then what are dual belongers aiming for? Is the Buddhist-Christian attempting, in vain, to follow two paths which lead in different directions? There is a Japanese saying which nicely encapsulates the worry: 'Those who chase after two rabbits will catch neither'. If dual belongers are pulled in different directions by their religious commitments, this may render them incapable of fully committing to either tradition and, therefore, of fully realising the insights of either. Perhaps Catherine Cornille, a sceptic about the possibility of authentic dual belonging, is right that, in the final analysis, '[t]he problem with multiple religious belonging is ... not merely one of conflicting truth claims or theological incompatibility, but rather one of arrested spiritual development and growth'.[3] So, *are* Buddhist-Christians chasing two rabbits?

---

[2]   This chapter summarises some of the key arguments found in Chapter 5 of Drew, *Buddhist and Christian? An Exploration of Dual Belonging*.

[3]   Cornille, C., 'Many Masters? Multiple Religious Belonging in Practice and in Principle', 14 (this paper was originally delivered at a consultation in Basel in 2007 and a German translation was subsequently published in Bernhardt, R. and Schmidt-Leukel, P., eds, *Multiple religiöse Identität Aus verschiedenen religiösen Traditionen schöpfen* [Zürich: TYZ, 2008], 15–32. The original English version used here was kindly provided by the editors).

Two Distinct Aims?

The hypothesis that Buddhists and Christians, respectively, pursue different objectives, in this sense following different paths to different destinations, has been argued for by a number of contemporary thinkers, most notably S. Mark Heim (from a Christian perspective) and John Makransky (from a Mahāyāna Buddhist perspective). Heim offers a theory of multiple religious ends which depends on the notion that ultimate reality is complex and, therefore, capable of supporting this diversity of ends. Christians hope for communion with God, says Heim, and this end is attainable; Buddhists hope for nirvana and this end is also attainable.[4] But, as *final states*, these goals 'exclude each other'.[5] One's religious thought and practice can condition one for the achievement of one of these ends, thinks Heim, but not both. Moreover, these distinct ends are not equal, as far as Heim is concerned. The Christian end is superior to all others; the Buddhist end, while achievable, is a lesser aim which is not completely salvific.[6]

Makransky agrees with Heim that ultimate reality can support a variety of aims and that the Buddhist and Christian aims differ, but Makransky argues from his Mahayana Buddhist perspective that it is the *Buddhist* end which is superior: only this end is completely liberative.[7] And on this basis, he takes Buddhist practice to be soteriologically superior to Christian practice. So, both Heim and Makransky see Buddhists and Christians as pursuing different goals and each takes the other's goal to be inferior to his own.

Dual belongers hope to be faithful Buddhists *and* faithful Christians. What they seem to require, then, is a way of endorsing *both* the Christian *and* the Buddhist claim to be concerned with the ultimate spiritual goal. Is there any sense, then, in which Buddhism and Christianity can be legitimately understood as having a single aim?

---

[4]   Heim, S. Mark, *Salvations: Truth and Difference in Religion* (Maryknoll, NY: Orbis, 1995), 151–2.

[5]   Heim, S. Mark, *The Depth of the Riches: A Trinitarian Theology of Religious Ends* (Grand Rapids, MI/Cambridge: William B. Eerdmans Publishing Company, 2001), 288.

[6]   Heim, *Salvations*, 160; and Heim, S. Mark, 'The Depth of the Riches: Trinity and Religious Ends', *Modern Theology* 17:1 (January 2001): 28, 44.

[7]   Makransky, J., 'Buddha and Christ as Mediators of the Transcendent: A Buddhist Perspective', in Schmidt-Leukel. P., ed., *Buddhism and Christianity in Dialogue*, The Gerald Weisfeld Lectures 2004 (London: SCM Press, 2005), 191–2.

A Single Aim?

The notion that different religious traditions are orientated towards a single goal has been argued for most famously by John Hick. According to Hick, both Buddhism and Christianity are concerned to bring about a transformation from self-centred existence to an existence centred in ultimate reality, however conceived, and, in this sense, these traditions indeed share an ultimate goal. '[T]he generic concept of salvation/liberation, which takes a different specific form in each of the great traditions', says Hick, 'is that of the transformation of human existence from self-centredness to Reality-centredness'.[8] Elaborating, he explains that in Theravāda Buddhism this transformation is conceived of as 'the realization of the non-substantiality of the self, bringing a loss of the ego point of view and a nirvanic transformation of awareness'. In Mahāyāna Buddhism 'it's likewise a transcendence of the ego point of view, culminating in the discovery that the process of *samsara* (ordinary human life with all its pain and suffering), when experienced completely unselfcentredly, is identical with *nirvana*'.[9] Turning to Christianity, Hick draws on St Augustine's language to describe how this transformation is conceived – as one 'from a heart curved in upon itself to a heart open and responsive to the love of God'.[10]

Hick does not deny that, in the Christian case, the doctrine of the atonement has meant that this salvific transformation has often been presented, not so much as salvation itself, but as a *result* of salvation – a salvation *constituted* by Jesus Christ's death and resurrection.[11] He argues, however, that this is problematic, not least because the notion that Jesus' death was necessary in order to atone for our sins is unsupported by the portrayal of Jesus in the synoptic gospels. 'Virtually the whole weight of Jesus' message', says Hick, lies 'in the summons to his hearers to open their hearts now to God's kingdom, or rule, and to live consciously in God's presence as instruments of the divine purpose on earth'. There is, he insists, 'no suggestion in Jesus' recorded teaching that the heavenly Father's loving acceptance of those to whom he was speaking was conditional upon his own future death'.[12] He points out, moreover, that whereas the various

---

[8]   Hick, J., *An Interpretation of Religion: Human Responses to the Transcendent* (New Haven, CT: Yale University Press. First published in 1989 by Macmillan), 36.

[9]   Hick, J., *A Christian Theology of Religions: The Rainbow of Faiths* (Louisville, KY: Westminster John Knox Press, 1995. First published by SCM Press in 1995 as: *The Rainbow of Faiths*), 107–8.

[10]   Hick, *A Christian Theology of Religions*, 107.

[11]   See Hick, *An Interpretation of Religion*, 44.

[12]   Ibid., 44–5.

forms of the atonement doctrine are theoretical constructs, 'the new reconciled relationship to God and the new quality of life arising within that relationship are facts of experience and observation'.[13] The reality of Christian salvation is 'no juridical abstraction', but rather 'an actual and concrete change from sinful self-centredness to self-giving love in response to the divine grace'.[14]

Hick is not alone in rejecting the idea that Jesus' death and resurrection *constitute* salvation, though the issue is a hotly contested one. Constitutive Christologies tend to imply Christian superiority. Growing awareness of religious diversity has led some Christians to feel increasing dissatisfaction with many traditional expressions of Jesus' role in salvation for this reason. Roman Catholic Roger Haight, for example, suggests instead that salvation be seen as *demonstrated* or *illustrated* by Jesus' life and death.[15] Such interpretations are controversial. Indeed Haight's 'Spirit Christology' has been explicitly condemned as heretical by the Congregation for the Doctrine of the Faith. But we need not conclude, therefore, that such interpretations are unavailable to dual belongers – or at least to Roman Catholic ones – unless we assume that alignment with the current Vatican on all theological matters is essential to authentic Roman Catholic belonging. Here, let us simply note that imposing such a criterion might very well risk denying the majority of single belonging, self-identified Roman Catholics their claims to belong. A more nuanced approach would, I suggest, be to see Roman Catholic identity as something which is negotiated and renegotiated in a continuous conversation between the Vatican and all those who self-identify as Roman Catholic. And given that this conversation is always in progress, the boundaries of Catholic identity are inevitably fuzzier and more accommodating of a diversity of views than are the boundaries of orthodoxy as inscribed in current Vatican pronouncements.[16]

Evidence of the idea that there is one salvific/liberative transformation which both Christianity and Buddhism foster, but conceptualise differently, could be found in the thought of most, if not all, of my interviewees. Habito, for example, suggests that both traditions 'function in a way that liberates human beings from

---

[13]   Ibid., 44.

[14]   Ibid., 46.

[15]   See Haight, R., *Jesus – Symbol of God* (Maryknoll, NY: Orbis Books, 1999) and Haight, R., 'The Case for Spirit Christology', *Theological Studies* 53 (1992): 257–87.

[16]   For more on this issue, see Drew, R., 'Christian and Hindu, Jewish and Buddhist: Can You Have a Multiple Religious Identity?' in *Controversies in Contemporary Religion: Education, Law, Politics, Society, and Spirituality* (Santa Barbara, CA: Praeger, 2014): 246–71, esp. 264. For more on the Christological (and Buddhological questions) to which dual belonging gives rise, see Drew, *Buddhist and Christian*, 86–107.

whatever leads to their dissatisfaction and selfishness and ... to the suffering of one's self and others, [and] towards a life of liberation and of compassion,'[17] and Reis Habito reflects that she probably thinks in terms of one transformation that is expressed differently in each tradition, a crucial aspect of which, in both expressions, is getting rid of selfishness.[18]

We must, however, test this understanding of Buddhism and Christianity as fostering a single salvation/liberation. Define any two things generally enough and one can say that they are the same, so let's consider some of the specific features of the salvific/liberative transformation as described in these two traditions, so as to be sure that this interpretation really provides the coherence the Buddhist-Christian needs. We will start with the question of what we are supposed to be being saved or liberated *from*.

1. What Are We Being Saved/Liberated From?

From a Buddhist perspective, our predicament is one of *dukkha* – of suffering, dissatisfaction, disease. We fail to see that nothing within samsara – including one's own *self* – is substantial and enduring. And so we grasp at – and become attached to – what is fluctuating, transitory, insubstantial. And this grasping and attachment causes us to suffer and, ultimately, keeps us tethered to the cycle of rebirth and re-death. The problem, from this perspective, is one of *ignorance* or *mis-knowing* (in Sanskrit: *avidyā*, which Makransky defines, from his Mahāyāna perspective as 'the deluded consciousness that reifies and grasps to a substantial sense of self and world, giving rise to grasping, fear and consequent suffering'[19]). As Makransky explains, Mahāyāna Buddhists construe our bondage as the result of 'patterns of thought that construct, reify and cling to an autonomous sense of "self" and "other".'[20] From this Mahāyāna perspective, it is our discriminative, dualistic way of perceiving the world that is the problem.

From a Christian perspective our predicament is one of sin. Christians seek salvation from sin, understood as broken relationship with God; our bondage is thought to be the result of our having turned away from God. As Harold Coward explains, after Jesus, it was Paul's understanding of the human predicament

---

[17] Habito, R.L.F. in Drew unpublished transcripts, 193.

[18] Reis Habito, M. in Drew unpublished transcripts, 479.

[19] Makransky, J., 'Buddha and Christ as Mediators of the Transcendent: A Buddhist Perspective', in Schmidt-Leukel, ed., *Buddhism and Christianity in Dialogue*, 210.

[20] Ibid., 195.

which had the most influence on the Christian tradition.[21] Paul understood all humans to be in a state of sin as a result of Adam and Eve's disobedience to God; our moral corruption and physical death results from our having inherited their disobedience. Able to control neither body nor will, we find ourselves divided: the will, made to love God, has turned in upon itself in *self*-love. Thus, human nature as Paul sees it, is 'turned away from God and toward ignorance and death'.[22]

Makransky argues that, although Buddhists and Christians are concerned with one ultimate reality (conceived of as God by Christians and as Nirvana or the *dharmakāya* by Buddhists), and although both seek the freedom of salvation/liberation, because they understand differently the predicament from which we require freedom, they seek that freedom in different ways. He takes this difference in how our predicament is understood to be one reason that Buddhist and Christian practices are differently targeted, hence one reason why these practices 'may function differently enough to make a real difference in salvific qualities realized and the type or degree of liberation attained'.[23]

But while Christians and Buddhists clearly do characterise the predicament from which we require freedom differently, it is also the case, as Paula Cooey notes, that both traditions 'clearly see egocentricity as the root of suffering and damage – an egocentricity that can be transformed'.[24] Might it not be, then, that, rather than fundamentally disagreeing, Buddhism and Christianity simply come at this problem of egocentricity or self-centredness from different angles?

Let's get back to basics and consider the Eden myth for a moment. If a literal interpretation of the story of Adam and Eve is rejected, Christians are faced with a question: as Ninian Smart puts it, '[i]f the first Adam is imaginative myth, then what does Christ's salvation amount to? From what? In the light of evolutionary theory the whole story has ... to be retold'.[25] Smart suggests the fall from innocence be construed as the stage in evolution when we gained 'a self-centredness which is the first stage to freedom', but which also lead to our alienation from God. This alienation, suggests Smart, may have as much to do

---

[21]   Coward, H., *Sin and Salvation in the World Religions: A Short Introduction* (Oxford: Oneworld, 2003), 31.

[22]   Ibid., 43.

[23]   Makransky, J., 'Response to Perry Schmidt-Leukel', in Schmidt-Leukel (ed.), *Buddhism and Christianity in Dialogue*, 210.

[24]   Cooey, P.M., 'Response to Alan Sponberg's "The Buddhist Conception of an Ecological Self"', in King, S.B. and Ingram, O., eds, *The Sound of Liberating Truth: Buddhist-Christian Dialogues in Honor of Frederick J. Streng* (Richmond: Curzon, 1999), 130.

[25]   Smart, N., *Buddhism and Christianity: Rivals and Allies* (London: Macmillan, 1993), 110.

with *ignorance* as faults in our *will*, that is, sinfulness.[26] Similarly, Adrian Smith interprets the Eden myth as being about an inevitable 'evolution ... to a state of self-consciousness'.[27] What the myth tells us, contends Smith, is that humans 'found their identity, their individuality, through recognising their separateness, their opposites'. He sees Genesis 3:7 – 'The eyes of them both were opened and they realised that they were naked' – as describing the awakening of humans 'to otherness, to difference'.[28] If the myth of the Fall is interpreted along these lines, then powerful resonances begin to emerge with the Buddhist understanding of our predicament, as stemming from grasping to a substantial sense of self (from the conceit 'I am') and, particularly, with the Mahayana contention that dualistic thinking is our problem.

Large parts of Mahayana Buddhism[29] identify our discriminative consciousness which conceptually divides the world into self and not self, me and you, this and that, good and bad as a deluded way of apprehending reality which causes us to suffer. The Eden myth seems to echo something of this analysis but to the extent that it does, what in the myth is referred to as 'Knowledge' seems akin, ironically, to what Buddhists refer to as 'ignorance' or '*mis*-knowing' (*avidyā*): it is eating from 'the tree of the Knowledge of good and evil' which causes Adam and Eve to become *self*-conscious; to experience themselves as separate from God and from each other and hence to perceive themselves as naked, to cover themselves, to hide and, ultimately, to suffer and die. Thus the 'Knowledge' gained in the Garden of Eden seems to have similar connotations to the '*mis*-knowing' Makransky defines as the 'deluded consciousness that reifies and grasps to a substantial sense of self and world'.

This possible parallel is not lost on Buddhists. Buddhadāsa, for example, suggests that the underlying meaning of God's forbidding Adam and Eve to eat from the tree of the Knowledge of good and evil is that '[a]ny suffering that arises in man is a result of his getting attached to what is considered good and evil', since this attachment 'generates desire and craving and illusion'.[30] Having eaten the forbidden fruit, Adam and Eve underwent a spiritual death, says

---

[26] Ibid., 110.

[27] Smith, A.B, *The God Shift: Our Changing Perception of the Ultimate Mystery* (London: New Millennium, 1996), 207.

[28] Ibid., 197.

[29] 'Dualism' is denounced primarily in *Yogācāra* and large parts of Zen and – to some extent – in Tantric Buddhism.

[30] Buddhadāsa, *Christianity and Buddhism, Sinclaire Thompson Memorial Lecture* (Bangkok: Karn Pim Pranakorn Partnership, 1967), 89. Although a Theravādin, Buddhadāsa is influenced by Mahayana thought and the identification of dualistic thinking as central to our difficulties.

Chasing Two Rabbits? 21

Buddhadāsa, as they 'began to think in dualistic terms ... to the point that their minds were flooded by indescribable sufferings. ... Death, in the original-sin sense', says Buddhadāsa 'occurs whenever we partake of the fruit of dualism'[31] and, as individuals, we begin to partake of this fruit from early childhood.[32] As an English monk put it in a Dharma talk I attended at Suan Mokkh (the Thai Monastery founded by Buddhadāsa), what we need to realise, then, is that we are in fact in the Garden of Eden now; we just fail to see it. In Pure Land Buddhist terms: we are in the Pure Land now.

This idea that our task is to realise that we are, metaphorically speaking, in the Garden of Eden now, ties in with those strands of both traditions which emphasise that the spiritual task is not so much a quest for something we do not yet have, as a realisation and acceptance of what already is (strands strongly emphasised by a number of my interviewees). In Mahayana Buddhism we find the notion that there is no difference between samsara and nirvana and the idea that our minds are originally pure insofar as our truest nature is Buddha Nature. And, from a Christian perspective, the Genesis myth can be read as telling us that our original nature – 'original' in the sense of truest or most fundamental, rather than first – is pure. Habito argues that the term 'original sin' is, in this sense, 'a gross misnomer' since 'our original condition is a state of grace. Being the image of God is what is "original" in our created being – not sin', says Habito.[33] Habito thinks in terms of our need for healing, and feels that the Buddhist characterisation of our predicament in terms of *dukkha* – 'a state of dis-location, dis-ease, and of being out of touch with being itself' – is very much resonant with 'the Christian understanding of cosmic woundedness due to sin'.[34]

2. What Is the Most Crucial Aspect of the Transformation?

But even if there are ways of understanding Buddhist and Christian characterisations of the predicament from which we require salvation/liberation which resonate with each other, Makransky argues that Buddhists and Christians disagree over the main principle which brings about the salvific/liberative transformation: from a Mahayana perspective, it is non-conceptual, non-dual

---

[31]   Buddhadāsa, *Me and Mine: Selected Essays of Bhikkhu Buddhadāsa*, ed. Swearer, D.K. (Albany, NY: State University of New York Press, 1989), 149–50.

[32]   Ibid., 155.

[33]   Habito, R.L.F., *The Healing Breath of Zen* (Boston, MA: Wisdom Publications, 2006), 17.

[34]   Ibid., 17–18.

realisation of emptiness which liberates people, and this realisation can only be gained in full measure through properly targeted practices, argues Makransky. '[T]he results of spiritual practice', insists Makransky, 'depend not only on the nature of ultimate reality but also upon the ways that specific practices render persons receptive to different aspects and qualities of that ultimate reality'.[35] Proper *methods* are needed for the development of the 'wisdom-emptiness' aspect of participation in ultimate reality. (In Mahayana Buddhism, the realisation of emptiness is the realisation that nothing has own-existence, that, ultimately, none of the entities individuated by our concepts have any substantial existence. All the distinctions we impose on reality are *thought-made* and do not correspond to reality itself.) Wisdom practices, explains Makransky, foster direct insight into the lack of own-existence; and, as one realises the *thought-madeness* of all aspects of ordinary existence, the deepest patterns of self-grasping are eradicated.

From his Mahayana Buddhist perspective, this 'wisdom-emptiness' aspect of participation in the ultimate reality is 'the centre of soteriology, the very source of liberation';[36] 'fullest realization of ultimate reality (active *nirvāṇa, dharmakāya)*', emphasises Makransky, '*is* fullest, non-dual insight into the *emptiness of all conceptualized appearances* and active compassion for all who have not realized the freedom of such insight'.[37] From this perspective, it is fully developed *wisdom* upon which liberation hinges. This wisdom, explains Makransky, in turn, informs Buddhist teachings of unconditional compassion and love: 'Deepest compassion', says Makransky, 'is non-dual awareness suffused with a tone of compassion that has transcended even the distinction of "self" and "other"'.[38]

Christians, on the other hand, understand redemption to come 'mainly though the power of God's grace in communion', says Makransky.[39] But while reliance on God's grace – expressed through the life of the Church, the practice of the sacraments, prayer and so on – certainly increases love, devotional communion and even wisdom to a limited extent, thinks Makransky; reliance on grace does not allow for the full development of wisdom which sees the non-dual

---

[35] Makransky, J., 'Response to Perry Schmidt-Leukel', in Schmidt-Leukel, ed., *Buddhism and Christianity in Dialogue*, 210.

[36] Makransky, 'Buddha and Christ as Mediators of the Transcendent', 195.

[37] Makransky, J., 'Buddhist Inclusivism: Reflections Toward a Contemporary Buddhist Theology of Religions', in Schmidt-Leukel, ed., *Buddhist Attitudes to Other Religions* (St Ottilien: EOS, 2008), 61.

[38] Makransky, 'Buddha and Christ as Mediators of the Transcendent', 196.

[39] Ibid..

Chasing Two Rabbits? 23

emptiness of all phenomena.[40] For Christians, salvation implies the repair of the human-divine relationship which is witnessed in a person's deep participation in God's unconditional love (*agape*) which pervades all creation. It is this *love* upon which the salvific transformation hinges, from a Christian perspective, and this love, says Makransky 'is a love within relatedness, ... involving distinctions between poles of relatedness that are irreducible, not non-dual'.[41] 'If, as most Christians are taught', says Makransky, 'someone relates to ultimate reality as a personal God most fully accessed by communing with Him through Christ in the Spirit, then the conceptualized poles of separation between oneself and God necessary for such communion are grasped as ultimate. The aim is not to *transcend* the conceptualization of such a dualism between self and God in Christ, but to adhere to that dualism as ultimate'.[42]

Makransky and Heim, though taking different views of which tradition is superior as a result, agree on this distinction. Heim takes right relationship with God and others to be the highest goal and insists that essential to this end is love within duality:[43] '[t]he salvation Christians anticipate', insists Heim, 'is a personal communion of distinct creatures with God their maker'.[44] Makransky and Heim agree that in the final analysis, their soteriological goals are incompatible with each other.

However, the characterisation of Christianity as resolutely affirming and accepting attachment to an ultimate dualism between self and God is not one which reflects the experience of most of my interviewees, none of whom would – I think – recognise their intention, as Christians, as being to adhere to the 'dualism between self and God ... as ultimate'. It would be easy to assume that this is because their Buddhism, rather than their Christianity, is normative with respect to this issue, and there may be some truth in this. Yet this characterisation may – on *Christian* grounds – be considered misleading.

The Christian affirmation of God's immanence and the idea that all people have the divine within them as Spirit suggest that the poles of relationship between ourselves and God might not be absolute and irreducible, but rather that God is on a continuum with us – greater than, but not separate from us. Certainly, in the Christian mystical tradition we find accounts of monistic or unitive experiences in which the poles of separation between self and God are not experienced as ultimate. It is not surprising that, as Perry Schmidt-Leukel

---

[40]   Ibid., 194–9.

[41]   Ibid., 196.

[42]   Makransky, 'Buddhist Inclusivism', 62.

[43]   Heim, *The Depth of the Riches*, 203–4.

[44]   Ibid., 203.

points out, although when it comes to the criteria of wisdom and meditation, most Buddhists find Christianity seriously wanting, the exception to this is its mystical or contemplative tradition.[45]

Makransky, however, argues that when Mahayana Buddhists talk about the realisation of emptiness as the end of the path to liberation, 'emptiness' (*śūnyatā*) should not be understood as 'an apophatic union with God attained by rare persons whose special vocation is mysticism'. Rather, what Buddhists mean by emptiness, says Makransky, is 'the insubstantial nature of all aspects of ordinary experience'.[46] But can we be sure that the Buddhist's direct awareness of emptiness and the Christian's transformative experience of apophatic union with God are not relevantly equivalent? Certainly it is very difficult to make judgements of equivalence when comparing experiences within different traditions on the basis of what is said about them within those traditions, but can it not be equally difficult to be sure that two experiences are *not* in some sense equivalent? Even if less emphasised, might not the 'wisdom-emptiness' aspect of participation in ultimate reality be present in Christianity but in a different guise?

This is perhaps suggested by Reis Habito's reflections on a pivotal experience of hers in Zen meditation, an experience authenticated by a Japanese Zen Master as a genuine *kenshō* experience, that is, as an initial awakening experience of non-dual awareness. When speaking about this experience from her Christian perspective, Reis Habito puts it in terms of the walls between herself and God – or between herself and the Absolute – becoming more transparent.[47] There is, she says, the more literal level of truth with which one begins – 'where you are down here and God is out there ... and you direct your devotion to something that is outside yourself' – and then there is another level, the level which Mahayana Buddhists call 'non-duality'. At this level, says Reis Habito, 'there is no outside and inside, so to speak; there is no self and other ... you can't distinguish anymore ... These things are difficult to describe', she says; 'in the final result, it all depends on interpretation: on the words that we use for certain experiences'.[48]

In response to reflections such as Reis Habito's, however, Makransky *might* argue that there's a difference between claiming, as he does, that the duality of self and other is overcome in the salvific/liberative transformation, and claiming

---

[45]   Schmidt-Leukel, P., 'Buddhist Perceptions of Jesus: Introductory Remarks', in Schmidt-Leukel, ed. (in cooperation with Götz, T.J. and Köberlin G.), *Buddhist Perceptions of Jesus. Papers of the Third Conference of the European Network of Buddhist-Christian Studies* (St Ottilien 1999) (St Ottilien: EOS-Verlag, 2001), 27–8.

[46]   Makransky, 'Buddha and Christ as Mediators of the Transcendent', 195.

[47]   Reis Habito, M. in Drew unpublished transcripts, 499.

[48]   Ibid., 481–2.

that at some stage in that transformation (or at least in some salvific/liberative experiences) it simply becomes *difficult to distinguish* between self and other. In other words, Buddhism and the Christian mystical tradition may converge to some extent in their accounts of the experience of practising the path, but they do *not* agree about what the final destination of that path will entail.

Let us turn, then, to this eschatological question – the question of where the transformation ends.

3. Where Does the Transformation End?

For Christians, the end hoped for is heaven. Now, whether the notion of 'heaven' is expressed in terms of the worship of God or in terms of 'a beatific vision of the divine Reality', it signifies the idea of perfected human personalities enjoying an existence completely orientated towards God.[49] Christian soteriological thinking, even at its most tentative and open-ended, has tended to assume that, in the eschaton, a person, even if radically transformed, in some way retains his or her individual personhood as distinct and separate from God and other persons. As Hick says, Christianity's eschatological emphasis 'has been firmly upon the value of the individual human soul, as an object of God's love, and upon the perfecting of finite personality and its eternal preservation in the divine presence'.[50] And, as he acknowledges, this is in contrast to the emphasis of Buddhism, in which the individual personality is seen as a temporary bundle of transitory elements which, in the salvific/liberative transformation, is dismantled by the negation of the craving for existence which holds it together.[51] Hick argues, however, that the eschatologies of both traditions are 'pointers beyond the known which do not profess to delimit the boundaries or describe the contents of that towards which they point'. Buddhists *and* Christians, says Hick, look 'towards an ultimate human destiny which ... can only be conceived in the most general terms; and ... we observe these lookings to be oriented in the same direction'.[52]

Concurring with this, my interviewees clearly saw Buddhism and Christianity as effecting the same *orientation*. Following these two traditions is not a question of being lead in 'two different directions', insists Habito, for example;[53]

---

[49]   See Hick, J., *Death and Eternal Life* (London: Collins, 1976), 202.
[50]   Ibid., 426.
[51]   Ibid., 427.
[52]   Ibid., 427–8.
[53]   Habito in Drew unpublished transcripts, 161.

'Buddhists use the term "nirvana" and Christians use the term "heaven"', says Habito, 'but, if we get stuck on the conceptual imagery of these terms, then we will be limiting ourselves ... [I]t's something that keeps pointing beyond ... [I]t is ... a way of expressing ultimate destiny'.[54]

But despite believing that their Buddhism and their Christianity orientate them in a single direction, most of my interviewees nevertheless felt unable to state with certainty that Christianity and Buddhism definitely share an ultimate end; and nor did they feel able to judge that these traditions are equally efficacious with respect to *final* salvation/liberation. King, for example, explains that one of her most fundamental commitments is to be honest with herself about what she knows and what she does not know.[55] Asked what she takes the eschaton to be, she is emphatic: 'I have no idea. No idea';[56] 'I can't really affirm ... definitively [that] they're ... headed to the same place; I can't affirm that until I'm there. I don't see how that's possible'.[57] She reflects, however, that both Buddhism and Christianity 'inspire', and provide encouragements, incitements and concretely helpful structures and practices which are all efficacious for her.[58]

Provided dual belongers find that Buddhism and Christianity orientate them in a single direction, is it necessary that they decide whether the Buddhist or the Christian characterisation of the final state is most accurate in order to be able to move in its direction through their practice of both traditions? Makransky and Heim take each other's goals to be inferior, yet even their views leave room to affirm the possibility that Buddhist and Christian practice might be, to some extent, mutually supportive of progress towards the goal each recognises as ultimate.[59] Crucially, however, what distinguishes King's position – and that of most of my interviewees – from Makransky's or Heim's positions is that she does *not* take one tradition to be inferior to the other. She does not *deny* the salvific/liberative equality of Buddhism and Christianity; she just does not feel she has sufficient evidence to positively affirm it. This position leaves open both the possibility that Buddhism and Christianity are equally efficacious and the possibility that one will turn out to be superior. For as long as both traditions are *experienced* by the dual belonger to be equally efficacious, neither tradition is undermined since neither's claim to full salvific/liberative efficacy is denied.

---

[54] Habito in Drew unpublished transcripts, 195.
[55] King, S.B. in Drew unpublished transcripts, 404.
[56] Ibid., 395.
[57] Ibid., 371–2.
[58] Ibid., 371.
[59] See, for example, Makransky, 'Buddhist Inclusivism', 63.

Interestingly, the Dalai Lama takes it to be possible for Christians to take Bodhisattva vows,[60] and to 'progress along a spiritual path and reconcile Christianity with Buddhism'. But, he says, 'once a certain degree of realization has been reached, a choice between the two paths will become necessary'.[61] Regardless of whether the Dalai Lama is right that a choice will at some stage be necessary (and remember, he is speaking from his experience as a Buddhist, not from experience of practising both Buddhism *and* Christianity over time), his position demonstrates that even those who *do* assume a choice will be necessary can nevertheless accept that a person can be fully and beneficially committed to the practice of both traditions for as long as both are found to be helpful.

Now, it is true that the position of most of my interviewees involves a degree of uncertainty about what the end of the path they are treading will entail, hence, one could argue that this implies a less than full commitment to these traditions. But if one sees both traditions as emphasising that the end of the path should not be one's focus, then this uncertainty looks unproblematic. None of my interviewees tended to think in terms of the ultimate *end* of the path, not primarily because of uncertainty about what precisely that end would entail, or about which tradition would prove most efficacious in helping them reach it, but due to a conviction that the appropriate focus of the spiritual life, from both a Buddhist and a Christian perspective, is the *here and now*.

They were most concerned with what was transformative in their present experience. For example, asked what she takes the eschaton to be, Reis Habito says: '[t]o answer this question I just think about what Jesus says: the Kingdom of Heaven is right here'; she links this to the Mahayana claim that nirvana is samsara.[62] What matters, thinks Reis Habito, is not what salvation means in future terms, but what it means right now. And this, she says, is also the case from a Buddhist perspective: 'it's the here and now that counts, not what you think about ultimate salvation'.[63] Similarly, King says: 'Heaven and nirvana ... it's right here; if I don't see it that's my shortcoming. So it's not an *end*. I can't think of it as an *end* at the end of the path. ... How could I think of that? That's immense. ... I don't even think in terms of [an] "end". I think in terms of non-dualism, so ends and means are the same'.[64] And Corless says: '[I]t is not up to me to figure out

---

[60]   Dalai Lama, *Beyond Dogma: Dialogues & Discourses*, Anderson, A. (trans.) (Berkeley, CA: North Atlantic Books, 1996. Originally published in French in 1994 as: *Au-dela des Dogmes*), 157–8.

[61]   Ibid., 155.

[62]   Reis Habito in Drew unpublished transcripts, 483–4.

[63]   Ibid., 468.

[64]   King in Drew unpublished transcripts, 395.

where it is going'; 'what happens to me is none of my business ... I strive to be authentic at the moment and ... presume it will ... somehow, work out'.[65]

From this perspective, the important question facing dual belongers is not 'where does the transformation end?' nor 'which is best with respect to that end?' but, rather, 'can I live in the here and now according to the teachings of both traditions; *are* Christian conditioning and Buddhist conditioning compatible and mutually supportive?'

Is Christian Conditioning Compatible with Buddhist Conditioning?

Although Buddhism tends to place greater emphasis on wise non-attachment than loving involvement, and Christianity, greater emphasis on loving involvement than wise non-attachment, in both these traditions non-attachment and love are understood as developing in a relationship of mutual dependence. And this makes it possible, from a Buddhist and a Christian perspective, to see the respective emphases of these two traditions in terms of an existential complementarity and beneficial internal dialogue.

To the Buddhist, for whom insight into the nature of reality, leading to the relinquishing of all grasping and attachment, is definitive with respect to liberation, the Christian might say: that is all to the good, but have you fed the hungry, clothed the naked and visited the sick and imprisoned? As Paul says, even if I understand 'all the mysteries there are', and know everything, even '[i]f I give away all I possess, piece by piece, and ... even let them take my body to burn it, but am without love, it will do me no good whatever' (1 Corinthians 13: 1–3).

Conversely, to the Christian, for whom loving engagement with one's neighbours (conceived of as anyone in need) is definitive with respect to salvation, the *Buddhist* might say: that's all to the good, but unless you develop penetrating insight into the nature of reality, unless you cultivate the wisdom which sees that all is not-self and directly perceive the emptiness of phenomena, thus relinquishing all grasping and attachment, then even your most generous dealings with others will be tarnished by subtle manifestations of self-interest and you will continue to suffer and cause suffering to others.

And so, for the dual belonger, Makransky's critique of Christianity's lack of focus on the development of wisdom becomes one side of an internal dialogue in which each perspective continually critiques the other, thus sustaining the

---

[65] Corless, R.J. in Drew unpublished transcripts, 74.

creative tension between non-attachment and love which both traditions recommend and encouraging critical self-reflection and development on both sides. Sustaining this creative tension can sometimes be a source of spiritual struggle for Buddhist-Christians. But there may be comfort in Aloysius Pieris's contention that '[i]t is the dialectical interplay of wisdom and love that ensures a progressive movement in the realm of the human spirit'.[66]

Conclusion

Our investigation suggests, then, that there is no need to suppose, as Cornille does, that dual belonging hinders spiritual progress, since there's enough convergence between the Buddhist and Christian understandings of what the salvific/liberative transformation requires in the here and now to make it possible to pursue a single salvific/liberative path informed by both traditions, even if one is uncertain about the precise nature of the final destination of that path, about how many lives one may have in which to pursue it[67] and about which – *if either* – tradition will turn out to be more efficacious in its final stages.

Somewhat surprisingly, given his contention that Buddhism and Christianity foster a single salvific/liberative transformation, in *An Interpretation of Religion* Hick appears to deny the possibility of dual belonging.[68] One reason for this might be that he sees religious traditions as akin to different paths to the summit of a mountain. This analogy makes dual belonging impossible virtually *by definition*, since one cannot reach the summit of a mountain by simultaneously walking up two distinct paths. Although this analogy sees both Buddhism and Christianity as offering valid routes to salvation/liberation, on the model of religious *belonging* it suggests, the possibility of a dual belonger reaching the summit can only be accounted for if he or she is understood as forging a new Buddhist-Christian path, that is, as embracing a new 'Buddhist-Christian' religion which is necessarily distinct from Buddhism and Christianity.[69]

---

[66] Pieris, A., *Love Meets Wisdom: A Christian Experience of Buddhism* (New Delhi: Intercultural Publications, 1988), 9–10.

[67] For a detailed discussion of the question of rebirth, as faced by the dual belonger, see Drew, *Buddhist and Christian?*, 145–61.

[68] Hick, *An Interpretation of Religion*, 373. Later in life, Hick became more open to the possibility of dual belonging (see Drew, *Buddhist and Christian?*, 162).

[69] This seems to be Heim's contention regarding those who practice within more than one tradition. See Heim, *Salvations*, 178.

But what the 'paths up a mountain' analogy fails to capture is that it is not *religious traditions* which are saved/liberated, but *individual persons*. The analogy is, therefore, misleading: it does not recognise that every person forges his or her own path up the mountain and no two paths are the same. Schmidt-Leukel agrees, pointing out that the route one takes up the mountain is one's actual life, 'and religions should be instrumental in helping us to live it'.[70] He suggests, therefore, that religions be compared, not to paths, but to 'different maps or hill-walking guides'.[71] Unlike the former analogy, Schmidt-Leukel's analogy accommodates the possibility of an individual integrating ideas and practices from more than one tradition. The fact that maps can be drawn from different perspectives, with different considerations in mind, to different scales, and using different points of reference and different keys – such that one cannot be simply 'mapped' onto the other – recognises both the fact that the language of one tradition cannot be easily translated into the language of another, and the possibility that having two very different kinds of map could be useful to someone who has learnt to read both and who is undertaking a difficult journey.

Recalling the Japanese saying which encapsulates the possible objection to dual belonging which we have been addressing, 'those who chase after two rabbits will catch neither', Habito reflects: 'perhaps in declaring my aspiration to live as a Buddhist, and my aspiration to live as a Christian, ... I am ... rendering myself unable to live up to either in a faithful and authentic way'.[72] He does not, however, feel that this objection is warranted: 'what I have learned from Buddhism and what I have learned from the Christian tradition, somehow, tend to confirm one another', says Habito. 'They may challenge one another on occasions or from certain angles but, in that mutual challenge, there's also a mutual enrichment and a mutual transformation';[73] 'they're not two different paths pulling away and tearing me apart', he explains, but '[o]ne path, informed by those two traditions'.[74]

---

[70]   Schmidt-Leukel, P., *Transformation by Integration* (London: SCM Press, 2009), 54. For examples of perspectives within different religious traditions which concur with this emphasis on the uniqueness of every individual's spiritual journey, see *Transformation by Integration*, 55–8.

[71]   Schmidt-Leukel, P., 'The Impact of Inter-Faith Dialogue on Religious Identity', 6 (unpublished paper given in Leicester 8 May 2005).

[72]   Habito, 'Being Buddhist, Being Christian', 179.

[73]   Habito in Drew unpublished transcripts, 166.

[74]   Ibid., 162.

Chapter 2

The Question of Salvation/Liberation: A Double-Belonger's Perspective

Paul F. Knitter

Let me begin with a defensive, but also clarifying, manoeuvre. I want to first define clearly the goals I have set for myself, as well as both my presuppositions and my limitations in trying to attain those goals. Really, this is an effort both to fend off, but also to help focus, critical responses.

1. First of all, I am speaking as a *double-belonger* – therefore as someone who is drawing on his own efforts to practice and to study both Buddhism and Christianity. That means I am going to be speaking as someone who is trying to figure it all out, trying to understand what this effort to double-belong means and where it might lead. It is definitely what we call 'a work in progress' – therefore more suggestive than declarative.

So I am going to be speaking from the particular to the general, from my own experience to what might be the experience of others. I know this matter of evoking the general from the particular can be risky business. But that is the course I am following, cautiously but hopefully. I therefore am going to offend normal protocols for projects such as this one and will, to a great extent, be speaking and writing in the first person. I think that is more honest and more productive of critical, friendly conversation.

2. Also, I am speaking as a *scholar of Christianity* and a *student of Buddhism*. My formal and extensive training, including the requisite languages, has been in Christian systematic theology. I am both a newcomer – or at my age I should say late-comer – to the study of Buddhism; which does not mean I have not tried to learn as much about Buddhism as I can with the best translations and interpreters I can find.

3. I am also a *comparative theologian*. Therefore I believe (or trust) that one of the most fruitful ways of understanding one's own religion is to compare it (bring it into dialogue) with another religion, and that such an endeavour is possible because there is something that 'connects' or 'is common to' the religions. However different religious languages truly are, I believe that some

degree of translation is always possible.[1] Therefore, the real, incorrigible, often incommensurable differences between the religions do not overwhelm what they have, or can have, in common. In other words, I am urging that the 'dominance of diversity', which has been proclaimed by postmodern or postliberal theologians, can and must give way to the 'solidarity of differences'.[2]

4. As a chastened *child of the Enlightenment* I recognise that 'reason' is both universally available and culturally conditioned. True to my Enlightenment values (and my Christian beliefs), I trust that social conditioning does not prevent one from either making truth claims that extend beyond one's social conditioning or from understanding the differently socially conditioned assertions of others. I do believe in the possibility, indeed the necessity, of making claims of truth and value that are universal, that is, that apply cross-culturally, multireligiously, and internationally.

5. I am a *member of a particular church and a particular sangha*. This means that when, throughout this chapter, I make statements or offer interpretations of 'what Christians' or 'what Buddhists' hold true, I do not mean *all* Christians or *all* Buddhists; but I certainly do mean *many*. I intend to speak for or out of particular traditions within the multi-traditioned reality of Christianity and Buddhism. More specifically, I am speaking as a member of what might be called, for lack of better terms, the 'progressive branch of both Catholic and Protestant' Christianity and as a follower of the Mahayana and especially the Tibetan Nyingma school of Buddhism. When I announce that 'Christians affirm' or that 'Buddhists teach', those are the Christians and Buddhists I am referring to and trying to represent.

6. Also, I offer these reflections as a *liberation Christian theologian* and as a *socially engaged Buddhist* who, therefore, believes that unless religious teachings and values are able to address the daunting mass of unnecessary, humanly caused suffering that afflicts sentient beings and the planet, such teachings are, at best, of secondary interest. I also believe that all the surviving religions in humanity's history have done so because they do address such eco-human suffering.

7. I speak as an *inheritor and survivor of the insights and limitations of the historical-critical method* of New Testament exegesis, who at this advanced stage of my life, has concluded that what is most important for a follower of Jesus or Buddha is not to know for sure exactly what 'the historical Jesus' or 'the historical

---

[1] So does Catherine Cornille in *The im-Possibility of Interreligious Dialogue* (New York: Crossroad, 2008), 95–136.

[2] The original, and still enduring, proclamation of the dominance of diversity and incommensurability was made by George Lindbeck in *The Nature of Doctrine: Religion and Theology in a Postliberal Age* (Philadelphia, PA: Westminster Press, 1984).

Buddha' said and did, but, rather, to understand the multiple ways their stories and teachings have been interpreted – and to carry on those interpretations for my cultural and historical context. We are saved or liberated not by historical facts but by stories and symbols.[3]

8. Finally – and both honestly and perhaps surprisingly – I speak out of my newly confessed convictions as *an American pragmatist* who believes that a crucial – certainly not the only – criterion for determining the validity of double-belonging (or any new item in a religion's storefront) is to investigate whether it is capable of promoting greater well-being for humanity and planet. And yes, I recognise that there is no universal, unchanging definition of 'eco-human well-being' and that every understanding of it will be particular, relative, conditioned. Still, I believe that this question of 'well-being' or 'flourishing' is a concern around which a multireligious and multicultural conversation can begin and move on to yield fruit.[4] And it will be this question – does one's double-belonging yield fruits of eco-human well-being for self and others – that is a decisive indication of its validity and fidelity to the past.

So in what follows I would like to make a case that Jesus and Buddha, as they have been and are being understood by their followers, offer: 1) a common starting point in their quest for truth and liberation, 2) a shared diagnosis of the fundamental human problem, 3) differing remedies for this problem and 4) a complementary liberative praxis.

A Common Starting Point in a Common Problem: Suffering

As Jesus and Buddha have been remembered, they both had a common starting point for their preaching: the sufferings that all humans (though some more than others) have to face – the inadequacies, the perplexities, the insufficiencies, the diminishments, the pains and disappointments that darken human existence. Both teachers began their missions out of a concern for the sufferings of their fellow human beings.

Buddha's concern for suffering is encapsulated in the visions or encounters that led to his spiritual search, and also by the four Noble Truths that summarise what he discovered. The first three of his four encounters embody the existential

---

[3]   Here I am repeating, and I hope clarifying, a stance I took during the early days of my work as a theologian in 'Jesus-Buddha-Krishna: Still Present?' *Journal of Ecumenical Studies* 16 (1979): 651–71.

[4]   This is the case I tried to make in *One Earth Many Religions: Multifaith Dialogue and Global Responsibility* (Maryknoll, NY: Orbis Books. 1995).

questions that come out of the human condition: diminishments of sickness, ageing, death. *Dukkha*, or suffering, pervades all. His whole message can be summarised in his desire to provide 'liberation' and freedom from such suffering.[5]

Jesus' concern for suffering embraced the existential anxieties of sickness and fear, but was concentrated on the sufferings imposed on his people by the might of the Roman Empire. Here I am basically following the 'empire-focused' hermeneutic of recent New Testament scholars: Jesus was a Jewish prophet who was responding to the sufferings of his people under the oppression of the Romans. This historical-political context is essential for understanding his message, as well as the message of St Paul. [6] Especially from his home context in afflicted and rebellious Galilee, Jesus witnessed how his people, together with many people throughout the Empire, were hurting. Consistent with the job description of any Jewish prophet, he felt called to do something about it. Liberation theologians interpret this as his concern for justice, a concern that was particularised in what they call a preferential option for the oppressed.[7]

A Shared Diagnosis: The Substantial Self/the Selfish Self

If suffering might serve as the shared starting point in the practice and reflections of a Buddhist-Christian double-belonger, it leads to what seems to be a further shared diagnosis of the fundamental source of human suffering. The nub of humankind's problems has to do with what followers of Buddha and Jesus would call a misunderstood or a malformed self.

---

5   A concise and classical summary of the four Noble Truths can be found in Walpola Rahula, *What the Buddha Taught* (New York: Grove Press, 1974 revised ed.), 16–50. Also helpful is Peter Harvey, *An Introduction to Buddhism: Teachings, History and Practices* (New York: Cambridge University Press, 1990), 47–72.

6   Richard A. Horsley, *Bandits, Prophets & Messiahs: Popular Movements in the Time of Jesus* (Harrisburg, PA: Trinity International Press, 1999); id. *The Message and the Kingdom: How Jesus and Paul Ignited a Revolution and Transformed the Ancient World* (New York: Grosset/Putnam, 1997); John Dominic Crossan, *Jesus: A Revolutionary Biography* (San Fransisco, CA: HarperSan Francisco, 1994); Brigitte Kahl, *Galatians Re-imagined: Reading with the Eyes of the Vanquished* (Minneapolis, MN: Fortress Press, 2010).

7   One of the most poignant expressions of this 'preferential option for the poor' is offered in Jon Sobrino's *No Salvation Outside the Poor: Prophetic-Utopian Essays* (Maryknoll, NY: Orbis Books, 2008).

Buddhism: Original Ignorance

The Buddhist diagnosis of the cause of suffering focuses not on *the way things are*, but on *the way we think they are. Ignorance – avidyā –* is our fundamental problem and the root cause of our suffering. Ignorance of what? Of our true nature as *anicca* (impermanent) and as *anattā* (non-substantial or non-individual). We think we are enduring, individual entities – and that is what gets us into trouble. This diagnosis is contained in the classical Buddhist teachings on the *three poisons*. The poison of ignorance or *delusion* about what we really are will necessarily lead to the poisons of *greed* and of *hatred*.

- To protect and augment what we believe to be our ever-threatened identity, we amass and then cling to as much as we can. 'To be' is predicated on 'to have'. In our conviction that we must preserve our identities, we try to hold on to, or cling to, what we have; we seek to acquire more than what we have; we are intent on defending all that we have, for if we lose it, we will be diminished. What we have is not just our 'property', it is our '*private* property', ours to do with as we wish simply because it is ours.
- And then, 'to have' is maintained by 'to compete' and 'to win'. So easily, everyone is seen as a competitor. And when they threaten to out-compete us and menace our being-as-having, they become our enemies. Out of fear, or out of envy, we find ourselves hating them. Thus, competition trumps cooperation. Our human rights outweigh our human duties.

Contemporary Buddhists, like David Loy and Sulak Sivaraksa, are exploring how the three poisons, though they originate in the human mind, take on or are embodied in social structures that exist independently of the human mind. *Delusion* surrounds us in the *consumerism* and *advertising* that constantly tells us that we cannot 'be' unless we 'have'. *Greed* is built into *economic principles* that declare that only if everyone is selfish can everyone prosper. *Hatred* nurtures a military-industrial complex that is built on the conviction that our survival depends on conquering our enemies through weapons superior to theirs.[8]

So for Buddhists, we cause suffering and endure suffering because we do not know who/what we really are. The cause is in our minds; but the effects are very real, all around us.

---

[8] David Loy, "'Listening to the Buddha: How Greed, Ill-will and Delusion Are Poisoning Our Institutions", *Transformation: Where Love Meets Social Justice*, 12 May 2014: http://bit.ly/1wE0WL5. Sulak Sivaraksa, *The Wisdom of Sustainability: Buddhist Economics for the 21st Century* (Kihei, Hawaii: Koa Books, 2009).

Christians: Original Sin

For Christians, the diagnosis of humanity's fundamental problem has traditionally been linked with *original sin*. According to this doctrine, from early on – indeed, from the very beginning – something went wrong, got out of kilter, profoundly out of kilter. The product that God created was broken, so broken that it could no longer work the way it was intended to work. It would have to be repaired. This, basically, is how the story of Adam and Eve has traditionally been understood. From the very beginning, humans messed things up, so badly that they created a mess that all subsequent humans fall into. Indeed, Christians have held that the human condition, or human nature, is either *fallen* (in more Protestant terms) or severely *wounded* (preferred Catholic terminology).

So if Buddhists offer a diagnosis of the human problem that is more *epistemological*, located in what we think we are, Christians offer a diagnosis that is more *ontological*, describing the way things actually are. Whether fallen or wounded, humans are born into the world, we might say, with a 'heart problem' – what Augustine called the 'cor curvatum in se', or 'the heart turned in on itself'.[9] We are inherently selfish, not because God made us that way but because we have fallen away from God's original designs and have created a condition into which all humans are born. While traditionally, that fallen condition was thought to have been passed on through procreation and sexuality, today it is understood more sociologically or historically: we have fashioned cultures in which we are indoctrinated to believe that security comes through possessions, power and violence.[10]

A Shared Diagnosis

For both Buddhists and Christians, the cause of suffering has to do with a misunderstanding or a malfunctioning of what we really are. Our true identity and reality, and therefore our well-being, are to be found beyond our presumed or our constructed individual identities. In John Hick's analysis of the so-called religions of the axial age, both Buddhism and Christianity, from different analyses and along different paths, announce that for human beings to find their

---

[9]   See Matt Jenson: *Gravity of Sin: Augustine, Luther and Barth on Homo Incurvatus in Se* (London and New York: T&T Clark, 2007), 37–42.

[10]   Piet Schoonenberg, *Man and Sin: A Theological View* (South Bend: University of Notre Dame Press, 1984); Carl R. Trueman, 'Original Sin in Modern Theology', in Hans Madueme and Michael Reeves, eds, *Adam, the Fall, and Original Sin: Theological, Biblical, and Scientific Perspectives* (Grand Rapids, IN: Baker Academic, 2014), 167–88.

'truth' and their 'well-being', they need to shift from 'self-centeredness' to 'other-centeredness'.[11] We are to exist as part of a 'bigger picture'; we have to find our place and meaning within a larger reality.

My Buddhist teachers have symbolically pointed to this 'bigger picture' as *Emptiness* or *Inter-Being*, or as the infinite expanse of *Space* that is both primordially cognisant (aware) and unrestrictedly compassionate.[12] Christian 'fingers' that I believe are pointing (all we can do is point!) to the same moon are *God* as omnipresent and all loving *Mystery*, the *Ground of Being*, the *Interconnecting Spirit*.[13] Both Buddhist and Christian traditions diagnose our fundamental problem as having to do with an overly individualised self that needs to be reconnected, notionally or actually, with what I as a Buddhist-Christian would call the reality of a larger, real Self, a groundless Ground of Being.

Differing Remedies: The Bodhisattva and the Reign of God

Buddha's Remedy: The Bodhisattva – Wisdom that Bears Compassion

Buddha's remedy for the ignorance at the root of our suffering is contained in the Mahayana ideal of the bodhisattva. We are all called to be bodhisattvas – persons who have awakened (or begun to awake) to a wisdom that includes compassion for all sentient beings. This is a process in which we wake up to our Buddhanature, to the Inter-Being that contains us all, to a non-dual Reality in which we are vitally connected to each other and to everything.

This is the wisdom of Inter-Being that naturally and necessarily becomes and is a compassion for all beings. The subject-object difference is removed; we are all subjects with each other. We are all held in, part of, a Spaciousness that is all-pervasive, aware and compassionate. In this awakening, we see the natural goodness in all beings. And in affirming and responding to this goodness in them

---

[11]   John Hick, *An Interpretation of Religion* (New Haven, CT: Yale University Press, 1989), 36–54.

[12]   Tsoknyi Rinpoche, *Carefree Dignity: Discourses on Training in the Nature of Mind* (Rangjung Yeshe Publications, 1998), 35 ff. and 148 ff. Id. *Fearless Simplicity: The Dzogchen Way of Living Freely in a Complex World* (Rangjung Yeshe Publications, 2003), 211–68. John Makransky, *Awakening through Love: Unveiling Your Deepest Goodness* (Somerville, MA: Wisdom Publications, 2007), 33–68 and 157–200.

[13]   See Paul F. Knitter, *Without Buddha I Could Not Be a Christian* (Oxford: Oneworld, 2011), 18–23. Rita Gross, 'Of Fingers, Moons, and Rafts', in *Religious Diversity: What's the Problem?* (Eugene, OR: Cascade Books, 2014), 101–17.

and as them, we enable them to recognise and affirm it in and as themselves.[14] We see others in their true, original nature, no matter how much that nature may be caught in ignorance and in the poisons that spring from ignorance. And no matter how much others may hate and hurt us, we cannot bring ourselves to hate and hurt them. That would be 'contrary to nature'; it would contradict what we know and feel we and they are: we are each other.

Such compassion, of course, will call the bodhisattva to action that addresses the suffering of others. Shantideva has offered us some of the most simple yet compelling declarations of what the bodhisattva naturally feels:

> May the pain of every living creature
> Be completely cleared away.
> May I be the doctor and the medicine
> And may I be the nurse
> For all sick beings in the world
> Until everyone is healed.

> May I be an island for those who seek one
> And a lamp for those desiring light,
> May I be a bed for all who wish to rest
> And a slave for all who want a slave.[15]

Jesus' Remedy: The Reign of God/Abba – Compassion that Calls for Justice

Jesus' remedy for our confined and fearful selves was rooted in his experience of the God of Israel as *Abba* – a personal God who embraces us with tender, parental love. Jesus knew that the love he felt from this Abba was extended to all creatures. His Father was our Father. And he, Jesus, was understood by his followers to be the vehicle, the embodiment or enfleshment of that parental love. 'As the Father has loved me, I have loved you ... That they may be one as you, Father, and I are one' (John 15: 9, 17:21).

And yet, this Father-God is not the fullness, or the distinctiveness, of Jesus' remedy. For him, 'God' could not be separated from 'the Reign of God'. God without the Reign was for Jesus not the real God. Such a God would be a false God for him.[16] The God Jesus the Jew experienced is a God who wants to bring

---

[14] Makransky, *Awakening through Love*, 69–93.

[15] Shantideva, *Bodhicaryavatara* 3: 6–7, 18.

[16] Jon Sobrino, *Jesus the Liberator: A Historical-Theological View* (Maryknoll, NY: Orbis Books, 1993), 67–104.

about a *Basileia*, a different way of being on this earth, a different social order, a different way of structuring society. For Jesus, God and the Reign of God are distinct but inseparable. God is that which seeks the Reign; the Reign is the expression of God. Here, analogies with the Mahayana understanding of Emptiness and Form resonate with Jesus' message: as Emptiness includes Form, God includes the Reign of God, and vice versa.

Consistent with the message of the Jewish prophets, this new social order will be marked by *justice*. To know God, as Jeremiah tells us, is to do justice (Jeremiah 22: 15–16). If for Buddhists, wisdom calls for compassion, then for Christians, compassion calls for justice. And it will be justice especially for those who have been treated unjustly, the *anawim*, the poor and the marginalised. The Jewish God of Jesus is a God who is alert to the way some human beings take advantage of other human beings, and how such unjust acts are translated into unjust policies, unjust laws, unjust economic systems. Compassionate toward all, this God had a 'preferential care' for the oppressed. As Sri Lankan liberation theologian Aloysius Pieris, S.J. puts it: Jesus announced and was 'God's defense pact with the poor'.[17]

The necessity of bringing about justice in the face of injustice is an explicit call to action – action that will go beyond compassion and will seek to change the way society or the world works: it is a call for structural change. So if the compassion of the bodhisattva calls for an action addressed to those who are suffering and who are victims of injustice, the concern for justice felt by the disciple of Jesus calls for action addressed to the perpetrators of injustice. To express compassion for the oppressed, one must confront the oppressors.

Clarifying the Differences

Both Buddhists and Christians, we can conclude, prescribe *compassion* as the necessary remedy for humankind's ailments. But each tradition writes that prescription in different ways.

Buddha and his followers, I would suggest, are especially concerned with *how we come to compassion*. There can be no real, no lasting compassion without wisdom. Therefore, they stress the need to train our minds. Spiritual practice is essential. Here Buddhism shines with a wide variety of meditational (or for Pure Land Buddhists, devotional) practices. Buddhism not only holds up compassion-producing-wisdom as a potential for all humans, it offers the practical means

---

[17] *God's Reign for God's Poor: A Return to the Jesus Formula* (Sri Lanka: Tulana Research Centre, 1998), 35–44.

Buddhist-Christian Dual Belonging

for achieving such wisdom: one must sit daily, have a teacher, form the habit of mindfulness in all one experiences and does.

Jesus and Christians show particular concern for *how we practice compassion*. By itself, compassion is not enough. Compassion must take historical-social form. It must change reality. It must devise policies and take political action that will bring this world a little closer to the Reign of God.

Such differences between Buddha and Jesus (as they were remembered by their followers) are illustrated, I suggest, in two popular stories: Buddha's response to Kisa-Gotami with her dead baby and Jesus' response to Jairus with his dead daughter.

When the bereaved mother Kisa-Gotami, who had just lost her infant son, implored the Buddha for help, he directed her to gather mustard seeds from every family in the village that had not experienced the death of a loved one. This became an effective means of changing her awareness and acceptance of transience. Gautama was responding to her immediate need by seeking to change her way of thinking about her suffering. And it worked.[18] Jesus brings the daughter of the bereaved Jairus back from her apparent death (Mark 5: 35–43). He seeks to change the reality, not just one's attitude toward suffering but the cause of suffering.

This is not to say that one response is better than the other. (The daughter of Jairus will eventually die and he will be in Kisa-Gotami's shoes.) But they do signal differences in how Buddha and Christ engage the reality of suffering. Buddha stresses the need to respond to those who are suffering; Jesus calls us also to respond to those who are causing the suffering. The difference between the two is illustrated, I suggest, in the action of Jesus in the Cleansing of the Temple. He calls for a change in the political-cultic practices and the way the Jewish oligarchy were working with the Romans (Matt. 21: 12–17). I know of no such expression of anger and action on the part of Buddha in Buddhist scriptures.

A Complementary Buddhist-Christian Liberative Praxis

As we have seen, there are clear differences in what I am calling the 'remedies' that Buddhists and Christians bring to the reality of human and planetary suffering. For the most part, I find these differences to be profoundly, even necessarily, complementary. In trying to explain what I mean by 'complementary', I arrive at

---

[18] See Sacred Texts: http://www.sacred-texts.com/bud/btg/btg85.htm (accessed 31 May 2014).

the practical core of this chapter – how a Buddhist-Christian double-belonging can contribute to the *liberation and healing of our world*. Here is where both traditions can foster a dual-identity and a dual liberative praxis that is, through their duality, more effective in realising the goals of both Buddha and Christ: to liberate people and all sentient beings from suffering.

How Christian Praxis Complements Buddhist Praxis: The Necessity of Justice and of the Preferential Option for the Oppressed

The necessity of justice: As already noted, although the fundamental cause of suffering is found in individual, personal ignorance, the results of ignorance go beyond the individual. The actions that follow upon my lack of awareness of my nature as *anattā/not-self* are not only *my* actions; they become, slowly but inevitably, *society's* actions. The personal, as feminists tell us, becomes the political, the cultural. My own ego-centred attitudes and acts become embodied in social forms; they incarnate themselves, as it were, in the way society works. My ego-clinging actions become enshrined in economic policies that further greed; or in military institutions whose existence is dependent upon enemies and the hatred of enemies. We have already noted how some contemporary Buddhists are recognising that individual karma becomes social karma.[19]

But if this is so – if the personal is the political, if individual karma becomes social karma – then we must also face the reality that the social and political offspring of individual self-centredness grows up to be, as it were, bigger, stronger and more enduring than its progenitors. Sinful or greed-filled structures remain even after individuals have been enlightened. To transform the structures of one's awareness and thinking does not necessarily change the structures of society. Indeed, it seems that one can be enlightened and full of compassion for all sentient beings without realising how one remains a part of an economic or military system that continues to cause suffering to others.

Here we can understand the oft-made – and I think to some extent justified – criticism of Buddhism in the West: that it all too often serves the stressed-out well-off as a spiritual refuge that enables them to mindfully reduce their stress but at the same time anaesthetises them to the way their way of life is causing stress to so many others, including the planet.[20] Self-care so easily becomes a distraction from other-care. Of course, many Christian churches are equally, or

---

[19]   David Loy, see footnote 7.
[20]   Maria Reis Habito, 'Buddhism in the West: Self-Realization or Self-Indulgence?' Website of Maria Kannon Zen Center, http://bit.ly/1yMSjOl. Accessed 3 December 2014.

much more, deserving of such a criticism; churches that are prompt to take up collections for the poor are reluctant to support policies calling for universal health care or an increase of the minimum wage.

But it does seem that Jesus and his liberation-theological followers make the point more clearly, and loudly, than Buddhists: transforming oneself is different from – and should not become a substitute for or distraction from – transforming society. This implies that compassion, though necessary, is insufficient. It can even be dangerous. Justice is also necessary. If compassion calls us to feed the hungry, as we saw in the citation from Shantideva, justice urges us to ask why they are hungry. It addresses the causes of hunger. It asks why there are so many unmet needs in this world, why there are so many people suffering from hunger.

For Christians, justice identifies how ignorance and ego-clinging produces social, economic, political systems that enable some people to take advantage of other people, and that, therefore, bring about an unequal and an unjust sharing in the goods of this earth. If we are not aware of these exploitative, unjust systems, our compassion can assuage suffering, but it cannot cure it. We will apply a bandage, but the wound will not heal. The further danger is that the satisfaction we naturally feel in applying bandages may distract us from the further need of healing the wound. In the sense of achievement in giving food to the starving child, we forget that she will be hungry again tomorrow.

The Christian insistence on justice reminds Buddhists that as necessary as the stress-reducing achievement of mindfulness is for living a life of inner peace and compassion for others, it is not enough to fashion a world in which all can have peace. We also need social mindfulness as to how our reified, egocentric thoughts and fears become reified social or political systems. What Buddhists call *mindfulness* needs to be enhanced by what Christian liberation theologians call *social analysis*.

The hermeneutical privilege of the oppressed: If Buddhists are to effectively extend their practice of personal mindfulness to include social mindfulness and analysis, they will also have to take seriously the Christian liberationists' call for a 'preferential option for the oppressed'.[21] The necessity of a preferential option for the oppressed calls upon all spiritual seekers to be sure that their quest includes, as an integral element, the effort to become aware of the reality and of the experience of those who have been pushed aside in one's society or culture, those who 'do not count', who do not have a meaningful voice in the deliberations

---

[21] See Daniel G. Groody, ed., *The Option for the Poor in Christian Theology* (Notre Dame, IN: University of Notre Dame Press, 2007).

and decisions of state or school or neighbourhood. Our 'mindfulness' must also include them, their reality, their experience and feelings and perspectives.

And this mindfulness of the oppressed, Christian liberationists insist, has to play a certain 'privileged' role in our spiritual practice. Why? Because it will tell us things we cannot know by ourselves; it will alert us to realities that in our well-off or middle-class lives, we simply do not see. This is a privileged mindfulness also because it can correct and convert attitudes we previously had about how our society or sanga or church works.

This is what the liberation theologians mean by the 'hermeneutical privilege of the poor'.[22] From their experience, from their position of suffering and exploitation, the oppressed can see the world in ways that the powerful or the comfortable cannot. If we are among the established comfortable or powerful, the poor and oppressed can enable us to expand our mindfulness and awareness in ways that are not available to us if we practice mindfulness only of our own experience. The mindfulness we practice on our cushions or in our pews must be balanced and expanded by the mindfulness gained on the streets. In fact, our social mindfulness will have the privilege of correcting our personal mindfulness.

How Buddhist Praxis Complements Christian Praxis: The Priority of Wisdom-based Compassion

When I speak of a 'priority' for wisdom-based compassion, I do not mean a chronological priority: first 'A' and only then 'B'. Rather, I am trying to describe an inner, sustaining priority – something like a *sine qua non*: '*that* without which *this* cannot really thrive'.

In my practice of double-belonging, I have found that Buddhists are pointing me to the priority of inner-personal transformation over social-political transformation.

Buddhists remind Christians of something they should know from their own tradition but often don't: namely, that if, as Christians insist, we must all be agents of societal change that will bring this world closer to the Reign of God, we will not be able to bring about such change around us unless we are also, even *a priori*, working on change within ourselves. As Gandhi put it: 'You

---

[22] Lee Cormie, 'The Hermeneutical Privilege of the Oppressed', in *Catholic Theological Society of America Proceedings* 33 (1978): 155–81; Jean-Pierre Ruiz, 'The Bible and Liberation: Between the Preferential Option for the Poor and the Hermeneutical Privilege of the Poor', in *Readings from the Edges: The Bible and People on the Move* (Maryknoll, NY: Orbis Books, 2011), 24–33.

must be the change'.[23] Yes, the three poisons take on a systemic reality that exists independently of personal poisons. But I am not going to be able to change anything in the system's poisons unless I am working on the poisons in my own consciousness. This is not an entirely new or strange reminder for Christians. They have heard its basic message before – in the call to combine contemplation with action; or even more profoundly, in the Pauline insistence that grace must precede good works.

And yet, I have come to suspect – to the point of a growing conviction – that the Buddhist insistence on the priority of inner experience, which I am here calling the 'priority of wisdom-producing-compassion', is indeed pushing, or luring, Christians toward a more profound – that is, a more ego-transcending – inner transformation.

But just what do I mean by 'inner transformation'? To pick up on what I tried to describe earlier (on the Buddhist remedy for suffering), I would describe this inner transformation as an experience of the non-dual unity between Emptiness and Form, between Inter-Being and all impermanent beings, between what Jesus called Abba and all humanity. Buddhism, I believe, is providing me, and my fellow Christians, with an opportunity to enter more profoundly, more self-transcendingly, more apophatically into the unitive experience signalled in John's description of Jesus as 'one with the Father' and 'one with us' (John 14), or in Paul's description (I would dare say 'definition') of a Christian as someone who exists 'in Christ' (Gal 3: 21).

This is an experience of the Abba-Mystery (expressed and incarnate in the Christ-Mystery), in which the Abba-Mystery and the finite are, like Emptiness and Form, distinct but inseparable. I have found that my Buddhist Tibetan practice, under the guidance of my teacher, is luring me more deeply into this kind of non-dual, mystical experience. What I mean by 'more deeply' is found in the creative tension between the Christian preposition '*in*' and the Buddhist copulative '*is*': while St Paul or St John speak of my being '*in* Christ' or '*in* the Father', my Buddhist teachers call me to *be* the Space' or they tell me that my 'Form *is* Emptiness'. I am being called to experience, and then to reflect on, a deeper and more mysterious non-duality between God and World, between Ultimate and Relative. (If they are non-dual, both have to be capitalised!)

And when I try to bring this non-dual inner transformation (for me, not complete but, I hope, in process) to my efforts at, and understanding of, social transformation, I discover that it affects, and often changes, how I perceive and

---

[23] For the difficulties in determining the original source of this statement, see: http:// www.compassionatespirit.com/Be-the-Change.htm (accessed 15 January 2015).

The Question of Salvation/Liberation   45

how I relate to the world of suffering – both those who suffer and those who cause suffering, the oppressed and the oppressors. The presence of the Abba-Mystery – or in the language of my Nyingma tradition, of all-containing, conscious and compassionate Space – pervades, animates, contains everything and everyone. This is the *wisdom* gained in inner transformation, a wisdom that naturally and spontaneously blossoms in *compassion* for *all* sentient beings.

Such an awareness of Abba-Mystery or of Spacious Presence I have found to be *necessary* – a *sine qua non* – for my liberative engagement with the suffering world.

Why is it necessary? In trying to answer that question, I will draw particularly on the teachings and writings of my Buddhist teacher, Lama John Makransky.[24] Summarising and somewhat recasting his reflections, I believe that Lama Makransky offers three pivotal reasons why, as he puts it, 'social activists' need the inner transformation of awakening to wisdom in order to carry on, perseveringly and effectively, their efforts to heal the sufferings of our world. These reasons can be gathered under the rubrics of *stamina*, *humility*, and *compassion*.

1) Stamina: from my own experience as a social and political activist (especially during the years of the brutal, US sustained civil war in El Salvador during the '70s and '80s) and from what I hear from my wife and her younger colleagues in social work, one of the greatest problems in such work is the danger of running out of gas. In their efforts to change the world and heal its wounds, activists exhaust their energies. They burn out.

The reasons for burn out are varied, but they seem to fall into two general categories: a) you cannot break through human conditioning and b) you cannot beat city hall. It is so difficult, often apparently impossible, to help people to change patterns and addictions that have, as it were, become part of their DNA through social conditioning – through what Buddhists would call their causes and conditions. At the same time, one has to confront the power of the moneyed establishment and the way it determines policy and opinion through its control of the media and government. Because of these two obstacles – and certainly many more – the job description of a social activist or liberationist seems to hold up an impossible goal. This is why people burn out.

---

[24] John Makransky, 'How Contemporary Buddhist Practice Meets the Secular World in Its Search for a Deeper Grounding for Service and Social Action': and 'Compassion Beyond Fatigue: Contemplative Training for People Who Serve Others'. Available at website of the Foundation for Active Compassion (http://www.foundationforactivecompassion.org/). Id. 'A Buddhist Critique of, and Learning from, Christian Liberation Theology', *Theological Studies* 75 (2014): 635–57.

This is where some kind of a spiritual practice that will foster and sustain our inner transformation and resources seems imperative. To have begun the process of awakening to the cognisant, compassionate Space of Inter-Being, or to what Jesus experienced as the unconditional love of the Abba-Mystery, can assure us that our efforts are not just our own efforts. Having tasted of the wisdom that reveals to us that all our efforts are 'Forms' of 'Emptiness', or that it is the Abba-Mystery that is active in and as us, or that we are doing what our Buddha-nature or Christ-nature necessarily brings us to do – then, as the Bhagavad Gita tells us, the value of our actions are not determined by their fruits. The value of our actions are in our actions themselves, for they are also the actions of Abba. They are Forms of Emptiness.

This deeper experience of the non-duality between the Abba-Mystery and the world that Buddhism has offered me can remind me and other Christians that even though my efforts to bring the world closer to the Reign of God fail, the Reign is still already here, right now. Yes, we must seek the Reign of God and work while the light is with us, but at the very same time we are assured that the Reign of God is already, *already*, among us. In both success and failure, the Reign of God is already alive among us.

2) *Humility*: perhaps one of the most difficult virtues for social activists to practice is humility. In struggling for justice, in resisting those who oppress others, one needs to be clear, firm, resolute. Human lives and human rights are at stake.

And so agents of social justice can be so sure about what needs to be done, about which policies are causing the exploitation, about who are the 'bad guys'. In their commitment to 'speaking truth to power', activists are so sure that they have the truth and those in power don't. I suspect that most people involved in social activism know what I am talking about. We become so certain of our own analysis and our own programs that we end up not listening to others and missing better opportunities, better programs. And so it can and does happen that the 'liberators' end up making the situation just as bad as, or even worse than, it was under the oppressors.

The practice of awakening to an inner transformation alerts activists to how they cling to their thoughts and feelings and how this can lead them to absolutise their own ideas and programs. The Buddhist practice of mindfulness can warn activists that as long as they are still clinging to ego-identity and their own ideas, there's a little (or big!) oppressor hiding in every good-willed liberator. The wisdom that comes from waking up can remind activists that if they have to 'speak truth to power', they have to be as humble about what they say as they are strong in saying it. Only if we do not cling to our truth can we – and others – experience its power.

3) *Compassion*: here I take up what I believe is one of the most urgent, but also one of the most sensitive, challenges that my Buddhist contemplative practice has offered my Christian liberation practice. It has to do with the Buddhist claim that just as inner transformation has a certain priority over social transformation, *compassion has a certain priority over justice*. And I have come to realise that this priority of compassion applies especially to the way I carry out my 'preferential option for the oppressed'.

What I am getting at has been gently but sharply stated by Thich Nhat Hanh in his little book on *Living Buddha, Living Christ* when he informs Christians that for a Buddhist, God does not have favourites.[25] Therefore, the preferential option for the poor that is so central to liberation theology can be dangerous. Nhat Hanh is reminding Christians that just as there is a relationship of non-duality between Emptiness and Form, or between Abba-Mystery and us, so there is a non-duality between oppressed and oppressor. Both – in what each is doing and in what each is experiencing – are expressions of and are held in and by Inter-Being and Abba-Mystery. The actions of oppressor or oppressed are clearly different. But their identities are the same. That means, also, that *my own* identity is linked to both oppressed and oppressors.

Therefore, we do not respond to the oppressed out of compassion and to the oppressor out of justice. No, we respond to *both* out of compassion! Compassion for both the oppressed and the oppressor. But compassion for the oppressor will be expressed differently than compassion for the oppressed. It is the same compassion, but, as it were, in different packages. As Lama Makransky puts it, the compassion shown to the oppressor will be *fierce*. It will be compassion that confronts, that challenges, that calls for change. It will name the poisons that cause so much suffering: greed, hatred, ignorance.[26]

But the primary motivation for such confrontation will not be the necessity of justice, but the necessity of compassion. It will be driven by a compassion for the oppressor and by the desire for his/her well-being, by the desire to free him/her from the illusions that drive him/her to greed and to the exploitation of others. So yes, we want to liberate the oppressed. But, *just as much*, we want to liberate the oppressors. Buddhists are telling liberation Christians that compassion has no preferences. We love the oppressor as much as we love the

---

25 New York: Riverhead, 1995, 79.
26 Makransky, 'A Buddhist Critique', 648.

oppressed. Our calls for justice intend the well-being of the oppressor just as much as the well-being of the oppressed.

Lama Makransky puts it this way:

> To defend those who suffer most intensively against depredations of the powerful is not to decide for the powerless over the powerful but to choose the fuller humanity in both, and so to confront both differently – challenging the powerless to discover their power, challenging the powerful by working to stop actions that not only hurt the poor but also impede their own fuller humanity.[27]

And when the oppressor sees this, when s/he realises that s/he is indeed being confronted but that the confrontation arises out of compassion, respect, cherishing, when s/he hears from his/her confronter not only that s/he is wrong, but also, and primarily, that s/he is loved – then, perhaps only then, we have the possibility of changing the structures of injustice, for then there will be the possibility of a change of heart in the oppressors. Such a non-preferential option for compassion that extends equally and clearly to both oppressed and oppressors will be the foundation on which justice can be built, on which structures can be changed.

Conclusion

So, is my experiment with Buddhist-Christian double-belonging reputable and valid? Is it faithful to the two traditions that took their origins from Gautama and Yeshua? I am not sure. But I think so. I – along with many other double-belongers – have tried to go about my experiment with academic and spiritual care, as a scholar and a seeker. And so far, I do believe my efforts are yielding fruits of well-being for myself and I hope for others. But only time and the kind of conversations we are pursuing in this book will tell.

---

[27] Op. cit. 649.

Chapter 3

Creation, Dependent Arising and Dual Belonging

Ross Thompson

Perhaps the most obvious conflict in Buddhist-Christian dual belonging – the conflict that in many people's minds makes the very idea of a Buddhist Christianity nonsensical – is between the theism of Christianity and the atheism of Buddhism. On the face of it these two faiths have to be regarded as irreconcilable, since for Christianity salvation is seen in terms of reconciliation and friendship with one's Creator, whereas for Buddhism, though the notion of deities is not ruled out, the question of a *creator* God is either regarded as irrelevant to salvation, or explicitly argued against. Hence Strange's chapter in this volume regards dual belonging as an act of infidelity, turning away from the God who reveals his glory in creation and redemption. As our sole origin and goal, God justly demands our sole allegiance.[1] And from the Buddhist side, Tilakaratne argues that the Buddhist account of liberation is premised on the fact that 'the world is protection-less; there is no overlord'.[2] If there were a creator or provider the obvious path would be to seek his help; it is because such a being is absent that one has to pursue, by one's own great effort, the eightfold way. Both writers would agree on this point: if there is a Creator God, then follow the path he has provided – for not doing so would represent an idolatrous turning away to self-reliance – but if there is not, Buddhism represents a clear-sighted pathway whilst theistic faiths are grounded in illusion. The dual belonger therefore has the double misfortune to be in Christian terms idolatrous and in Buddhist terms deluded![3]

This chapter cannot tackle all the manifold issues at stake here, but takes as its starting point a significant exchange between Perry Schmidt-Leukel – an Anglican who wishes to embrace a lot of Buddhism – José Cabezón – a convert from Roman Catholicism to Tibetan Buddhism – and Paul Williams – a well

---

[1]   Cited on p. 100 in this volume.

[2]   *The Middle Length Discourses of the Buddha*, cited 101.

[3]   J.P. Williams' chapter in this volume presents a more positive evaluation of the contradiction between affirming and denying God; for her, contradictions in religious truth can be affirmed ([**225.**]), while for me they are a starting point for exploration.

50 *Buddhist-Christian Dual Belonging*

known convert in the opposite direction.[4] Their debate focuses on four questions: whether Buddhism is really atheistic; whether it affirms a transcendent reality; whether Christianity and Buddhism are divided on the matter of creation and how and why the universe exists; and whether ultimate reality can be characterised as personal and loving. This chapter focuses on the third question: whether it is possible to reconcile the very different accounts Christianity and Buddhism give of the basis of reality in terms respectively of creation and dependent arising. This question gets most attention from the three writers themselves, and it seems to me to be the most fundamental question, in that once it is answered it becomes easier to answer the other three.

The debate on this matter introduces my own discussion of what kind of causality could make sense in reference to creation. Three understandings are rejected, but another is affirmed: a notion of 'metacausality' is developed with the help of a triadic model relating matter, consciousness and conceptuality. This model enables us to see the Christian understanding of God as creator (in the sense of metacause) and the (varied) Buddhist understandings of dependent arising, as well as other options, as alternative ways of seeing the same reality. Creation and co-arising could then be the same actuality described and hence seen in conceptually opposed ways, so that the seeming conceptual conflict would not be ultimately irreconcilable. This would be analogous to the way the same quantum reality, light, can be validly described in terms of particle or wave, which in other contexts are incompatible concepts. It follows that each way of describing and imagining may legitimately challenge and refine the other, leading potentially to new ways of describing, imagining and practicing each religion without fundamentally departing from its content. Of course, this would have to be established in the case of other doctrines than the two considered here. The present chapter represents only the beginning of a much wider project of relating the Buddhist and Christian doctrines to integrative perspectives that are – crucially – not imposed from elsewhere, but emerge from the questions the religions pose to each other in dialogue, including the inner dialogue of the dual belonger.

---

[4]   John D'Arcy May, ed. *Converging Ways? Conversion and Belonging in Buddhism and Christianity* (Klosterverlag Sankt Ottilien: EOS, 2007). Other works referred to as significant for this discussion are Williams's 'Aquinas meets the Buddhists: Prolegomenon to an authentically Thomas-ist Basis for Dialogue', *Modern Theology*, 20.1, January 2004: 91–121, and his *The Unexpected Way* (Edinburgh and New York: T&T Clark, 2002) which provoked the discussion.

The Debate about Creation and Causality

Schmidt-Leukel argues, and Williams denies, that the Christian God can be identified with Buddhist nirvana, as being the transcendent ground and goal of our salvation. Schmidt-Leukel argues that nirvana is sometimes misconceived as a personal state.[5] But in a famous passage from the *Udāna* (8.3) and *Idivuttaka* (43) it is defined as the not-born, not-originated, not-made and not-conditioned reality that alone enables release from the samsaric world of birth, change, decay and conditionality.[6] The *Anguttara Nikaya* moreover refers to our 'plunging into nirvāṇa', so 'nirvāṇa must exist whether someone plunges into it or not'.[7] Schmidt-Leukel concedes that the Buddhist arguments against God as an *efficient* cause are valid. If God is an efficient cause, he is part of the samsaric universe, part of what dependently arises. But for Buddhists, nirvana can be identified as the *final* cause of the universe, that is, the purpose for which it exists. Here, and at greater length elsewhere, Schmidt-Leukel argues that the Buddhist universe with its karmic causality is oriented toward the attainment of this goal, in a way that could be described in Christian terms as providential.[8] Meanwhile the understanding of creation to be found in Aquinas and the Christian mainstream tradition affirms God as the final rather than the efficient cause of the world, so answering the Buddhist critique. God then means for Christians what nirvana means for Buddhists.

Williams retorts that this is certainly not the mainstream Christian understanding of creation. God in the Christian tradition is 'both the *alpha* and the *omega*'.[9] 'God is for Aquinas ... the creator in the sense that he answers the question "Why is there something rather than nothing?"' Buddhists reject this as a conceivable answer, and even reject the question.[10] But Christians like Aquinas urge that the contingency of the world must be grounded in a non-contingent, necessary being that chooses to make it exist, by some kind of efficient causality, albeit unlike natural causality.[11]

---

[5] Tilakaratne, in this volume, presents strong arguments against the kind of understanding of nirvana presented by Schmidt-Leukel; for him it is indeed a personal state not an ineffable goal.

[6] *Converging Ways*, 72.

[7] Ibid., 73.

[8] See especially *Buddhism, Christianity and the Question of Creation* (Aldershot: Ashgate, 2006).

[9] *Converging Ways*, 123.

[10] Ibid., 125.

[11] 'Aquinas meets the Buddhists', 106, 111.

Cabezón meanwhile believes, for the traditional Buddhist and for other reasons, talk of a necessary being or ground raises more problems than it solves. He can understand 'ground' in the sense that

> the earth is the 'ground' of the sprout. Without the earth as a cause, the sprout could not come about. But what does it mean to say that there is some 'ground' for the sprout separate from the things that define it and separate from its causes – some ethereal principle that explains why the sprout should exist at all?[12]

Nevertheless Cabezón does offer a Buddhist candidate for a necessarily existent reality that grounds the contingent existence of everything. 'The universe exists because sentient beings (beings with minds) create karma ("actions") and karma brings the universe into existence as the place where the results of that karma are experienced'.[13] Cabezón is referring to the Buddhist alternative account of how the world arises: through *pratītya samutpāda*, often translated 'dependent origination' or 'dependent arising'. Minds are necessarily existent, because 'a universe – existence – without minds is not logically possible. Why? Existence is, by definition, "that which is cognised/imputed by minds"'.[14] Williams counters that though a world without minds is inconceivable, it is not logically contradictory; minds are not necessarily existent.[15] He therefore rejects the idea that minds can fulfil the role Christians have ascribed to God as the necessary ground of existence.

What Kind of Causality Could Creation Involve?

Regarding the traditional Christian understanding of creation, Williams is surely right to argue against Schmidt-Leukel that God is both alpha *and* omega, the originating as well as the final cause of the universe. It is in any case questionable whether final causality makes sense without efficient causality. To describe the universe, or anything, as having a purpose, is to invoke the analogy of being made by some agent for that purpose.

This is precisely what is denied by Buddhists. Nirvana may for Buddhists be the end of the universe in the sense that samsaric existence can end no other way, but to my knowledge it is never described as the reason why the samsaric

---

12   *Converging Ways*, 101.
13   Ibid., 99.
14   Ibid., 99–100.
15   Ibid., 143.

universe exists. Samsara does not stand in relation to nirvana as means to end; rather, nirvana is conceived of as the alternative to samsara. Rather than being what gives samsara purpose, it is the sheer purposelessness of samsara that impels us to make nirvana our purpose. Schmidt-Leukel equates God and nirvana by making both too like the Platonic form of the good, which indeed is our *telos* without being our origin.

But is Williams's positive understanding of the causality involved in creation tenable? Following Aquinas, he answers the question of why anything exists at all in terms of the Uncreated God, operating not only as the final cause of the cosmos but as literally (albeit analogically)[16] its efficient cause. Does this make sense?

I propose three understandings of causality which do *not* make sense when applied to God's creation of the world, before in the next section moving on to one that may make sense so applied. Crucially I shall argue that this legitimate sense correlates well with Buddhist notions of dependent arising. This will demonstrate the crucial point, that the best way we can make sense of creation in the Christian sense is by invoking the kind of causality that from a Buddhist perspective is described as dependent arising.

a. **Covariance**: As David Hume famously argued,[17] we never directly observe a case of causation. What we actually observe is what he called constant conjunction, but might better be termed the covariance of cause and effect. For Hume, we know x causes y when in the absence of x there is no y, and in the presence of x there is. These ideas are not just Hume's; a primary Buddhist formula for dependent arising runs 'This existing, that exists; this arising, that arises; this not existing, that does not exist; this ceasing, that ceases'.[18]

Now both Hume and the 6th-century-Buddhist Dharmakirti[19] argued that we cannot establish a causal relation of this kind between God and creation. To do so we would have to show that God's existence co-varies with the world's existence: that is, whenever God exists, there is a universe, but also whenever God does not exist, there is no universe. However, if God can fail to exist, God is contingent and himself in need

---

[16]   132. For Aquinas, analogical predication is a case of literal, not metaphorical meaning. I am inclined to agree – see my *Holy Ground* (London: SPCK, 1991), 74–7.

[17]   *A Treatise of Human Nature*, 1.3.6–10.

[18]   For example *Majjhima Nikāya*, 115, *Samyutta Nikāya*, 55.27.

[19]   Cf. Schmidt-Leukel, *Buddhism, Christianity* ...,125.

of a causal explanation. But if God cannot fail to exist, God cannot cause the world in the sense of covarying with it.

b. **Action**: Constant conjunction was probably never a serious candidate for God's causing of the world, but then, intuitively we feel that causality is more than covariance. Hume noted the way we (groundlessly in his view) construe causality as imparting a 'natural necessity'. The effect not only always does follow the cause, but we feel the cause means that it *must* happen: the cause somehow forces the effect to occur, by a natural law. Arguably we do so on the analogy of our experience of making things happen. And obviously, when people think of God making the world, the analogy of human making is close at hand. God is thought of as relating to the world as agent to action. On this understanding, the being of things is the doing of God, the work of the divine artist.

But can such an analogy apply to God, if, on the understanding that has prevailed since the second century,[20] God is the creator of all things out of nothing – the eternal, aspatial and immaterial creator of time, space and matter? In our actions, intentions temporally precede actions, and are in spatial contiguity with the actions and their effects. These features seem to be essential to the very concept of causal action, and therefore not aspects that can be 'stretched' to describe analogically a subject in whom those features are negated. The notion of a timeless efficient causality operating *ex nihilo*, in which time and space are created along with everything else, is not even analogically like the kind of causality whereby we intend things and make them happen within time and space.

c. **Logical Basis or Ground**: Here we move closer, perhaps to what Williams has in mind – though away from what might be called efficient causality. We observe that all things are contingent; logically they might not have existed. Thus far Buddhists agree: nothing is *svabhāva*, self-explanatory or self-existent. Causal explanations like those offered by science can only trace the existence of one contingent thing to another contingent thing or set of things. So if we are not simply to accept (as many Buddhists and scientists do) that there is no final answer to the question why anything exists at all, we need another kind of explanation that can logically

---

[20] Though there are many Old Testament anticipations, notably in deutero-Isaiah, it has been argued that the notion of creation *ex nihilo* became mainstream Christian doctrine as part of the development of second-century apologetics. See Gerhard May, *Creatio ex Nihilo: The Doctrine of 'Creation out of Nothing' in Early Christian Thought* (Edinburgh: T&T Clark, 1994). This view of creation has been disputed, but this chapter has to focus on what is undoubtedly the mainstream Christian tradition.

Creation, Dependent Arising and Dual Belonging   55

ground the existence of things in something that is self-existent and self-explanatory; something which logically could not not have existed, and which has made things exist, grounding their contingency in the divine necessity.

This last alternative might seem to have more to offer. The notion of God as necessary being – as the One who could not fail to exist – is central to Aquinas' arguments for God's existence as well as the ontological argument of Anselm. But it poses many problems, of which here are three. In finding a way to resolve these problems, however, we will find a way to turn the weaknesses of the above causal accounts of creation into the strengths of our alternative.

1. **What kind of causality could connect a necessary and eternal being to a contingent world?**[21] Can the kind of causality we observe operating contingently and spatiotemporally in the world constitute any kind of literal analogy for a logical grounding (whatever that may mean) of contingent beings? The difficulty noted above, in using our human action as analogy for the divine, applies *a fortiori* when the relation involves not any kind of activity at all but a logical necessitating.
2. **Does the idea of a necessary being itself make sense?** A statement is necessarily true if and only if its denial involves a contradiction.[22] In Thomist terms the denial of the existence of God is indeed contradictory; but that is because Thomists define God as *ipsum esse*, existence itself. Outside this particular frame of reference, the statement 'God does not exist' involves no evident contradiction, and is coherently believed by many, including Buddhists.
3. **Why delegate the mystery?** If the idea of necessary being does make sense, why does only God qualify, and not something else, like the universe, or as we shall see, mind?[23] The God who allegedly explains the world, and the sense in which he is necessary or self-explanatory, seems darker and more baffling to the intellect than the universe itself. So what

---

[21] A similar argument is made by the Buddhist Śāntideva (*Bodhicharayavatara*, 9.122 ff).

[22] Cf. Hume, *Dialogues concerning Natural Religion* (Indianapolis, IN: Hackett, 1980) Part 9.189.

[23] See ibid., Part 9.190.

is actually gained by delegating the mystery of the universe to the even greater mystery of God?[24]

For these and other reasons, talk of God as the cause of the world in any of these senses presses analogy beyond the point at which it makes sense, as innumerable Buddhist and Western sceptics bear witness.

Emergence and 'Metacausality'

I now turn to a concept that may describe the kind of creativity we witness in the world without such catastrophic stretching of language. Metacausality is my own term, denoting the kind of causality associated with emergence. Emergence is a term widely supported though not universally accepted in philosophy, systems theory, science and art, naming 'a process whereby larger entities, patterns, and regularities arise through interactions among smaller or simpler entities that themselves do not exhibit such properties'.[25] When systems reach a certain degree of complexity, new qualities and causal and other relations emerge which transcend those that hold between the parts, and are spoken of as operating on a new and higher 'level'.

Philosopher David Chalmers usefully distinguishes between strong and weak emergence. In weak emergence 'truths concerning the [high-level] phenomenon are unexpected given the principles governing the low-level phenomenon'.[26] He believes examples are to be found in the evolution of new forms of life, in the development of intelligent behaviour in the more complex animals and computers and in the surprisingly complex and evolving forms generated from the simple rules of the computer game called 'Life'. In strong emergence, by contrast, 'truths concerning that [higher level] phenomenon are

---

[24] I make this point in *Buddhist Christianity: A Passionate Openness* (Winchester: O-Books, 2010), 224. Richard Dawkins makes a similar point in *The Blind Watchmaker* (Harmondsworth: Penguin, 1988), 316–17 – though I reject his assumption that God would have to be more *complex* than the universe he explains.

[25] Wikipedia entry on 'Emergence'. The term was coined by philosopher G.H. Lewes in 1895. Other useful introductions include Philip Clayton and Paul Davies (eds), *The Re-Emergence of Emergence* (Oxford: Oxford University Press, 2006); Stuart Kauffman, *At Home in the Universe* (New York: Oxford University Press, 1995); Ilya Prigogine and Isabelle Stengers, *Order out of Chaos* (New York: Bantam Books, 1985).

[26] 'Strong and Weak Emergence', http://consc.net/papers/emergence.pdf (2002), also printed in Clayton and Davies (previous note), 1.

Creation, Dependent Arising and Dual Belonging 57

not *deducible* even in principle from truths in the lower-level domain'.[27] The higher level operates on laws distinct from those of the lower levels. Chalmers offers reasons for regarding consciousness as a case (perhaps the only case) of strong emergence, though many would disagree.[28]

However, for our purposes it is not necessary to establish whether Chalmers is right about which cases of strong and weak emergence apply to the world we live in. What is significant for us is that the question of the metacause takes two different forms, equally pertinent. In the case of weak emergence there is the question: 'What causes the simple physical laws to be such that they are capable of giving rise to such complex entities and behaviour?' In the case of strong emergence there is the question: 'If the lower-level laws do not cause the higher level reality (e.g. consciousness) to arise, what does?' And there is a third question which combines the other two: 'Why are things subject to mathematical laws; why are physical things so regularly and reliably constructed that conscious minds can know, predict and use them?' Or in the inverted format in which Stephen Hawking famously asked this question, 'What breathes fire into the equations and makes a universe for them to describe?'[29]

A metacause is therefore a 'cause of causality', an explanation of explicability itself. Since to exist contingently is to be caused to exist by other things, Williams' quest for a ground of our contingency is a quest for the cause of things in their caused-ness: the metacause.

This is not to be confused with the question what causes things to be as they are, which is answerable (in principle) in terms of efficient and final causes. A metacausal question cannot be adequately answered in such terms. To invoke a 'papal neuron'[30] – or Descartes' pineal gland – as the physical entity that causes consciousness would be to confuse levels. To invoke an *élan vital* or life force to explain life, or a *res cogitans* to explain thinking, is to invoke the *explanandum* in the *explanans*, so explaining nothing. We need to move decisively away from such dualistic confusions,[31] in two directions.

The first is to emphasise that it is the whole organism, not some part of it that operates on the higher level. There is no extra force that comes in to create a new life, or consciousness. The chemicals in the cell and the neurons in the brain do

---

[27] 'Strong and Weak Emergence', 1.

[28] David Chalmers, *The Conscious Mind: In Search of a Fundamental Theory* (Oxford: Oxford University Press, 1996).

[29] Stephen Hawking, *A Brief History of Time* (New York: Bantam, 1988), 174

[30] I am unsure of the origin of this elegant phrase.

[31] Though Christian tradition has often framed itself in dualistic terms, this is now widely regarded as a distortion of its Hebrew inheritance.

it all of their own accord, between them, in interdependence with one another, not dependence on one other.[32] The elements work together democratically, we might say, rather than hierarchically, in a manner that suggests the Buddhist 'dependent co-arising'.

The other direction arises from considering Aquinas' description of the final cause as 'cause of causes':

> The end is not the cause of that which is the efficient cause, but it is the cause of the efficient cause being an efficient cause ... Therefore we say that the end is the cause of causes *(finis est causa causarum)* because it is the cause of the causality in all causes.[33]

The end does not then cause the efficient cause itself, but uses the efficient causal operation to achieve the end. As an example to bring this abstract idea down to earth, when I knock a billiard ball down a hole with my cue, I am not causing the cue or the ball to exist, or adding an extra cause to the causal interaction of arm, cue and ball, but rather using their own immanent, efficient causal interaction to finally cause the ball to achieve my desired end, the hole.

So metacausality is on the one hand thoroughly immanent in the interplay of parts in the whole, and on the other hand presupposes development toward a transcendent end. Metacausality is a two-sided coin, one 'Buddhist', one 'Christian'. To see how, we need deepen our understanding of the Buddhist notion, or notions, of *pratītya samutpāda*.

Mind out of Matter, Matter out of Mind

The Mahayana Buddhist monk Thich Nhat Hanh translates this as 'interdependent co-arising', explaining it as follows:

> Cause and effect co-arise *(samutpāda)* and everything is a result of multiple causes and conditions ... In the sutras, this image is given: 'Three cut reeds can stand only by leaning on one another. If you take one away, the other two will fall'. For a table to exist, we need wood, a carpenter, time, skilfulness, and many other causes ...

---

[32] Daniel Dennett provides one of the best arguments to this effect in *Consciousness Explained* (Harmondsworth: Penguin, 1993).

[33] *De Principiis Naturae*, tr. R.A. Kokourek (http://dhspriory.org/thomas/DePrincNaturae.htm) Cap 4.

If we continue to look in this way, we'll see that ... everything in the cosmos has come together to bring us this table.[34]

Elsewhere Thich Nhat Hanh uses the term 'interbeing'. On this broad interpretation, which stands in the Madhyamaka tradition (of which more soon), beings bring one another into existence in an all-pervading chain of causality that has no beginning and no ultimate ground. The idea of spontaneous self-organisation of parts in wholes is applied to the universe, which is seen as one emergent, interdependent whole. Everything in the cosmos stands and falls together like the three reeds, nothing being firmly self-existent (*svabhāva*).

In dialectical relation to this tradition, however, stands a different though not necessarily opposed emphasis developed by the Yogācāra or Mind-Only school of Mahayana Buddhism. This tradition carries through the implications of the early Theravāda texts which describe dependent arising as a process involving 12 *nidānas*, a series of causes of which the original one is ignorance. Ignorance is defined in terms of the duality of consciousness and object, as a falling away from the original unity of *citta*, mind. A familiar Zen *kōan* explains this:

Two monks were arguing about a flag. One said: 'The flag is moving'.
The other said: 'The wind is moving'.
The sixth patriarch happened to be passing by. He told them: 'Not the wind, not the flag; mind is moving'.[35]

As the wind is the cause of the flag's moving, mind is the non-dual cause of the perception of this causality: the flag, the wind and the perception are grounded together in mind.

Now following Cabezón against Williams, mind seems to be a valid candidate for the necessary existent that grounds all other existents. Williams may be right to argue that the idea of a universe without consciousness is not a straightforward contradiction in terms. But there would be a kind of contradiction in knowing that you were in a mindless universe, or in the statement 'I know there is nothing in the universe capable of knowing anything'. There would be an epistemic contradiction (as we might call it) not between the terms of the assertion itself, but between the basis of the assertion and its content – rather as in saying to the person next to you 'I am not here'. The term 'real' includes ideas like truth

---

[34] Thich Nhat Hanh, *The Heart of the Buddha's Teaching* (New York: Three River Press, 1999), 121–2.

[35] Mumon, *The Gateless Gate* no. 29, in Paul Reps, ed. *Zen Flesh, Zen Bones* (Harmondsworth: Penguin, 1957), 117.

and in-principle-knowability, such that a mindless, unknowable universe could not be real. Mind is the basis of our being able to know truths about things; it is what we might call in brief the 'epistemological ground' of things. We have no good reason to believe in things' existence, or affirm any truths about them, unless minds have experienced them or deduced them by (mental) reasoning from experience.

Yogācāra teaches that what we call physical reality is a product of conscious representation (*vijñapti*) plus convention or conceptualisation, which structures our experience into the seemingly solid objects 'out there' which we can describe to ourselves and others. We imagine we see the flag and hear and feel the wind, but the colour of the flag and the sound and chill of the wind are in the mind. Science teaches us that 'out there' is only a movement of particles and waves without colour or sound. Yogācāra would probably go further, and note that the particles and waves are also mathematical, mental constructs. Those familiar with the British empiricist tradition, especially the idealism of Bishop George Berkeley, may feel on familiar ground here.

But as well as being the epistemological ground of existence, mind might qualify as the metacause of why things are as they are, and have the causal laws they have. Cosmologists have begun to wonder what makes the universe so right for the evolution of life and consciousness. The chance of getting just one of these factors (the balance strengths between the basic forces) right for life to form has been calculated as 1 followed-by-60-zeroes.[36] This represents the chance that a blindfolded sniper would hit a one-inch bull's-eye on a target set up at the opposite end of the known universe![37] To explain this amazing just-rightness, cosmologists invoke various forms of the 'anthropic principle'[38]

The most popular, 'weak' form of this invokes the kind of epistemological necessity we have been considering. The universe we observe must be just right for us to evolve because otherwise we would not be here to observe it. In one version of this weak form, a multiverse – an infinity of universes – exist, most without minds; it is then no coincidence that we happen to find ourselves in the one that is right for us to evolve in it! The 'strong' version invokes final causality: a conscious being made the universe just right because he wanted

---

[36] Paul Davies, God and the New Physics (Harmondsworth: Penguin, 1984), 179.

[37] Paul Davies, *The Mind of God: Science and the Search for Ultimate Meaning* (Harmondsworth: Penguin, 1992), 178.

[38] The classic discussion is J.D. Barrow and F.J. Tipler, *The Anthropic Cosmological Principle* (Oxford: Oxford University Press, 1988).

us to evolve in it. And the 'participatory' version developed by John Wheeler[39] invokes the strange kind of backwards causality that (on one interpretation) is involved in the mysterious collapse of the quantum wave function, whereby observation turns an array of possibilities into a specifiable reality. Wheeler argues that the interdependence of the universe is such that it may be regarded as a single quantum system. If so, then it too needs consciousness to collapse it into a determinate reality. The cosmos is therefore like a closed causal loop in which mind emerges (as in conventional science) from matter, but also matter emerges from the quantum collapse generated by mind. If this is so, then there is a physical as well as philosophical basis for regarding mind as constitutive of physical reality.

For our purposes it does not matter which form of explanation we adopt. We can simply propose that the necessarily existent which brings this among all possible worlds into being is something we all experience very directly: mind. The universe and its laws have to be fine-tuned the way they are, so that minds can emerge to know them and so ground their reality. Mind can be described as the metacause of the universe.

Whether this metacause is understood in terms of 'weak' epistemological necessity, 'strong' final causality or 'participatory' quantum causality does not affect the argument. It will, however, influence the 'angle' we take on mind and the universe. In the terms soon to be invoked, a 'weak' understanding will predispose us to either a materialist or an 'emptiness' understanding whereby the universe is a self-sustaining mystery. A 'strong' understanding will lead to an understanding in terms of divine creation. And a 'participatory' understanding will lend support to a 'mind-only' viewpoint, though it is not the only way of getting there.

'Mind' and Minds

First, however, we need to clarify 'mind' and 'consciousness', terms we have used rather impressionistically, perhaps too easily conflating them with Buddhist *citta*. Do we mean by these terms the individual mind, some kind of collectivity of human and perhaps other consciousnesses, or a supreme divine Mind as ultimate subject of all consciousness, thinker of all possible thoughts, and ground of all

---

[39] See Paul Davies, *The Goldilocks Enigma: Why is the Universe Just Right for Life?* (London: Penguin Books, 2007). Also from a more Buddhist perspective, Graham Smetham, *Quantum Buddhism: Dancing in Emptiness* (Brighton: Shunyata Press, 2010), 241–76.

things including those we do not and perhaps cannot know?.[40] And do we mean experience, awareness and consciousness, or thought, conceptualisation and reason? These ambiguities pervade the notion of the quantum collapse – where it is not always clear what counts as an 'observation' – as well as the Yogācāra understanding. In the latter the focus is on the 'mindset' of the meditating individual, and has connotations of will and emotion as much as cognition. But the notion that the individual's mindset is the basis of everything would colossally aggrandise the ego, the very delusion from which the meditator is seeking release. *Citta* must mean, as noted in connection with the *kōan*, that which falls through ignorance into duality, resulting in a fragmented mindset subject to egocentric striving after supposed objects. Conversely, mind is what apprehends reality as it is, non-dually, after the cessation of ego and striving in nirvana? Mind is therefore much wider than the ego's limited consciousness. Hence Buddha-hood is often linked with divine-sounding attributes like omniscience.

What a Western heir to Greek and Enlightenment rationalism, or even a Postmodernist exalting the primacy of language, might find missing in this Buddhist account, however, is the role of language, reason and dialogue in the movement from individual consciousness to something like a common mind. By mutual exchange through languages and cultures we create concepts, symbols and life practices which feed back into the way we structure and transmute our conscious experience into the experience of a common world.[41] Some of the languages we use, notably mathematics and scientific procedures, seem to be capable of generating a global consensus regarding how the world 'really is'. Others remain local cultural or religious worlds, lacking this global consensus, and often dismissed by the mathematico-scientific purists as purely imaginary, though real enough for participants. It is the conceptual worlds (pre-eminently the mathematical) that Plato regarded as more supremely real than the physical, and which Karl Popper has rehabilitated with his notion of a 'World 3' alongside Worlds 1 (matter) and 2 (subjective consciousness).[42]

---

[40] George Berkeley famously invoked God to secure the continued existence of things that nobody is currently experiencing. Keith Ward, in Berkleyan but also Augustinian and Thomist tradition, argues that concepts – including those we that are beyond our own conceiving – are realities existing in the mind of God (*Pascal's Fire*, Oxford: Oneworld, 2006, 87–8).

[41] This has been noted by innumerable philosophers, pre-eminently Merleau-Ponty among continentals, and Wittgenstein in the Anglo-Saxon tradition.

[42] Karl Popper, *Objective Knowledge: An Evolutionary Approach* (Oxford: Clarendon Press, 1972) Chapter 3.

Creation, Dependent Arising and Dual Belonging   63

The mind-matter loop then is an oversimplification. To consciousness and matter we need to add a third arena, which is the conceptual world in all its variety. The loop then becomes a threefold cycle involving (in Chalmers' sense) the strong emergence of worlds. Mathematician Roger Penrose describes the three 'mysteries' involved:

> There is the mystery of why such precise and profoundly mathematical laws play such an important role in the behaviour of the physical world. Somehow the very world of physical reality seems almost mysteriously to emerge out of the Platonic world of mathematics ... There is the second mystery of how it is that perceiving beings can arise from out of the physical world. How is it that subtly organised material objects can mysteriously conjure up mental entities from out of its material substance? ... Finally, there is the mystery of how it is that mentality is able seemingly to 'create' mathematical concepts out of some kind of mental model.[43]

Four Angles on a Threefold Mystery

It is now not difficult to see how Buddhist dependent co-arising and Christian creation represent different angles on the fundamental threefold mystery. The mystery is rather like an Escher picture[44] in which stairs rise from one another in turn, such that, though some levels are higher than others, there is no ultimately bottom or top level. When looking at the picture we can treat one level as foundational, and the others as arising from it, but then after a while we notice the stairs rising to that level from the others, and the Gestalt shifts to a different perspective. There are likewise several ways in which we can reduce the threefold mystery to a manageable perspective. Here are four ways that are relevant to our argument.

a. **Materialism**: The familiar linear story, well broadcast on the TV channels, in which physical matter, originating in a mysterious big bang, evolves

---

[43]   Roger Penrose, *Shadows of the Mind: A Search for the Missing Science of Consciousness* (Oxford: Oxford University Press, 1994), 413–14. Penrose describes the conceptual world mainly in terms of mathematics, whereas I would also emphasise the 'worlds' evoked by culture, religion and art.

[44]   I have in mind especially works like *Relativity* (1953) and *Ascending and Descending* (1960). These and other Escher prints are discussed extensively as a model of reality in Douglas Hofstadter, *Gödel, Escher, Bach: An Eternal Golden Braid* (Hemel Hempstead: Harvester Press, 1979).

into life, the world of genes. This in turn gives rise to consciousness, and consciousness produces the world of 'memes': ideas, art, religion and mathematics; the world of all possible worlds which we could justly call a 'multiverse'. The 'cut' in the loop that gives rise to this linear progression, however, the mystery that is suppressed, is how the multiverse of conceptual worlds collapses into this particular universe, which organises itself just so as to give rise to life, consciousness and the multiverse itself. Buddhists and Christians alike reject materialism as an all-encompassing metaphysic, but it represents a widely held story with which both need to engage.[45]

b. **Mind-Only**: This is the opposite approach, cutting the loop at the point where consciousness emerges from matter, so as to render consciousness the fundamental reality – consciousness which through primordial ignorance loses its original nirvanic non-duality to generate a world of individual ego-minds and desired objects. Hence the world is logically constructed out of and teleologically informed by mind, mind that will achieve its full dimensions only when released into nirvana. Most Christians and many Buddhists would not wish to follow the metaphysics here all the way; but many would affirm that it rings profoundly true in the practice of meditation.

c. **Emptiness**: Here the cycle of mysteries is accepted for what it is. Consciousness, concept and matter rest on one another like the three reeds. All depend on one another and ultimately there is nothing that grounds them and gives anything *svabhāva*, self-existence. The loop between mind and object is left as a closed circle:

> The object is an object for the subject,
> The subject is a subject for the object;
> Know that the relativity of the two
> rests ultimately on one emptiness.[46]

The Madhyamaka School relate co-arising to the notion of emptiness (*śūnyatā*,) – the transience and bottomless-ness of all that is – and *tathātā* – generally translated suchness or just-so-ness. There follows a simple, but often joyful, acceptance of the world's contingency.

---

[45] It figures for me personally as a third dialogue partner with Buddhism and Christianity, but not as a kind of umpire to which the others must give account.

[46] Huang Po (third Zen patriarch), *On Trust in the Heart*, 13 (Cited Christmas Humphreys, *The Wisdom of Buddhism* (London: Rioder, 1970), 178).

d. **Creation through Metacausality**: Here again the whole cycle is present, but with emphasis on the conceptual worlds, conceiving of God as the Mind that is conscious of all such worlds.[47] God creates this particular world, not as some unfathomable kind of efficient cause, but rather as cause of space, time and causality: as metacause, understood, in this perspective, as a kind of final cause. The physical world is created such that it will give rise to minds capable of communing intersubjectively with one another and with the Mind of God.

In this context the idea of God creating the world through a free act of choice becomes an appropriate analogy. It is through choice that an array of possibilities reduces to a particular path of action. But we need to be clear how the concepts need to be stretched to fit the infinite and eternal God. As creator of time, God makes, loves and knows the world from eternity. Moreover the making, loving and knowing cannot be distinguished. Within time a making involves an idea in the mind prior to its realisation in the world. An act of knowing involves an idea in the mind subsequent upon the known reality in the world. An act of loving involves a co-presence of lover and beloved. But if God is eternal there can for Him be neither prior nor subsequent, neither before nor after. As eternal mind, God creates in and through knowing and does both through loving.[48]

I suggest that through being understood in terms of the threefold pattern, each of the four alternatives is improved by being brought into the kind of relation to the others that enables transformative dialogue. Buddhism and Christianity are enabled to become what Daniel Strange in his article calls the 'subversive fulfilment'[49] of each other, in his sense of giving ultimate answers to questions the other religion asks but cannot answer in its own terms.

For example, (d) resolves difficulties encountered in formulating the divine causality, answering the three questions posed above.

1. Metacausality is a kind of causality that could *connect a necessary and eternal reality to a contingent world*. Mind itself is necessary and eternal (measuring time from physical regularities in its contents) and imparts necessity to the way the world is, as necessary for its own existence. The sun does not just always rise each day; it *must* rise each day, because

---

[47] See note 40.

[48] Some readers will be reminded of Augustine's analogy of the Trinity, as-co inherent knowledge, love and will.

[49] See 86.

Buddhist-Christian Dual Belonging

without this and a host of other regularities on which mind depends for its knowing, mind would not be. And then the sun would not be either.

2. *The necessary existence of mind makes sense*, because, as argued above, the mind-less universe is by definition thought-less and in that sense unthinkable: an epistemic contradiction.

3. *There is no delegation to a greater mystery.* Mind is something we all experience and partly understand, though of course mind is also very mysterious and intangible. It is at once personal (since having mind, including thought, feeling, intention, communication, distinguishes what is personal) and impersonal (since mind is only realised by transcending the ego). Mind operates in the universe, and we all know it because we all have a share of mind. We do not need to deny that God, as Mind, is real and personal; but our reality, as Aquinas put it, adapting Plato, arises from our own participation in God as minds in Mind.

To complete the argument we would need to show not only that some Christian conundrums are resolved by thinking of creation in a more Buddhist way, but that some Buddhist ways of thinking are likewise resolved by a more Christian approach. It might be shown, for example, that the threefold model enriches and corrects a certain simplification involved in the concepts of duality and non-duality. The concept of World 3 as a third term beyond the physical-mental duality might enable us to affirm more fully the beauty and reality of conceptual worlds, including both mathematical and religious worlds. Though profoundly imaginary and 'constructed', these are not to be dismissed as mere delusion.[50]

Conclusion

I suggest our threefold model enables us to see the differing Buddhist and Christian (and secular-scientific) understandings as differing perspectives on 'how things are'. Each has strengths and weaknesses. But each could be true, while none represents the only right way to state the whole truth. And while the model might be criticised for promoting the 'three mysteries' as the exclusive

---

[50] On the other hand as Cabezón argues (*Converging Ways*, 112ff.), in practice the Mahayana Buddhist emphasis on the imaginary and constructed nature (in ultimate terms) of *all* we take for reality offers a way of stressing the reality (in conventional terms) of imagined worlds. The many Buddhas, Bodhisattvas, Meditation-Buddhas, Deities and Pure Lands, in Mahayana and especially Tibetan Buddhism, are as conventionally real as we are, and we ultimately as imaginary as they.

truth, it involves no Procrustean bed, but openness precisely to mysteries. Clarity only appears in the four perspectives.

The threefold model helps overcome the widespread misconception of the religions as impermeable parallel universes, offering a framework for a robust dialogue which could both reaffirm and challenge traditional understandings. For example, it might suggest new, 'polydox'[51] ways of reading both the Christian Trinity and the Mahayana *trikāya* (three 'bodies' of Buddha), both of which already have many interpretations, so as to negotiate a bridge between them.[52]

It is true that I have focused very specifically on just one Buddhist doctrine, *pratītya samutpāda*, and one Christian doctrine, creation. But these doctrines inform the other teachings, with which there are in both religions close interconnections. So I suggest the framework just established might also liberate dialogue concerning other dichotomies between Buddhism and Christianity. It is not hard to begin to apply it to different ways of looking at salvation and nirvana, say, or the eternal soul and *anattā*.

The dialogue may take place within the mind of a dual belonger. Most dual belongers seem to find it impossible to enter imaginatively into both Buddhist and Christian perspectives at once; they describe themselves as undergoing perspective shifts between the two.[53] Our model offers a way of welcoming this shift in viewpoint, because it is not a prevarication or evasion of reality but a grasp of something 'Escherian' in the way things are. The logical reasons advanced for choosing just one perspective have lost their initial appearance of rigour.[54] There is sufficient convergence on the crucial issues concerning creation and co-arising at least to make for the kind of rich and coherent life practice in the here and now for which Drew argues in this volume. The different perspectives form a continuum, a bridge of visions across which a Buddhist-Christian can roam with integrity. There may be other viewpoints that could be incorporated or generated too, and there is much room for creative exploration by Buddhists, Christians and Buddhist-Christians alike.

---

[51] See Catherine Keller and Laurel Schneider, eds, *Polydoxy: Theology of Multiplicity and Relation* (London: Routledge, 2011).

[52] Consider the 'Inscendent Trinity' proposed in Thompson, *Buddhist Christianity* (see note 23), 262–9.

[53] Rose Drew, *Buddhist and Christian? an Exploration of Dual Belonging* (London and New York: Routledge, 2011), 211ff.

[54] That is not to say there may not be worthy reasons of other kinds – cultural, personal, aesthetic, ethical and so on – for making a choice; but may there not also be worthy reasons of these kinds for *not* making a choice?

PART II
Challenges

Chapter 4

'There Can Be Only One': The Impossibility and Idolatry of 'Dual Belonging'

Daniel Strange

I currently inhabit a rewarding but uncomfortable dual belonging. I 'live and move and have my being' in a confessionally conservative evangelical theological seminary. On occasion, however, I choose to breathe in the air of a very different religious world of which this symposium, in my *alma mater*, has been an instance. Part of the discomfort concerns the utter incredulity amongst my students and colleagues that not only might there be a category of 'multiple religious' belonging, but that it is populated! Having mapped out the terrain of the theology of religions, got to grips with typology and its problems, both understood and critiqued various positions, we now discover that we need an updated map which has a territory marked liminality. Of course this incredulity works both ways, for I know that for most taking part in our symposium, the argument I propounded would be novel and scandalous not because it was new and original, but precisely because it was not: There are people who still believe this?

Knowing therefore the nature of these two theological communities so often hermetically sealed from each other, part of the reward in participating in a project like this, was that mutual understanding and plausibility could be increased, caricatures torn down and friendships established: which I hope they were. While I recognise that my conclusions concerning dual belonging are strongly negative, I hope I am not rude, ungracious or aggressive in the way I tackle these important issues. Apart from my previous interactions with Paul Knitter, the phenomenon of dual belonging has been relatively new to me and so it has been immensely helpful in getting to grips with the area by interacting first hand with the other participants in this symposium. Similarly, for these other participants, while I in no way claim to represent the 400 million or so professing evangelical Christians in the world,[1] I hope they are able to witness a cogent and clear articulation of my own stance on dual belonging within this tradition, a tradition which wishes to see itself as within the stream of historic orthodox Christian belief.[2]

To understand the claims I wish to make about dual belonging it is necessary to take up a little bit of space in some matters of prolegomena, although as I hope will be recognised, prolegomena which is in reality part of my argument proper.

I wish to define religions, religious traditions and their adherents in terms of the concept of 'worldview'. As David Naugle has pointed out, defining 'worldview' depends upon one's worldview![3] My definition of worldview is set within the grand Christian metanarrative of Creation – De-Creation – Re-Creation. For our purposes here, *creation* bespeaks a certain commonality and continuity, and *de-creation*, a radical discontinuity and difference.

With this context in mind let us return to worldview and bring in our theme of dual belonging. The first claim I wish to establish concerns the coherence and possibility of dual belonging,[4] given the radical difference and dissimilarity

---

[1] This is the figure of those in churches affiliated to the *World Evangelical Alliance*. Other surveys tend to range from between 300–600 million depending on whether charismatic/Pentecostal Christianity are included as evangelicals or not.

[2] Academic evangelical engagement with the explicit topic of 'multiple religious belonging' has not been voluminous. One evangelical who has engaged specifically with dual belonging is Kang-San Tan. See his 'Dual Belonging: A Missiological Critique and Appreciation from an Asian Evangelical Perspective', *Mission Studies* 27 (2010): 24–38; 'Can Christians Belong to More than One Religious Tradition?', *Evangelical Review of Theology* 34:3 (2010): 250–64. See also Prabo Mihindukulasuriya, 'Without Christ I could not be a Buddhist: An Evangelical Response to Christian Self-understanding in a Buddhist Context', *Current Dialogue* 51 (December 2001): 73–85. More implicitly, evangelicals have been engaging for quite some time with the issue of 'multiple religious belonging'. This is evidenced in two areas. The first concerns 'C5/insider movements' within Islamic settings. For a comprehensive literature review of this area see Matthew Sleeman, 'The Origins, Development and Future of the C5/Insider Movement Debate', *St Francis Magazine* 8:4 (August 2012): 498–566, available at: http://www.stfrancismagazine.info/ja/images/stories/SFMAugust2012-6.pdf. The second area concerns the relationship between Israel and Christian theology with obvious applications in terms of Jewish-Christian relationships and dialogue. For an introduction into this discussion see Adam Sparks, *One of a Kind: The Relationship between Old and New Covenants as the Hermeneutical Key for Christian Theology of Religions* (Eugene, OR: Pickwick, 2010), 73–117.

[3] David Naugle, *Worldview: The History of a Concept* (Grand Rapids, IN: Eerdmans, 2002).

[4] Recognising the many different types of dual belonging (DB) which Catherine delineates in her essay and which were helpfully teased out further during our time together at the symposium.

of religious worldviews. This is a variation of a theme (in)famously laid down Hendrik Kraemer in 1938:

> In the first place, religion is nowhere in the world an assortment of spiritual commodities, that can be compared as shoes or neck-ties. This sounds frivolous, nevertheless it is a point of such overwhelming importance that it can hardly be over-estimated. It ought never to be forgotten in the treatment of religious subjects – but it constantly is – that religion is the vast and desperate effort of mankind to get somehow an apprehension of the totality of existence, and therefore every religion is an indivisible, and not to be divided, unity of existential apprehension. It is not a series of tenets, dogmas, prescriptions, institutions and practices, that can be taken one by one as independent items of religious life, conception or organization, and that can arbitrarily be compared with, and somehow related to, and grafted upon, the similar item of another religions. Every religion is a living indivisible unity. Every part of it – a dogma, a rite, a myth, an institution, a cult – is so vitally related to the whole that it can never be understood in its real function, significance and tendency, as these occur in the reality of life without keeping constantly in mind that vast and living unity of existential apprehension in which this part moves and has its being.[5]

Religious worldviews can be likened to trees with roots (ultimate presuppositions) that feed trunks (metanarrative), branches (ontology, epistemology, ethics and aesthetics) and fruit (doctrines, praxis and ritual).[6] Given the systemic/organic totalitarian nature and function of worldviews, there is simply no liminal space for the dual belonger to occupy which does not fatally compromise their two or more 'belongings'. When it comes to Christian-Buddhist dual belonging, and when it comes to the topic of 'God', we have an instance of this incompatibility at possibly its most acute. To put it starkly, there is an explicit, root and presuppositional theocentricity to the Christian worldview which is all-pervasive – from theological method, to every doctrinal locus, to overall *telos* – which is inimical to Buddhism in all its various schools. This radical difference is denied in dual belonging which means that dual belonging itself must be denied.[7]

---

[5] Hendrik Kraemer, *The Christian Message in a Non-Christian World* (London: Edinburgh House, 1938), 135.

[6] See Ted Turnau, *Popologetics: Popular Culture in Christian Perspective* (Phillipsburg, NJ: P&R, 2012), 7–17.

[7] In terms of other contributions within this book, Tilakaratne confirms this point from the Buddhist side, but Thompson questions it as a Dual Belonger.

74 *Buddhist-Christian Dual Belonging*

This is not all however. As well as questioning dual belonging intellectually in terms of coherence, a second claim concerns the moral culpability of dual belonging. Unlike certain postmodern/postliberal trajectories in the theology of religions,[8] radical difference *does not* imply incommensurability between worldviews, suggesting an inability to judge between them. The Christian understanding of creation, unpacked in doctrines such as the *imago Dei* and the *sensus divinitas*, establishes a universal correspondence and accountability between the Creator God and all of created humanity (albeit a negatively de-creative idolatrous one),[9] and between the Christian faith and the Religious Other (albeit the latter being a false counterfeit of the former). Again, this is most acute when we come to the loci of God and ultimate reality. Christianity declares ultimate reality to be the transcendentally unique self-contained ontological Trinity revealed supremely in Jesus Christ.[10] To deny not only the existence of ultimate reality but the revealed exclusivity and particularity of this ultimate reality is not only ontologically and epistemologically incoherent, but is a denial of the *telos* of all things: the *soli Deo Gloria*. Moreover, dual belonging is ethically sinful for it is the claim that both the true and the counterfeit are equal. It amounts to an act of spiritual adultery from our covenantal betrothal to Christ, and therefore must be repented of. It is this theme of God and his glory which will act as an organising theme for my exposition.

A final introductory remark concerns the theological method with which I make such statements. Here we have our first instantiation of my theocentricity (or maybe better 'theo-dependence') point made above, for such bold claims are defensible and explicable only because of the ontological reality of the God I have just described. My *pou stō* (place to stand) is that of the divine biblical revelation and affirmation of *sola Scriptura*.[11] In other words even this

---

[8] As described by Paul Hedges in 'Particularities: Tradition-Specific Post-modern Perspectives', in Alan Race and Paul Hedges, eds, *Christian Approaches to Other Faiths SCM Core Text* (London: SCM, 2008), 112–35.

[9] I have expounded a detailed theology of religions in my recent monograph *For Their Rock is not as our Rock: An Evangelical Theology of Religions* (Nottingham: Apollos, 2014).

[10] It should be said here that my Christology from 'within' (that is within the promise/fulfilment structure of the Old Testament), equates the identity and action of the historical Jesus of Nazareth with the God of Israel. Jesus Christ is YHWH and Lord. See Larry W. Hurtado, *Lord Jesus Christ: Devotion to Jesus in Earliest Christianity* (Grand Rapids, IN: Eerdmans, 2003); Richard Bauckham, *God Crucified: Monotheism and Christology in the New Testament* (Grand Rapids, IN: Eerdmans, 1998).

[11] Being one of the *solas* of the Reformation. As Ward helpfully points out, 'The Reformer's conviction of *sola Scriptura* is the conviction that Scripture is the only infallible authority, the only supreme authority. Yet it is not the only authority, for the creeds and

point of epistemological prolegomena is *theo* soaked, for ontology precedes epistemology. The self-attesting, personal and ultimate authority of the Bible is precisely that because it is *theopneustos* from a God who is self-attesting, personal and absolute. This Living God 'speaks' and is one with whom creatures can have a covenantal I-Thou relationship. The Bible is replete with personal names, personal descriptions and personal actions of this God. One thinks of Barth's words here, 'The doubtful thing is not whether God is a person, but whether we are'.[12] Such an epistemology can be called 'transcendent foundationalism':

> The theory agrees with immanent Foundationalism that certain, beginning points are necessary for all human knowledge. The beginning point, however, is not found within the observable creation or neutral reason. All true thoughts begin within a relationship with the invisible Creator, his comprehensive truth system, and his true data points, which exist outside the human mind ... sin and incautious perception can distort perceived information. The Holy Spirit unbends and heals the distortion caused by sin ... .Therefore facts exists that are not first interpreted by human minds. God is the original Creator and interpreter. Humans must think God's thoughts after him in order to know certain truths and factuality.[13]

We note, of course, the 'analogous' and 'anthropomorphic' nature of all religious language, what Calvin evocatively called God's 'lisping'.[14] Such accommodation is testimony to our creaturely ectypal dependence upon and distinction from a totally independent Creator whose knowledge is archetypal. Thus both God's transcendence and immanence are affirmed in the doctrine of revelation. Indeed just to make sure we get the direction right, maybe referring to religious language as 'anthropomorphic' is misleading, since 'it is important to keep in mind that, according to the Scriptures, God created humanity in *his* image (*contra Feuerbach*). The human capacities to know, will and love are

---

the church's teaching function as important subordinate authorities, under the authority of Scripture'. Tim Ward, *Words of Life: Scripture as the Living and Active Word of God* (Nottingham: IVP, 2009), 149. I would want to locate my evangelical heritage as being faithful to a number of Reformation confessions and traced back further to the Ecumenical Creeds.

[12]   Karl Barth, *Church Dogmatics*, 4 vols (Edinburgh: T&T Clark, 1956–75), 1.1., 139.

[13]   Mark Kreitzer, *The Concept of Ethnicity in the Bible: A Theological Analysis* (London: Edwin Mellen, 2008), 426.

[14]   John Calvin, *Institutes of the Christian Religion*, Book I:13:1.

76 Buddhist-Christian Dual Belonging

themselves theomorphic: "God's unconditional concern for justice is not an anthropomorphism. Rather man's concern for justice is a theomorphism".[15]

Finally, even the qualities and character of Scripture is a reflection of a triune God for we see both unity-in-diversity and diversity-in-unity. Drawing on the intertextuality in literary theory of Plett, Bakhtin and Ricouer, Ward calls this 'canonically limited polyphony'.[16]

The epistemology just sketched out is antithetical to that of Buddhism where metaphysically ultimate reality is called into question. As The Dalai Lama has stated:

> The entire Buddhist worldview is based on a philosophical standpoint in which the central thought is the principle of inter-dependence, how all things and events come into being purely as a result of interaction between causes and conditions. Within that philosophical worldview it is almost impossible to have any room for an atemporal, eternal, absolute truth, Nor is it possible to accommodate the concept of a divine Creation.[17]

To a Christian, this is problematic and raises a number of apologetic questions which go beyond the remit of this chapter. What is pertinent though is how a dual belonger can affirm both theological methods and accounts of the nature of religious language, given the completely different starting points. A dual belonger like Paul Knitter attempts to do this in his affirmation of non-dualistic and impersonal Inter-Being, but to reiterate a point made in my previous (and lively) dialogue with Paul himself, how can this provide a solid authoritative basis for rationality, language, knowledge and ethics, not least the claim of the legitimacy of dual belonging?[18] I do not know how *'Biblia locuta, causa finita'*[19] (how Paul summarised my theological method) and *'Experienta locuta, causa finita"*[20] (how I summarised Paul's) can both be affirmed at the same time.

---

[15] Kevin Vanhoozer, *Remythologizing Theology: Divine Action, Passion, and Authorship* (Cambridge, CUP), 64.

[16] Timothy Ward, 'The Diversity and Sufficiency of Scripture', in Paul Helm and Carl Trueman, eds, *The Trustworthiness of God: Perspectives on the Nature of Scripture* (Grand Rapids, IN: Eerdmans, 2002), 214.

[17] His Holiness the Dalai Lama, *The Good Heart: A Buddhist Perspective on the Teachings of Jesus*, ed. Robert Kiely and translated by Geshe Thupten Jinpa (Boston, MA: Wisdom Publications, 1996), 82.

[18] See Gavin D'Costa, Paul Knitter and Daniel Strange, *Only One Way? Three Christian Responses on the Uniqueness of Christ in a Religiously Plural World* (London: SCM, 2011).

[19] 'The Bible has spoken, the case is closed'.

[20] 'Experience has spoken, the case is closed'.

In saying this I am aware of stamping (with big dogmatic boots!) all over Dupuis' contention that 'double belonging is a delicate field, in which theology ought to abstain from *a priori* pronouncements by way of deduction from accepted principles and traditional positions'.[21] I cannot see though, how my 'first theological act'[22] can be other than the 'from above' Scripture, for to start 'from below' would be to question my entire evangelical theological method. I do not believe such a method negates concrete experience and the fascinating qualitative research of someone like Rose Drew.[23] However such a method may well relativise it, giving a normative interpretative grid through which such experiences are to be ultimately evaluated. It is certainly a method which clashes head on with Paul's own theological method which is a form of American Pragmatism.

1. The God of Glory who Creates for His Glory

The Westminster Larger Catechism (1647), one of the touchstones of Reformed Christian belief, begins its 196 questions as follows:

Q. 1. *What is the chief and highest end of man?*
A. Man's chief and highest end is to glorify God, and fully to enjoy him forever.

The *telos* of the Christian Faith and of which all subordinate purposes and ends are ultimately subsumed, is solely focused on the Christian God and His glory – that is the manifestation of His infinite beauty, worth and perfection: his 'God-ness'. The alpha and omega of all existence is a 'somethingness' rather than a nothingness, indeed a personal 'someoneness' who reveals Himself as YHWH, the self-contained ontological Trinity, supremely revealed in His Son the Lord Jesus Christ, 'the radiance of the Father's glory and the exact representation of his being'.[24] I will describe in more detail this God shortly, but my opening point concerns the grounds for the intelligibility of this *telos* which is predicated on metaphysical concepts like creation and creature, and a basic 'outwardness' and 'exteriority' of this creation towards an ontologically real Creator. Without these basic concepts and building blocks, the Christian

---

[21] Jacques Dupuis, S.J. 'Christianity and Religions: Complementarity and Convergence', in ed. Catherine Cornille, *Many Mansions*, 68.

[22] Ibid., 69.

[23] Rose Drew, *Buddhist and Christian*: *An Exploration in Dual Belonging* (London: Routledge, 2011).

[24] Heb. 1:3.

worldview makes no sense and loses its identity as Christian. Even the *evangel* itself (and I say this as an 'evangelical') has this ultimate end, 'God's great and first design, in and by the gospel, is eternally to glorify himself, his wisdom, goodness, love, grace, righteousness, and holiness by Jesus Christ and in order to do this his great and supreme end, he hath designed the gospel'.[25] As the Lord Jesus Himself prays:

> Father, the hour has come. Glorify your Son, that your Son may glorify you. For you granted him authority over all people that he might give eternal life to all those you have given him. Now this is eternal life: that they know you, the only true God, and Jesus Christ, whom you have sent. I have brought you glory on earth by finishing the work you gave me to do. And now, Father, glorify me in your presence with the glory I had with you before the world began. (Jn. 17:1–5)

Before returning to the theme of glory, let us dwell a little longer on the metaphysics of the Christian God and His creation.

The Apostle Paul's Areopagus address in Acts 17 neatly distils for us not only a description of the Christian God in contradistinction to other 'gods', but the foundational importance of affirming this God for the coherence of the entire Christian worldview. Having been distressed by a city submerged in idolatry (v. 16),[26] he preaches the good news of Christ and the resurrection but is not understood. His subsequent address has the aim of providing a systematic and redemptive-historical metanarrative which makes sense of the gospel he has been proclaiming. Stripped back to the bare essentials, we note what makes a Christian worldview 'Christian'. Fundamental is the Creator-creature distinction, 'The God who made the world and everything in it is the Lord of heaven and earth' (v. 24). This is an elementary ABC of orthodox Christian belief and the opposite of any non-dualist metaphysic. Revelation 4:11 captures this well: 'You are worthy, our Lord and God, to receive glory and honor and power, for you created all things, and by your will they were created and have their being'.

God is distinctively a personal absolute and absolute personality. On the one hand He is transcendent (but not 'wholly other' to creation) in that he 'does not need anything' (v.25). The One who describes himself as YHWH is the transcendently unique self-contained ontological Trinity. The term 'transcendent uniqueness' comes from Bauckham:

---

[25] John Owen, *The Works of John Owen*, ed. William H. Goold, vol. 3: Pneumatologia: A Discourse Concerning the Holy Spirit (Edinburgh: T&T Clark, n.d.), 377.

[26] What forms the discursive framing for the whole narrative.

> The essential element in what I have called Jewish monotheism, the element that makes it a kind of monotheism, is not the denial of the existence of other 'gods', but an understanding of the uniqueness of YHWH that puts him in a class of his own, a wholly different class from any other heavenly or supernatural beings, even if these are called 'gods'. I call this YHWH's transcendent uniqueness. (Mere 'uniqueness' can be what distinguishes one member of a class from other members of it. By 'transcendent uniqueness' I mean a form of uniqueness that puts YHWH in a class of his own). Especially important for identifying this transcendent uniqueness are statements that distinguish YHWH by means of a unique relationship to the whole of reality: YHWH alone is Creator of all things, whereas all other things are created by him; and YHWH alone is the sovereign Lord of all things, whereas all other things serve or are subject to his universal lordship.[27]

This 'self-containedness', or independence (aseity) is inextricably related to God's unity, his triunity, and his sovereignty in that he is the 'all-conditioner'[28] not subject to any impersonal principles outside of Himself.

However, this same God is also immanent (but not identical to creation) in that 'he is not far from each one of us' (v. 27). He is God who reveals Himself and His glory: 'The heavens declare the glory of God; the skies proclaim the work of his hands. Day after day they pour forth speech; night after night they reveal knowledge' (Ps. 19:1–2).

While creation is not God, God reveals Himself in his creation both in His unity and diversity. Creation is both one and many. There is an ontological reality, physicality and 'giveness' to this creation which is created good. The apex of this creation are those made in the *imago Dei*, who are 'very good'.[29] In expounding the nature of this image, we can mention a revelational aspect being finite 'analogues' of God; and a representational aspect whereby we are tasked to be God's vicegerents, undertaking the cultural mandate[30] under God's norms and for his glory. However most relevant here might be the relational aspect. There is a relational ontology to human personhood which is not simply about human-to-human relations but most basically our covenantal relationship to the

---

[27] Richard Bauckham, 'Biblical Theology and the Problems of Monotheism', in Craig Bartholomew, ed., *Out of Egypt: Biblical Theology and Biblical Interpretation* (Grand Rapids, IN: Zondervan, 2004), 211.

[28] Cornelius Van Til, 'Why I Believe in God', in Greg Bahnsen, *Van Til's Apologetic: Readings and Analysis* (Phillipsburg, NJ: P&R, 1998), 130.

[29] Gen. 1:31.

[30] The commission in Genesis to fill and subdue the earth, and to tend and keep the garden.

triune God. Humans are *homo adorans*, dependent upon and responsible not to a generic deity but to this triune Creator God, and with wholistic God-given appetites and desires which when rightly directed are to be enjoyed in God's physical creation and under God's ethical norms.

Is not this brief sketch in complete contrast to the Buddhist metaphysical concepts of *dukkha*, *anattā*, *anicca* and *nirvana*, and even after attempts to try and 'Christianise' them in some way?

2. Idolatry as the Failure to Give God Glory

If we are to measure all things from the *telos* of God's glory then we should not be surprised to see a recurring theme throughout Scripture that YHWH is rightly jealous of his own name, and acts for the sake of His name and reputation, for His name is inextricably linked with His glory: 'I am the Lord; that is my name; my glory I give to no other, nor my praise to carved idols' (Is 42:8).[31]

As Bauckham writes, 'We may have difficulty with this picture of God desiring and achieving fame for himself, something we would regard as self-seeking vanity and ambition if it were said of a human being. But this is surely one of those human analogies which is actually appropriate uniquely to God. The good of God's human creatures requires that he be known to them as God. There is no vanity, only revelation of truth, in God's demonstrating his deity to the nations'.[32] Moreover, to talk of God seeking his own glory can never be seen as an act of narcissism or solipsism for we are not speaking of a monadic ultimate reality but rather a trinity where the Father, Son and Spirit have been glorifying the other Persons from eternity.

If the doctrine of a Creator and a creation is a fundamental part of Christian belief, then so too is a 'Fall'. The essence of this doctrinal loci is not merely finitude or ignorance, but is rather theocentrically defined as not giving God the glory due his name,[33] a 'falling short of God's glory'.[34] There is an act of de-creation going on here, for sin can be defined as a blurring, unpicking or even denial

---

[31] See also Isa. 48:9–11.

[32] Richard Bauckham, *The Bible and Mission* (Carlisle: Paternoster, 2003), 37. I recognise that my understanding as to the nature of YHWH together with historical-critical issues of the 'evolution' of Israelite religion are very different from that of someone like Ross Thompson in *Buddhist Christianity*, 232–42. For a more detailed explanation of my position here see, *For Their Rock is Not as Our Rock*, 155–213.

[33] Rom. 1:21.

[34] Ibid. 3:23.

of the Creator-creature distinction, for it replaces the Creator with something created thus bringing God down to the level of the created and pushing ourselves up in place of God. As a result God is not glorified but creation. This is idolatry. Moreover, idolatry is an act of 'false faith' for it not only denies who God is in the revelation of Himself, but believes falsehood about him. Hence idolatry can be seen encompass not only displacement of the triune God but also distortion and denial. As Ovey writes:

> Such idolatrous lies falsify a person, obscuring and distorting who the person is. The lie destroys true relationship as humans stop relating to God as he knows himself to be, instead treating him as they have fashioned him. Idolatry strongly expresses human sovereignty, but sovereignty at the expense of true relationship. God is treated not as a person we encounter (a 'Thou' in Martin Buber's terms), but as an object (an 'It'), indeed a plastic, malleable one. Buber writes 'The *Thou* meets me'. Imposing identities on other persons risks not 'meeting' them – preventing them being a 'Thou'. The biblical God reveals he is not infinitely plastic and malleable. To treat him as that involves counterfeit, not true, relationship, with him. The price for being makers of God, albeit attractive, is that the God we make is not real. The true God is hidden, because we attempt to reduce him to an 'It' of our choosing. Buber notes: 'This selfhood ... steps in between and shuts off from us the light of heaven'.[35]

Any worldview which not only denies the Triune God and Jesus Christ as Lord,[36] but even shows indifference to His existence, is idolatrous.[37] On this account, Buddhism is idolatrous. Idols deprive the Living God of his glory, defame his Name and his jealously and indignation is rightly aroused.

---

[35] Michael Ovey, 'Idolatry and Spiritual Parody: Counterfeit Faiths', *Cambridge Papers* 11:1 (March, 2002): 3. The Buber quotations are taken from *I and Thou*, 2nd edn (Edinburgh: T&T Clark, 1958), 11; and *The Eclipse of God* (Atlantic Highlands: Humanities Press International, 1952), 129.

[36] 'Buddhists do not believe in the existence of God. There need be no debating about this. In practicing Buddhism one never finds talk of God, there is no role for God, and it is not difficult to find in Buddhist texts attacks on the existence of an omnipotent, all-good Creator of the universe'. Paul Williams, *The Unexpected Way: On Converting from Buddhism to Catholicism* (Edinburgh: T&T Clark, 2002), 25. See also, José Cabezón, 'A God, But Not a Savior', in Rita M. Gross and Terry C. Muck, eds, *Buddhists Talk About Jesus, Christians Talk About the Buddha* (New York: Continuum, 2000), 26. In this present volume, both Tilakaratne and Thompson agree that there is no Creator God in Buddhism.

[37] Interestingly, Williams in *The Unexpected Way*, notes that the claim that Buddhism is agnostic rather than atheistic is 'a modern strategy' (3).

This is precisely what the seminal passage at the beginning of the book of Romans is speaking of:

> The wrath of God is being revealed from heaven against all the godlessness and wickedness of people, who suppress the truth by their wickedness, since what may be known about God is plain to them, because God has made it plain to them. For since the creation of the world God's invisible qualities – his eternal power and divine nature – have been clearly seen, being understood from what has been made, so that people are without excuse. For although they knew God, they neither glorified him as God nor gave thanks to him, but their thinking became futile and their foolish hearts were darkened. (Rom. 1:18–21)

To reiterate here, there can be no appeal to 'sincerity' or 'ignorance' at this fundamental of the human predicament. While it may offend our autonomous sensibilities, God as Sovereign Creator has legitimate ownership and authority over his creatures, and failure to acknowledge this is culpable.

How is this related to the phenomenon of 'dual belonging'? Here we come to the complex anatomy of idolatry. Idolatry and idols are not created *ex nihilo* but are parasitic on truth and a good creation. The perpetuity of the *imago Dei*, God's common restraining grace and the sheer 'giveneness' of the created order means there will always be gaps and inconsistencies in non-Christian worldviews, and certain commonalities and continuities with the Christian worldview which are to be acknowledged as 'distorted truth', and which can be used missiologically. This is what I believe the Apostle Paul is doing in Acts 17, when he refers to the people of Athens as '*deisidaimonesterous*' (v. 22), translated in the NIV as 'very religious', (a *hapax legomenon*), and referring to their 'unknown god' (v. 23).

However, such practical continuity must be held with a spiritual and principial discontinuity. Idolatry is still idolatry. From Genesis to Revelation, Christian Scripture testifies to a fundamental bifurcation in the human race, which is generated from two antithetically related 'religious ground motives', which serve as the 'pre-pretheoretical spiritual core of each human',[38] one being rooted in the claim that YHWH/Jesus Christ is Lord and brings us into relationship with a Divine Father, the other being not according to Christ but according to 'hollow and deceptive philosophy, which depends on human tradition and the elemental spiritual forces'. (Col. 2:8). These two ways of being are described as being in enmity with each other and issue is a string of antithetical contrasts seen

---

[38] James Sire, *Naming the Elephant* (Downers Grove, IL: IVP, 2004), 87.

'There Can Be Only One' 83

throughout the canon of Scripture: holy and profane, light and dark, blind and sighted, dead and alive, in Adam/in Christ, sheep and goats and so on.

In Christian conversion, therefore, we witness a crisis and spiritual paradigm shift as by the Holy Spirit one's fundamental presuppositions are changed: a turning from idols to the Living God.[39] This turning is seen in the call not solely to faith in Christ but in faith *and repentance* as witnessed in the end of Paul's address to the Areopagus.[40] One may speak of universal religiosity, unknown gods and even quote from poets who inhabit other worldviews, but the final application is the call to repentance.

God's people are to have only a single belonging and a single citizenship.[41] There can be no hyphenation, liminality or hybridity. Rather than describing a more fluid process of 'passing over' and 'coming back', there is a divinely revealed 'fixity' in Christian identity. In the Old Testament this is seen with typological clarity in the moral, civil and ceremonial laws which separate Israel from the nations. Indeed it was precisely for mixing their religion with the religions of the nations, rather than a simple abandonment of the Lord, that they were exiled (2 Kings 17: 7–23; 33–4; 41). The affirmation of the incomparability and uniqueness of YHWH means incomparability uniqueness of the covenant community. There is no other covenant community like them, and there is no other community with a history like theirs because the incomparable and unique God has covenanted with them alone and intervened salvifically on their behalf alone. As already noted, God's glory is displayed in creation. However, it is especially revealed through the mercy of His redemptive and saving acts whereby God's glory is particularly focused:

> When our ancestors were in Egypt, they gave no thought to your miracles; they did not remember your many kindnesses, and they rebelled by the sea, the Red Sea. Yet he saved them for his name's sake, to make his mighty power known. (Ps. 106:6–7)

> For he chose us in him before the creation of the world to be holy and blameless in his sight. In love he predestined us for adoption to Sonship through Jesus Christ, in accordance with his pleasure and will – to the praise of his glorious grace, which he has freely given us in the One he loves. (Eph. 1:4–6)

---

[39] 1 Thess. 1:9.
[40] Acts 17:30.
[41] Cf. Phil. 3:20.

84 *Buddhist-Christian Dual Belonging*

What makes this magnification larger is that it is a sovereign work not only *ex nihilo* as in creation, but in regards to the idolatrous Other is a work *ex oppositione*, 'the God who gives life to the dead and calls into being things that were not'.[42] Rather than a magnification, dual belonging would seem to diminish God's glory here, as where is the *ex oppositione*?

The new Israel of the church are 'a chosen people, a royal priesthood, a holy nation, God's special possession', declaring the praises of him who called them out of darkness into his wonderful light.[43] On the question of belonging, the question most often posed is not so much 'where do you belong?' but 'to whom do you belong?' Jesus Himself speaks of the impossibility of serving two masters (Matt. 6:24).[44] Christians are to 'flee from idolatry'[45] to 'keep themselves from idols'.[46] The Apostle mirrors his Lord when he says to those under his pastoral care: 'I am jealous for you with godly jealousy. For I have betrothed you to one husband, that I might present you as a chaste virgin in Christ'.[47]

At the end of *Without Buddha I Could not be a Christian*,[48] Paul Knitter asks candidly if his dual belonging is 'a kind of religious promiscuity',[49] a 'cheating on Jesus'.[50] Sadly, I have to say that it is. To give one's devotion to the Other claiming it makes one love Jesus more, does not stop it from being adulterous.[51] Moreover, who is the Jesus that Knitter (and other dual belongers) is loving more? What account of the Christian faith are they claiming to uphold? As I read Christian dual belonging accounts of God, humanity, fall, Christ, salvation and so on, I do not recognise the Christ I am devoted to, but someone other. Such

---

[42] Rom. 4:17.

[43] 1 Pet. 2:9. Note once again the *telos* here of God's glory.

[44] I realise that Thompson interprets this verse differently to me. See *Buddhist Christianity*, 16. While I think Thompson is right that the immediate context is that of 'money', there is a more general point regarding fundamental allegiances that holds and fits in with the exclusivity (not 'tyrannical' *pace* Ross) of the rest of the Biblical witness. In Col. 3:5, greed is referred to as 'idolatry'.

[45] 1 Cor. 10:14.

[46] 1 Jn. 5:21.

[47] 2 Cor. 11:2. This marital model was criticised by some at the symposium. Ross pointed out that it is only used corporately – God and Israel, Christ and the Church and so not related to individual belief. While in a letter like 2 Corinthians Paul is certainly writing corporately, it is to a local congregation made up of individual believers. I do not think corporate and individual can be separated so markedly here.

[48] Oxford: Oneworld, 2009.

[49] 231.

[50] 214.

[51] I should note that in terms of the other contributors in this volume, Cornille supports this marital analogy, while Velez questions it.

morphing is perhaps predicable given the stark difference between Christianity and Buddhism, and the need for an intellectual 'keeping of the peace' between the lovers. However, the result, ironically but inevitably (for in reality we are all single belongers where there can be only one ultimate commitment), is exclusive commitment to a new lover, unrecognisable from both Christianity and Buddhism. She has been named previously by Gavin D'Costa as modern neo-pagan Unitarianism.[52]

3. Saved by the Gospel of Christ for God's Glory

Where does this stress on and call for religious monogamy to Christ leave us?

Although straying outside my brief, it is worth noting what such exclusivity to *this* God means for missiological inculturation and contextualisation. Monogamy does not mean cultural monochromaticity, for triunity bespeaks of unity and diversity. To carry on the illustration, the gospel of Christ is never 'wedded' to one cultural expression, which leads to extractionism.[53] The eschatological picture we have is of God being glorified by people 'from every nation, tribe, people and language'[54] On the other hand, this diversity must never be religiously syncretistic. I have found J.H. Bavinck's model of *possessio* helpful here:

> The Christian life does not accommodate or adapt itself to heathen forms of life, but it takes the latter in possession and thereby makes them new. Whoever is in Christ is a new creature. Within the framework of the non-Christian life, customs and practices serve idolatrous tendencies and drive a person away from God. The Christian life takes them in hand and turns them in an entirely different direction; they acquire an entirely different content. Even though in external form there is much that resembles past practices, in reality everything has become new, the old in essence has passed away and new has come. Christ takes the life of a people in his hands, he renews and re-established the distorted and deteriorated; he fills each thing, each word, and each practice with a new meaning and gives it a new direction. Such is neither 'adaptation' nor 'accommodation'; it is in essence

---

[52] Gavin D'Costa, *The Meeting of the Religions and the Trinity* (Maryknoll, NY: Orbis Books, 2000), 39. This is explicitly in reference to Knitter.

[53] Where people are pulled out ('extracted') from their own cultural/ethno-linguistic background, and have to adopt another culture.

[54] Rev. 7:9.

the legitimate taking possession of something by him to whom all power is given in heaven and on earth.[55]

Moreover, recognising the religious Other as truly Other does not cancel out but encourages the God-given commands and impetus to show the love of God and Christ-likeness: to love our enemies, to welcome the alien and stranger, to always show hospitality, to be tolerant (in the true sense of the word) of the Other. Our exclusive commitment to Christ must never lead to a vain glory or malice for both Israel and the Church are chosen by the sheer grace of God to display His glory.

Finally, despite human sin, idolatry and unfaithfulness, the 'good news' of the *evangel* is of the Christian God's provision of the Saviour Jesus Christ, to be received by faith. The antithetical relationship of the Christianity to the religious Other means that dual belonging will always be deeply problematic and illegitimate and should be repented of. However as God's creatures, made in His image to worship Him, communication and contact is always possible between Christ and the Religious Other, but a relationship where the gospel is the 'subversive fulfilment' of Buddhism and indeed of dual belonging. Salvation and liberation is not to be found in any teaching, in the refuge of the self or in detachment. Rather salvation is found in another, in an attachment to Christ by faith union in whom we are justified, sanctified and, yes, glorified.

Conclusion

In this chapter focusing on the doctrine of God, I have attempted to articulate from my Evangelical tradition, that dual belonging is anathema both intellectually and morally. In doing this, I think I add credence to Catherine Cornille's 'rough-and-ready axiom' that 'the more encompassing a religion's claim to efficacy and truth, the more problematic the possibility of multiple religious belonging'.[56]

Given my stark conclusions, where might we go from here? Have we reached an impasse already? As is always (and should be) in discussions like this, we come back sooner rather than later to matters of theological method, presuppositions and the authorities on which we build our theological constructs. For those

---

[55]   J.H. Bavinck, *Introduction to the Science of Missions* (Phillipsburg, NJ: P&R, 1960), 179.

[56]   Catherine Cornille, 'Introduction: The Dynamics of Multiple Belonging', in Cornille, ed., *Many Mansions: Multiple Religious Belonging and Christian Identity* (Eugene, OR: Wipf and Stock, 2010), 2.

of us claiming any belonging to the Christian tradition then maybe there is a way forward here. For those claiming a Protestant heritage like Thompson and Williams, it might be instructive to investigate how dual belonging 'fits' into the canons and formularies of their own Anglican tradition, for example the Thirty-Nine Articles. I know that Gavin, Paul and the other Catholic participants will want to be (and have been for a long time) engaged in similar intra-tradition-specific discussion. For both Protestant and Catholic traditions, although there are important differences in the level of 'authority', both recognise that the Bible has some role to play in these discussions and so maybe a constructive next step might be to look at the various exegetical and hermeneutical issues which lead some of us to have diametrically opposed stances on the legitimacy or illegitimacy of dual belonging. Certainly as one committed to the ultimate authority of Scripture, I would welcome such engagement which could be fruitful and challenging.

Chapter 5

The Ultimate Buddhist Religious Goal, Nirvana and its Implications for Buddhist-Christian Dual Belonging

Asanga Tilakaratne

In this chapter, I discuss the nature of the Buddhist religious goal, namely, nirvana, with a view to examining the viability of Buddhist-Christian dual belonging. The discussion is not a comparative study between the Buddhist concept of nirvana and the Christian concept of a heavenly Kingdom. Rather the approach will be to present, following the Pali canonical discourses which are considered to be the oldest available sources for the teaching of the Buddha, a picture of nirvana as the ultimate goal upheld in Buddhism, and then, in the concluding section, to investigate in this light the possibility, or otherwise, of dual belonging between the two religious traditions.

Nirvana, the Goal of the Buddhist Path

The basic meaning of the Pali term *nibbāna* (nirvana: Sanskrit) derives from the metaphor of blowing out the light of a lamp (ni+va to blow). In this sense, nirvana refers to the extinguishment of fire. The Buddha says that people are burning with the fires of attachment, aversion and delusion,[1] and the extinguishment of these fires is called nirvana. Another sense derives from analysing '*nibbāna*' as ni+vr (to cover), extinguishing fire by covering or depriving the mind of fuel, by not feeding it any further. What is noteworthy in these analyses is that they have direct reference to some obviously negative characteristics of mind, and that nirvana is defined in terms of their termination. In line with this way of

---

[1]   *Saṃyutta-nikāya* IV (Pali Text Society [PTS] edition), 19–20. (Bhikku Bodhi, *The Connected Discourses of the Buddha*, Boston: Wisdom Publications, 2000, 1143–4).

understanding, nirvana is usually described as 'the extinction of attachment, aversion and delusion'.[2]

Two of the more important terms used in the discourses to refer to the ultimate goal of Buddhist religious life are purification (*visuddhi*) and liberation (*vimutti*). These concepts are significant because they refer to two very vital aspects of the ultimate goal, namely, its purified and free nature. The idea of purification presupposes impurities, or, in a more familiar Buddhist term, defilements (*kilesa*). Likewise, the concept of liberation implies a bonded nature of the human mind which is described in terms of being obsessed by influxes (*āsava*). These two concepts, defilements and influxes, capture two very important aspects of the state of mind of one who is yet to realise this ultimate goal.

Of the defilements that pollute the human mind, attachment, aversion and delusion, mentioned above, are fundamental. Even among them, what is singled out in the Four Noble Truth teaching, as the source of discontent, is attachment, characterised as 'thirst' (*tanhā*), signifying the ceaseless thirst people have for sensual gratification, continued existence and destructive sentiments. The reason for this emphasis on desire over the other two is the significant influence that it exercises on people's lives. Both attachment and aversion are ultimately rooted on the deluded nature of mind which is not ignorance in the sense of not knowing enough facts, but the lack of knowledge/understanding of the Four Noble Truths.

Defilements referred to here operate in the mind at different levels. For instance, although attachment, aversion and delusion constitute the fundamental forms of defilements, what are called the 'five hindrances' (*pañca nīvaraṇa*), namely, desire for pleasure, ill-will, sloth and torpor, restlessness and remorse and doubt, these function at a more basic level of hindering progress along the path. They are brought under control at higher states of concentration although they will be totally eradicated only at the level of full attainment. The practice intended to bring these hindrances under control is described in the following words:

> Abandoning covetousness for the world, he abides with a mind free from covetousness; he purifies his mind from covetousness. Abandoning ill-will and hatred, he abides with a mind free from ill-will, compassionate for the welfare of all living beings; he purifies his mind from ill-will and hatred. Abandoning sloth

---

[2] ' *rāgakkhayo dosakkhayo mohakkhayo nibbānam*': *Saṃyutta-nikāya* (PTS) iv. 251. (Bhikkhu Bodhi, 2000, 1294).

The Ultimate Buddhist Religious Goal, Nirvana and its Implications   91

and torpor, he abides free from sloth and torpor, percipient of light, mindful and fully aware, he purifies his mind from sloth and torpor. Abandoning restlessness and remorse, he abides unagitated with a mind inwardly peaceful; he purifies his mind from restlessness and remorse. Abandoning doubt, he abides, having gone beyond doubt, unperplexed about wholesome states, he purifies his mind from doubt. (Nanamoli and Bodhi 1995, 274–5)

This purificatory process continues through gradually ascending states of serenity and steps along the path until it reaches total purification in the state of arahanthood.

The freedom metaphor refers to influxes/taints (*āsava*) which flow into the mind and get established in it and enslave it. They are the influxes of sense desire, becoming and ignorance (and views added at some places making the total of four). While these are the primary forms of influxes, there are other influxes active in many different levels. In the well-known 'discourse on all the taints'[3] the Buddha classifies taints into the following categories: taints that should be abandoned by seeing, by restraining, by using, by enduring, by avoiding, by removing and by developing. Once this process is complete, all one's taints, including the four fundamental ones mentioned above, are gone. Consequently one achieves total freedom from these taints.

The concept of freedom (from) is best emphasised by such terms as fetter (*saṅyojana*), bondage (*bandhana*) and flood (*ogha*). These capture the enslaving character of taints. Fetters are enumerated as 10 and these culminate in ignorance (*avijjā*). These fetters are removed gradually by the practice of the path. They are totally eradicated at the fourth and the highest stage of the path, which is arahanthood.

It is interesting to note that the path to achieve the final goal is always characterised as the arising of knowledge or the eradication of ignorance/delusion. Delusion (in the defilement analysis) and ignorance (in the influx analysis), both of which provide direct reference to knowledge, are given as the focal points. Accordingly, the culmination of the path is described as a dawn of knowledge. In the 'Discourse on the Turning of the Wheel of the *Dhamma*',[4] considered to be his first sermon, the Buddha uses the following expressions, 'the

---

[3]   *Sabbāsava-sutta, Majjhima-nikāya (2)* ('All the Taints', Bhikku Nanamoli and Bhikkhu Bodhi, *The Middle Length Discourses of the Buddha* (Boston, MA: Wisdom Publications, 2001), 91–6).

[4]   *Dhammacakka-pavattana-suta, Saṃyutta-nikāya* V (PTS), 420–24. (Bhikku Bodhi, *The Connected Discourses of the Buddha* (Boston, MA: Wisdom Publications, 2000), 1843–7).

eye is born; knowledge is born; wisdom is born; "science" is born; and light is born': all denote knowledge. The non-mystical, clear character of this knowledge is described in the following passage:

> Just as if in the midst of the mountain there were a pond, clear as a polished mirror, where a man with good eyesight standing on the bank could see oyster-shells, gravel-banks, and shoals of fish, on the move or stationary ... Just so, with mind concentrated, purified and cleansed, unblemished, free from impurities, malleable, workable, established, and having gained imperturbability, he applies and directs his mind to the knowledge of destruction of the taints. He knows as it really is: these are the taints; this is the origin of taints, this is the cessation of taints, and this is the path leading to the cessation of taints. Through this knowing and seeing his mind is freed from the taints of sense desire, from the taint of becoming, from the taint of ignorance, and knowledge arises in him: this is freedom.[5]

Nirvana, the ultimate goal of Buddhist religious life, is the result of the purification of mind from defilements and its freedom from influxes. Nirvana is described as the highest happiness which an arahant experiences as a result of his inner purity and freedom. As monks and nuns who have accomplished this state of mind testify, their experience is one of being cool, [fires] extinguished and peaceful. Even though it would be good to conclude the discussion on nirvana at this point, it is not possible to do so because there is a lively debate among Buddhists themselves as to what nirvana is and, in particular, whether or not it constitutes a metaphysical state. This discussion would not be complete without even a cursory consideration of this age-old debate.

In spite of the testimonies of monks and nuns who became arahants and the statements of the Buddha providing a 'naturalist' picture of nirvana as a state of mind and an experience, there exist other statements which open possibilities to interpret nirvana as an objective reality with its own being. The much discussed U.80[6] affirms that there is 'unborn, unbecome, unmade and unconstructed', in the absence of which there will not be release from born, become, made and constructed. Although nirvana is not specifically mentioned in this analysis, it is understood that what is being referred to is nirvana. In agreement with this way of thinking, nirvana is named as the 'unconstructed element' (*asaṅkhata dhātu*).

---

[5] *Sāmaññaphala-sutta*, *Dīgha-nikāya* 2 (Maurice Walshe, *The Long Discourses of the Buddha* (Boston, MA: Wisdom Publications, 2012), 107–8).

[6] *Udāna*, a text included in the *Khuddaka-nikāya* of the Pali canon.

Another discourse classifies nirvana into two types, the element of nirvana with the five aggregates remaining and the other, without aggregates, remaining.[7] Here too nirvana is referred to as an element (*dhātu*), indicating some kind of objective reality. Marking the conclusion of this way of interpreting nirvana, Buddhaghosa, the leading commentator on the Pali canon, says that nirvana is not non-existent like a rabbit-horn and clearly affirms that nirvana really does exist.[8]

The ontological status of nirvana has been a persistent worry for some followers from the time of the Buddha. The oft-referred to four (so-called 'unanswered') questions on the post-mortem status of the arahant is an indication of this worry. What is at the heart of the issue is an individual's deep-rooted desire for existence which is described in the discourses as the 'thirst for existence' (*bhava-taṇhā*), one among the three aspects of the cause of suffering, namely, thirst. To those who criticised nirvana as an annihilation of a really existent being, the Buddha responded by saying that, in the first place, there is no such persistent person to be annihilated. To Sati, who believed that his consciousness persists on its own through samsara, the Buddha pointed out that one's consciousness is dependently arisen and that there is no consciousness in the absence of conditions.[9] The Buddha states that the notion of a continued person, 'I' or 'mine', is a myth constructed by desire, and in order to attain nirvana it is essential for one to understand that it is a false notion. There is no evidence that any of the arahants who realised nirvana were ever worried about his or her after-death status. Consequently it is clear that the answer given by the Buddha was not satisfactory to those who were anxious about their continued existence. But the Buddha, nevertheless, never intended to satisfy this desire by projecting nirvana as a form of everlasting existence. In fact, the Buddhist nirvana cannot be an attractive option for those who desire eternal life. This explains why eternal life in the Kingdom of God remains the preferred destination for many in the world. Even for a majority of the Buddhists in traditional Buddhist societies, nirvana is the last of the last to be realised after having enjoyed all the human and divine pleasures!

---

[7] Nibbānadhātu-sutta, Itivuttaka (PTS), 38.

[8] Bhikkhu Nanamoli, *The Path of Purification* [*Visuddhimagga*] (vol. II) (Shambala, 1976), 578.

[9] Maha-tanhāsaṅkhaya-sutta, *Majjhima-nikāya* 38; Bhikkhu Nanamoli and Bhikkhu Bodhi, *The Middle Length Discourses of the Buddha* (Boston, MA: Wisdom Publications, 2001).

It is not my intention, in this context, to go into details of this debate on the ontological status of nirvana which I have treated in detail elsewhere.[10] What is clear is that naturalist as well as metaphysical interpretations are possible to these debated texts. What seems to be the correct position is to apply the criteria of consistency and coherence to the texts and draw from these a conclusion accordingly. I would suggest that applying the criteria of consistency and coherence to the texts of the Pali canon results in the understanding of nirvana as the experience of total purification and freedom of mind.

Buddhist-Christian Dual Belonging

Taking this picture of nirvana as our point of reference, we can move on to examine how far and to what extent Buddhists and Christians can adopt each other's standpoints and ways of life. This cannot be done, however, without having an idea of its Christian counterpart – or 'homologue', to borrow from Fr Aloysius Pieris[11] – the Kingdom of God. Whether the Kingdom should be understood literally or metaphorically remains a contested issue. Leaving it to the experts in Christian religion, the best I can do is, as ordinary Christians do, to accept the traditional understanding of the goal as Heaven or Kingdom where one is born to enjoy eternal life in association with God who is the creator and redeemer according to traditional monotheistic religions. Not only here, but in the entire chapter, I use the term 'God' to refer to a god who is believed to have created everything out of nothing and who is held to be omniscient, omnipotent and all-good. The eternal life happens as a result of salvation which is 'a free gift flowing from a complete self-surrender to [such] God'.[12] The entire discourse on dual belonging arises because some are not satisfied with this plain and simple picture of God and the goal. Theologians insist that one must not take 'Kingdom' in its literal spatial sense. If so, what are the non-literal and figurative modes of understanding of such crucial concepts as 'Kingdom' and

---

[10] Asanga Tilakaratne, *Nirvana and Ineffability: A Study of the Buddhist Theory of Reality and Language* (Columbo: Postgraduate Institute of Pali and Buddhist Studies, 1993), 55–85.

[11] Aloysius *Pieris*, 'Prophetic Humour in Buddhism and Christianity: Doing Inter-religious Studies in the Reverential Mood', in *Dialogue* New Series vol. xxxi (Colombo: Centre for Study and Dialogue, 2004), 107–21.

[12] Claude Geffre, 'Double Belonging and the Originality of Christianity as a Religion', in Catherine Cornille, *Many Mansions? Multiple Religious Belonging and Christian Identity* (Eugene, OR: WIPF and Stock, 2002), 95.

The Ultimate Buddhist Religious Goal, Nirvana and its Implications 95

'God'? To answer this question means getting into endless theological debates, ancient, modern and contemporary. I would rather leave this task to those who are better qualified than I am. What I will do is to take a representative case of dual belonging and show how it is beset with some serious difficulties.

Accordingly, I will develop the remainder of my chapter as a response to Paul F. Knitter, who is a defender of Buddhist-Christian dual belonging. At the outset of this discussion I must admit that Knitter has become more tradition-specific since the publication of the work I am going to review. But I simply take Knitter as a representative case. In *Without Buddha I Could not be a Christian* (2009; 2013), Knitter argues and defends his case, honestly, candidly and passionately. In order to justify his position of dual belonging, Knitter develops a critique of traditional Christian understanding of such key concepts as God, Jesus, salvation and heaven. This critique is based on Buddhism, or to be more precise, what Knitter constructs as Buddhism. There are two questions to be raised on Knitter's exercise. The first, namely whether or not his interpretation of Christianity through the application of Buddhist concepts is tenable, I leave for Christian scholars to examine. The second, namely whether or not his representation of Buddhism is tenable, is what I now plan to address.

But before addressing these issues I wish to examine what Knitter considers to be Buddhism. It is well known that there exist three historical Buddhist traditions in the world today. The oldest extant is Theravāda, traditionally found in South and Southeast Asia. Taking an historical time-line, Mahayana, which is traditionally found in East Asia, comes next. Vajrayana, the last in this line, is traditionally found in Tibet and its surrounding regions. Although these traditions are not directly opposed to each other, and on the more positive side, share the fundamental worldview of the historical Buddha, one can observe that these traditions contain substantial doctrinal differences in addition to their cultural differences. Knitter moves through these traditions freely, and constructs a Buddhism drawing from all three traditions. He takes emptiness from the early Mahayana philosopher Nagarjuna, 'interbeing' from Thich Nhat Han (a contemporary Mahayana teacher), identity of samsara and nirvana from the later Mahayana and religious practices from his Tibetan teachers. Knitter does not appear to notice any problems with this approach because he compares the distinctions between Theravāda and Mahayana to those between Roman Catholicism and Protestantism respectively, and sees only 'smells and bells' as distinguishing characteristics of Vajrayana (107–8).

If we appreciate that Knitter has reconstructed his own personal version of Buddhism, drawing from these various Buddhist traditions, I do not believe that anyone can object so long as his reconstruction is internally consistent. But since Knitter states that it is what the Buddha said, there is a methodological problem in accepting these teachings, which have been hotly debated, taken from traditions belonging to different time periods, and then presenting them as belonging to the Buddha himself. In order to demonstrate this methodological difficulty let me discuss a few issues Knitter refers to:

1. The alleged identity between samsara and nirvana can be traced to Nagarjuna who, in the *Mūlamadhyamakakārika*, makes the following statement which can be considered as the source of this later claim: *na saṁsārasya nirvānāt– kiñcidasti viśeṣanam; na nirvānasya saṁsārāt kiñcidasti viśeṣanam.* Following D.J. Kalupahana,[13] I translate this in the following manner: samsara does not have anything that distinguishes it from nirvana; nirvana does not have anything that distinguishes it from samsara. Taking into consideration the occurrence of 'anything' (*kiñcid*) and also the context of the discussion, this statement can be interpreted as affirming the absence of any 'own-nature' (*sva-bhāva*) in samsara or in nirvana. This can be understood in the hyperbolic sense which Nagarjuna seems to enjoy, as saying that both samsara and nirvana are the same, from the perspective of absence of any own-nature whatsoever. To interpret this statement as affirming the identity of nirvana and samsara in an absolute sense is to misconstrue the direct meaning of this statement. If not meant as a hyperbolic device, the equation between samsara and nirvana is unimaginable for one who thinks in accordance with the philosophy in the Pali discourses.

2. Once the equation between samsara and nirvana is taken as established, the next step is to affirm non-duality between the two.[14] Although some Mahayanists seem to have accepted a concept of non-duality as a characteristic of the ultimate reality, it is not only hard to find in Pali discourses but also it is not a characteristic of nirvana as we described in the first part of this discussion. Non-duality of Atman and Brahman is the defining characteristic of the Vedanta view of liberation. In Vedanta non-duality, Brahman/Atman (subject) is retained as the ultimate reality while the object disappears. In Buddhist analysis neither samsara nor nirvana remains because both are ultimately empty in the sense of not having self-nature. Nor does emptiness exist over and above all empty

---

[13] David J. Kalupahana, *Nagarjuna: The Philosophy of the Middle Way* (New York: State University of New York Press, 1986).

[14] Paul F. Knitter, *Without Buddha I Could not be a Christian* (Oxford: Oneworld, 2013), 221.

things. For Nagarjuna emptiness (*śunyata*) is not a super-concept which remains when all other concepts are gone. It is only an aspect of the religious practice or an act of relinquishing all concepts/views.[15] Both the early discourses and Nagarjuna seem to uphold this position.

3. 'Bodhisattva' is another concept posing difficulties when used across traditions. In the Pali discourses 'bodhisattva' has been used to refer to the Buddha before his enlightenment. It is in the Mahayana tradition that bodhisatvahood became a distinct mode of following the path. In this new sense, a bodhisattva is one who gives up his own nirvana in favour of the liberation of others. It is believed that such a bodhisattva will not attain nirvana until the last sentient being also attains it. Considering the endlessness of samsara, this 'last sentient being' will never exist. This implies that the Bodhisatva himself will never attain nirvana for he will have to remain in samsara for ever. From a Theravāda point of view, this appears to be a compromise between samsara and nirvana providing a moral justification for the desire for continued existence (*bhava taṇhā*). Furthermore, obviously the bodhisattva path cannot have been meant for all for then there would arise the bizarre situation that there would not be anyone to be saved. If this is true, then it means that there are those who attain liberation without being bodhisattvas, a position that is not different to that of early tradition.

These are some of the difficulties that arise from trans-traditional construction of what is Buddhism. Apart from these initial methodological difficulties, Knitter's position is founded on several problematic premises which he adopts from earlier writings on interreligious dialogue. What I mean in this context are the following: (1) that all religions refer to one transcendental reality as their ultimate goal; (2) that the ultimate Buddhist religious experience is mystical; consequently, that it is ineffable; and (3) that the Buddha neither denied nor affirmed God, but remained silent on the subject. Although Knitter accepts all these premises almost as given, they are not: they are questionable. I have examined all these claims elsewhere, in detail, and hence I do not plan to repeat all that I have already said. Nevertheless, I need to make some analysis here.

The view that all religions ultimately refer to one transcendental state has been suggested by many. A representative case is by John Hick according to

---

[15] *śunyatā sarva dṛṣṭīnām proktā nihśaraṇam jinaih – yeṣaṁtu śunyata dṛṣṭih tan asādhyān babhāṣire* (*Karika* 13:8) The Buddhas have taught emptiness to be relinquishment of all views. If for anyone emptiness is a view, those are called incurables.

98   *Buddhist-Christian Dual Belonging*

whom all the major religions in the world are different responses to one ultimate principle which he calls 'the Real' or 'the Transcendental'. Some religions present this ultimate principle, says Hick, in personal idioms (*personae*) such as Yahweh, Allah, Krishna and so on and some other religions express it in such impersonal (*impersonae*) idioms as nirvana, *tathatā*, *satori*, *advaya* and so on. Whether personal or impersonal, ultimately all these refer to one and the same transcendental reality which he calls 'the Real'.[16] This view seems to get support from the ancient Rg Vedic statement the context of which is not exactly what it is popularly understood to be: 'The Real (*sat*) is one; sages describe it variously' (*ekan hi sat viprā bahudhā vadanti*[17]). The claim made here is not that all religions refer to some transcendental state or being, but is a much different and stronger one, namely, that all religions ultimately refer to one identical transcendental reality which is understood in a metaphysical sense. The concept of transcendence found in Pali discourses refers usually to the nature of the behaviour of the enlightened person. The following is an example:

> Just as a blue, red, or white lotus flower though born in the water and grown up in the water, rises above the water and stands unsoiled by the water, even so, though born in the world, and grown up in the world, I have overcome the world and dwell unsoiled by the world.[18]

When the concept of transcendence proper – *loka+uttara* = transcending the world – was introduced into the Theravāda tradition at a somewhat later period, it was still understood not in a metaphysical sense but in an experiential sense.[19] As I discussed toward the end of the first part of this chapter, there is a debate among Buddhist scholars as to whether or not nirvana is a transcendental reality. Even if we were to concede that nirvana is transcendental in this metaphysical sense, it is uncertain that such a transcendence will support Hick's transcendental interpretation of religion.

The next two inter-connected claims that nirvana is a mystical experience or state and that it is ineffable, these are the result of applying the popular generalisation of religion, which are based on the theistic model of religion, to

---

[16]   John Hick, *An Interpretation of Religion* (New Haven, CT: Yale University Press, 1989).

[17]   Rg Veda 1.164.46.

[18]   *Anguttara-nikāya* III (Bhikkhu Bodhi, *The Numerical Discourses of the Buddha* (Boston, MA: Wisdom Publications, 2012), 426).

[19]   *Path of Discrimination* (being a translation of *Paṭisambhidāmagga*) (London: Pali Text Society, 2002), 347–8.

The Ultimate Buddhist Religious Goal, Nirvana and its Implications 99

Buddhism. An early example of this general characterisation of religion based on the theistic model is found in Rudolf Otto who identifies 'numinous dread' (*mysterium tremendum*) as the essence of religion and further describes it as 'non-rational' or as unable to be conceptually defined or described or analysed.[20] It appears that subsequent scholars who discussed religion were influenced by this characterisation, and thus grouped all religions into one category having both mysticism and ineffability as defining characteristics.

Here I refer again to my analysis of nirvana in the first part of this discussion, namely, the analysis of the ultimate religious goal of Buddhism as involving a clear state of knowledge. This is meant to demonstrate that nirvana is not a mystical state or experience. It is also interesting to note that there exists not even one single place in the discourses where the Buddha has suggested that nirvana is ineffable,[21] or where arahants (those who realised nirvana) complain that language is unable to describe what they had realised. It is correct that ineffability has been upheld in the Mahayana tradition in the way in which Knitter has pointed this out. But the attribution of mysticism and ineffability to nirvana as understood in the Theravāda tradition suffers from these methodological issues referred to earlier.

The last claim that the Buddha did not assert or deny the existence of God and that he was silent about the whole issue is a highly problematic assertion that remains popular in the field of interreligious dialogue. Raimundo Panikkar[22] goes even further and claims that the Buddha was silent about God for he knew that God was absolutely ineffable. In Panikkar's view, the Buddha in his silence was even more faithful to God than some believers who tried to articulate in words their experience of God. Although there is a set of 10 or 14 issues on which the Buddha did not give a definitive answer, that list does not contain anything on the concept of God. So there is a simple factual error in this assertion. When T.R.V. Murti[23] used the concept of silence to refer to the phenomenon of unanswered questions, he has to be understood as using 'silence' in a figurative

---

[20] Rudolf Otto, *The Idea of Holy* (London: Oxford University Press, 1927), 1–6.

[21] The only remark that permits interpretation to that effect is '*atakkāvacara*' – 'not to be realized by logic' – (found in the *Majjhima-nikāya* 26) used by the Buddha to describe the *Dhamma* (teaching). Since logical reasoning is carried out by means of language, the term in its negative form has been interpreted as referring to a non-conceptual character of the teaching. What is meant by this term in this context seems the crucial need of practice, not mere rational analysis, in order to realise nirvana.

[22] Raimundo Panikkar, *The Silence of God: The Answer of the Buddha* (Maryknoll, NY, 1989).

[23] T.R.V Murti, *The Central Philosophy of Buddhism* (London: George Allen and Unwin, 1960), 48–9.

sense because, although the Buddha did not give a definitive answer to those questions, he was not silent about them either. Instead he explained the reasons why he did not answer, in a definitive manner, those questions.

In addition to some instances in the *Jātaka*[24] where arguments against the existence of God, based on the problem of human agency and the presence of evil, have been articulated, there are clear sutra references to the denial of the creator God. What is denied by the Buddha is what has been described often in the Buddhist texts as 'over-lord, doer and creator' (*issaro kattā nimmātā*), God understood as a person, not as an impersonal reality of the kind described in the later Indian traditions as *nirguna brahman* – Brahman without qualities. The following statement in *The Middle Length Discourses of the Buddha*: 'the world is protection-less; there is no overlord (in it)' (*attāno loko anabhissaro*[25]), clearly articulates the denial of such a God. The absence of a God is adduced by Raṭṭhapāla, the wealthy young man who decided to renounce his household life to join the monastic order, as one of the reasons behind his decision. In another discourse the Buddha identifies three views 'which, when questioned, interrogated and cross-examined by the wise, and taken to their conclusion, will eventuate in non-action',[26] one of which is the view that whatever one experiences is due to God's creation (*issara-nimmāna*). Discourses such as the *Ambaṭṭha* (*Dīgha-nikāya* 3) and *Tevijja* (*Dīgha-nikāya* 13) contain substantial discussions on the untenability of God. The philosophical basis for the denial of God is the Buddhist understanding of reality as causally conditioned and dependently arisen, according to which a transcendental and 'wholly other' God is just not possible.

In addition to these direct references to the denial of God, what I consider to be the most fundamental argument against the existence of God is the path to nirvana taught by the Buddha. All agree that the doctrine of the Four Noble Truths contains the essence of the Buddhist religious path meant to bring about the termination of suffering. It explains human suffering, its cause, thirst for pleasures, as a characteristic of human mind, and nirvana as the cessation of this suffering and the eightfold path as the path to be followed by practitioners on

---

[24] *Jātaka* V. 238 and VI. 208. Refer to K.N. Jayatilleke, *Early Buddhist Theory of Knowledge* (London: George Allen and Unwin, 1963), 410–11 for an English translation and a discussion.

[25] *Raṭṭhapāla-suttaṃ, Majjhima-nikāya* 82. (Bhikku Nanamoli and Bhikkhu Bodhi, *The Middle Length Discourses of the Buddha* (Boston, MA: Wisdom Publications, 2001), 686).

[26] *Aṅguttara-nikāya* I, 173 (Bhikkhu Bodhi, *The Numerical Discourses of the Buddha* (Boston, MA: Wisdom Publications, 2012), 266ff.).

The Ultimate Buddhist Religious Goal, Nirvana and its Implications

their own. The rationale behind this 'soteriological' scheme is the absence of God who saves beings from suffering. If God exists, one does not need to strive along the ethical path taught by the Buddha because one will be saved by God's grace. The Dhammapada states in no uncertain terms: 'Oneself, indeed, is one's saviour, for what other saviour would there be?'[27] As Raṭṭhapala reasoned out, one has to follow the path taught by the Buddha because the world is protection-less and God-less. The very nature of the path outlined in the first part of this discussion is based on the assumption that there is no saviour God. The Buddha's role with regard to the path is that of a teacher and guide who embodies what he has taught; not that of a saviour. Under these circumstances, it is difficult to maintain that the question of God is irrelevant to the Buddhist path for it is the very absence of God that has made the Buddhist path what it is.[28]

In discussing the ultimate goal and the path to it, the Buddha seems to have been quite conscious and assertive of the uniqueness of these phenomena. A statement in the 'Discourse on Lion's Roar'[29] is as follows:

> Only here [in his teaching] there is the first *samaṇa* ['ascetic'/religious practitioner]; only here is the second *samaṇa*; only here is the third *samaṇa* and only here is the fourth *samaṇa*. The doctrines of others are devoid of *samaṇas*.

What is meant by *samaṇa* here are the achievers of the four stages of the path, namely, the stream winner, once-returner, non-returner and the accomplished one, the fourth, and last, indicating one who has completed the path and won what the Buddha describes, to a naked ascetic named Kassapa, as 'the highest Aryan liberation' (*ariyā paramā vimutti*). The Buddha further adds to this: Kassapa, insofar as the highest Aryan liberation is concerned I do not see an equal. How could there be a superior? I am supreme in this regard, in super-liberation.[30]

---

[27] *Attā hi attano nātho – ko hi nātho paro siyā*: The Dhammapada 160. (Nārada Thera, *The Dhammapada* (Taipei: The Corporate Body of the Buddha Educational Foundation, 1993), 145).

[28] Paul Williams gets this point, namely, the atheistic character of Buddhism, and the resultant absence of God in the Buddhist path, straight. Refer to his: *The Unexpected Way: On Converting from Buddhism to Catholicism* (London and New York: T&T Clark, 2002).

[29] *Cūlasīhanāda-sutta, Majjhima-nikāya* 11. (Bhikku Nanamoli and Bhikkhu Bodhi, *The Middle Length Discourses of the Buddha* (Boston, MA: Wisdom Publications, 2001), 159–63).

[30] *Mahā Sīhanāda-sutta, Dīgha-nikaya* 8. (Maurice Walshe, *The Long Discourses of the Buddha* (Boston, MA: Wisdom Publications, 2012), 151–7).

These seemingly exclusivist statements and discussions by the Buddha have to be understood in their proper context. It is well known that the Buddha did not reject *in toto* the views and practices of other religions. In particular, he agreed with those who upheld the efficacy of moral actions (*kammavādi, kiriyavādi*). It is also known that the Buddha assimilated substantially from the religious traditions of his time. A particularly interesting example of his assimilation is what are known as material and immaterial *jhanas* practiced by religious people during his time. Consequently his emphasis in this context is solely on the final goal and the path. It is only on those grounds that the Buddha asserts his own authority and the uniqueness of the path and where he is not prepared to compromise. This could perhaps be an example of what Rose Drew identifies as 'irresolvable differences' among religions.

So what of dual belonging? The discussion up to this point should have shown that dual belonging between Buddhism and Christianity is impossible because the conception of Buddhism, as constructed by Knitter, suffers from a methodological deficiency and also that some of the basic premises of the argument are faulty. Even if dual belonging, as envisaged by Knitter, is impossible, it could still be possible to argue that there exists room for dual belonging within a different model but on different grounds. However, if my characterisation of nirvana and the arguments presented here are correct then they serve to support the view that the two religions are radically different at their cores and therefore that dual belonging at the level of the final goal and the path to it is hard to justify, even on other grounds.

Concluding Remarks

Let me address a few issues in order to conclude this discussion. Behind the discussion of dual or multiple belonging there remains the question: Should one be confined to one religion? Introducing the rich anthology of papers on multiple belonging, Catherine Cornille says:

> In a world of seemingly unlimited choice in matters of religious identity and affiliation, the idea of belonging exclusively to one religious tradition or drawing from only one set of spiritual, symbolic, or ritual resources is no longer self-evident. Why restrict oneself to the historically and culturally determined

symbols and rituals of one religious tradition amid the rich diversity of symbols and rituals presenting themselves to the religious imagination?[31]

What Cornille says fits very well with our globalised world context. And her opinions also make much sense in the present global reality of bitter rivalries among religions. If we are talking of being open to other religious traditions, deriving inspiration from the lives of different religious teachers, learning from rich and different cultural and historical contexts and the like, I see nothing but good in this proposal. In addition, I do not reject the possibility of piecemeal use of one religion while remaining within another, which the majority of dual belongers seem to be doing. The question, however, is: Can we really move from one religious tradition to another without leaving behind the former? Although externally a religion is a set of practices, rites and rituals, these are rooted in a system of beliefs which forms a consistent whole. In other words, a religion is a conceptual universe – a paradigm of its own. If we borrow from Thomas Kuhn,[32] movement from one to another religion requires a paradigm shift. The conceptual universe of one is not relevant to the other – although this may not be precisely so in the case of monotheistic traditions such as Judaism, Christianity and Islam, or, in some respects, between Buddhism and Hinduism.

Let me briefly discuss a particularly interesting case in Sri Lanka where Hinduism and Buddhism meet so frequently in rites and rituals. In particular what I refer to in this context is the Buddhist practice of asking for help from gods, most of whom are shared between the two traditions, in addition to some exclusive monopolies of two religions such as Kārtikeya and Durga for Hindus and Nātha and Saman for Buddhists. Buddhists believe in the existence of many gods (and other unseen beings) who are powerful and capable of granting favours or inducing harm to human beings. It is customary for many Buddhists to visit shrines of these gods and ask for favours for themselves or punishments for enemies. As an important part of the ritual, these gods are presented with fruits and so on and nominal cash. Decades ago these offerings were purely symbolic in that they presented these gods with a coin of low value to accompany their request or complaint. Today a typical offering costs a much larger sum of money. Other requisites depend on the riches of the participant. It is also interesting to note that Buddhists do not go to a shrine of the Buddha for these worldly purposes for they know he is no more. Having first paid homage to the Buddha,

---

[31] Catherine Cornille, *Many Mansions? Multiple Religious Belonging and Christian Identity* (Eugene, OR: WIPF and Stock, 2010), 1.

[32] Thomas Kuhn, *The Structure of Scientific Revolution* (Chicago, IL: University Press of Chicago, 1970, second edition).

then they proceed to the god's shrine to receive help in their day-to-day matters. Buddhists do not see this as contradicting their Buddhist practice for they make a clear distinction between the two domains, this-worldly and the other-worldly. As I have discussed elsewhere, Buddhists have distributed among several gods the functions of a single God, such as rewarding, punishing and protecting, and with attributes such as moral supremacy but – note specifically – *minus* the roles of being creator and saviour.[33] Believing in gods, getting favours from them or emulating them does not pose a problem for Buddhists so long as such a god is not God. This practice and similar practices in Southeast Asia are not to be understood as instances of dual belonging although they could belong in a sub-category of what D'Costa calls 'A' type.[34]

Heavenly worlds, as pleasurable abodes of divine beings, are very much a part of Buddhist religiosity. Buddhist discourses usually refer to *sagga* and *mokkha*, heaven and liberation, as goals of the religious life, usually the former for the householders who aspire to remain in samsara, and the latter, usually but not exclusively, for the renounced who aspire to escape from samsara. Except for the Christian belief that heaven and hell are eternal while their Buddhist counterparts are impermanent, both Buddhists and Christians have much to agree on this point. Nevertheless, what makes any possibility of dual belonging difficult is that a Buddhist, even one whose religious goal does not go beyond being born in a heavenly abode after his death, still has to ground his religious life in the larger picture of samsaric existence in a God-less universe.

The only way, perhaps, to belong to more than one religion would be to interpret one in line with the other or both in line with each other, which is what Knitter seems to do. But then the two have been made one or almost one. On the other hand, Knitter's Buddhism remains his own creation and so does his Christianity. The end result could be neither this nor that, but a new creation. In either instance, whether two or several traditions become together one or whether a creation of a new hybrid, the dual or multiple belonging loses any sense.

Finally, in the latest edition of his work (2013), Knitter, moving substantially from his earlier position of being a 'Buddhist Christian' (216), claims that both the Buddha and Jesus together come first in his religious practice and identity. In his earlier position he would have been more Christian and less Buddhist. But in this new position he is both Buddhist and Christian, each occupying 100 per cent of his religious space. (Knitter does not propose a name for this position.)

---

[33] 'Buddhist non-theism: Theory and Practice', in Ann Blackburn and Jeffrey Samuels, eds, *Approaching the Dhamma: Buddhist Texts and Practices in South and Southeast Asia* (Seattle, WA: Pariyatti Publishers, 2003), 125–49.

[34] See his chapter in this volume.

The Ultimate Buddhist Religious Goal, Nirvana and its Implications   105

It is plain that one cannot be both 100 per cent Buddhist and Christian unless there is total agreement between the two religious systems. Then 'two-ness' however loses its meaning. Hick's transcendental position, which holds that all religions ultimately refer to 'the One', seems to allow one to exist in all religions simultaneously, provided that one sufficiently accommodates the cultural differences which make different religions different.

Another possibility of 100 per cent dual belonging is to have two systems which are complementary to each other in the sense that one fills in with what is not found in the other. The characterisation of Christianity and Buddhism as (Christian) love vs. (Buddhist) wisdom by Fr Aloysius Pieris[35] may be taken as an example. According to him, these two terms are 'two irreducibly distinct languages of the Spirit, each incapable without the other of adequately mediating and expressing one's experience of God and the world'. Although Fr Pieris does not take this complementarity as a basis for dual belonging, one can argue that dual belonging is the logical conclusion of this method of characterisation[36] of the two religions. The point made by Fr Aloysius Pieris on the predominance of wisdom in Buddhism and of love in Christianity is true particularly on a practical level. In Buddhism, ultimately, wisdom plays a more important role because the ultimate goal is essentially a result of 'knowing and seeing'. Nevertheless, as Fr. Pieris himself has noticed,[37] Buddhism refers to loving kindness (*mettā*) as an essential virtue to be practiced along the path. To conduct oneself with actions, words and thoughts associated with loving kindness has been recognised as an important part of virtuous behaviour (*sīla*). In a somewhat different but not totally irrelevant context of discussing 'the balance of faculties', Buddhaghosa mentions how 'faith (*saddhā*/trust) and wisdom are to be particularly balanced:

> However, what is particularly recommended is balancing faith with understanding [wisdom] ... . For one strong in faith and weak in understanding has confidence uncritically and groundlessly. One strong in understanding and weak in faith errs on the side of cunning ... [38]

---

[35]   Alloysius Pieris, *Love Meets Wisdom: A Christian Experience of Buddhism* (New Delhi: Intercultural Publications, 1988).

[36]   Please refer to 'Aloysius Pieris on Interreligious Dialogue and Problems of Truth in Religion: A Buddhist Perspective', in Robert Crusz, Marshal Fernando and Asanga Tilakaratne, eds, *Encounters with the Word* (Columbo: Centre for Study and Dialogue, 2004), 381–400.

[37]   Pieris (1988). 177.

[38]   Bhikkhu Nanamoli, *The Path of Purification* (Columbo: Semage Brothers, 1956), 135 (iv:47).

What Buddhism demands of a follower is not necessarily a predominance of either of these states of mind but their balance. Discussing loving kindness, Buddhaghosa highlights the importance of having this virtue in a practitioner. But his account also suggests that in the actual practice loving kindness has been understood as a psychological virtue, rather than as an active involvement in social action. In this sense, Buddhist social activism has much to learn from Christianity. In his more recent writings, including his chapter in this volume, Knitter lays stress on this complementarity between Christian demand for justice and the Buddhist emphasis on understanding. Nevertheless, in order to learn this lesson and absorb it from Christianity, one may not need to go so far as to practice dual belonging. Perhaps the path to achieve this goal for Buddhists and Christians may be to be genuine friends (*kalyānamitta*) to each other.

Let me wind up this discussion by quoting Edmund F. Perry who wrote the following in 1980 when dual belonging was little heard of:

> In this new era of Buddhist Christian relations, Buddhists and Christians have the opportunity to do enormous good for the whole world by becoming to each other a *kalyānamitta*, a trusted friend for mutual spiritual advancement. The starved and neglected religious imagination of the masses of people throughout the world today need the epic grandeur of an announced conspiracy in which Buddhists and Christians work each for the other's eternal wellbeing and conjointly seek to transform the world with their tender care and clear thinking.[39]

---

[39] Edmund F. Perry, 'Can Buddhists and Christians Live Together as *Kalyana-mitta*?' in Somaratne Balasooriya et al., eds, *Buddhist Studies in Honour of Walpola Rahula* (London: Gordon Fraser, 1980), 201–12.

Chapter 6

A Roman Catholic Approach to Buddhist-Catholic 'Dual Belonging'

Gavin D'Costa

Definition of the Theological Question

The phenomenon of 'dual belonging' (DB for short) has been studied from within different disciplinary approaches: anthropological, sociological, phenomenological, feminist, philosophical and theological.[1] Indeed, some anthropologists and some feminists argue that all religions have been hybrid mixtures of religious traditions and DB and multiple belonging is hardly unique or novel.[2] They argue that DB is a belated recognition of what has always actually been the case in terms of religious identity. Just as one could be a parliamentary

---

[1]   See anthropologically: Premawardhana Devaka, 'The Unremarkable Hybrid: Aloysius Pieris and the redundancy of multiple belonging', *Journal of Ecumenical Studies* 46: 1 (2011): 76–101; phenomenologically: Catherine Cornille, 'Double Religious Belonging. Aspects and questions', *Buddhist-Christian Studies* 23 (2003): 43–9, with astute theological reflections in the conclusion; and Rose Drew, *Buddhist and Christian? An Exploration of Dual Belonging* (London: Routledge, 2011); in a feminist mode: Michelle Voss Roberts, 'Religious Belonging and the Multiple', *Journal of Feminist Studies in Religion* 26:1 (2010): 43–62. The theological treatment is quite extensive. The single best volume is Catherine Cornille, ed., *Many Mansions: Multiple Religious Belonging and Christian Identity* (Maryknoll, NY: Orbis Books, 2002) with mainly Catholic perspectives, but with some other Christian denominations represented. For an evangelical perspective the debate has been approached with an interest in 'insider movements', see especially, Paul Gordon Chandler, *Pilgrims of Christ on the Muslim Road: Exploring a New Path between Two Faiths* (Lanham, MD: Rowman & Littlefield, 2007), and Jonas Petter Adelin Jørgensen, *Jesus Imandars and Christ Bhaktas. A Qualitative and Theological Study of Syncretism and Identity in Global Christianity* (University of Copenhagen: PhD thesis, 2006).

[2]   Roberts, 'Religious Belonging and the Multiple'; and see also Jeannine Hill Fletcher, *Monopoly on Salvation? A Feminist Approach to Religious Pluralism* (New York, Continuum, 2005); Premawardhana, 'The Unremarkable Hybrid', and the most interesting interdisciplinary exchange between Premawardhana and Klaus Klostermaier, Peter Phan and Aimee Upjohn Light in *Journal of Ecumenical Studies*, 46:2 (2011); and David Cheetham, *Ways of Meeting and the Theology of Religions* (Farnham: Ashgate, 2013), 93–122.

member of the British Communist party, a Roman Catholic, a member of the Masters of Fox Hounds Association, a regular attendee of the local meditation centre, an opera buff and a mother of three all at the same time, so one is made up of constantly shifting multiple identities. In Asia it is quite usual for this kind of multiple identity construction to apply to religious belonging. Such are the complexities and thickets that lie before us.

However, to attempt to cut through the forest, I will focus exclusively on a Roman Catholic theological perspective on DB, informed by the recent teachings (post-1964) of the magisterium, here understood in descending order of authority as teachings emanating from: (a) the Second Vatican Council; (b) popes at encyclical level; (c) and dicasteries of the Vatican that are entrusted with teaching and safeguarding doctrine, such as the Congregation for the Doctrine of the Faith. *Magisterium* is a polyvalent term and here indicates the formal teaching authority that is vested in the bishops and the pope, speaking in communion, or the pope, speaking through his own office or through delegated offices (Roman dicasteries). All Christians share the 'magisterium' of scripture and since for Catholics, the ecclesial hierarchal magisterium's authority is limited to that which is given in the deposit of faith/scripture, my approach in this chapter is ecumenically intended. In effect, I assume that all teachings by a Council or popes or dicasteries are biblically grounded. Non-Catholic Christians should challenge this in any particular case and this can generate fruitful ecumenical discussion.

There is one problem with my plan. These different levels of the magisterium have never explicitly addressed the issue of DB. So is this chapter a waste of time? You may think so after reading it, but I would propose that the novelty of this chapter is to draw together various magisterial teachings to provide a tentative theological perspective on the matter in a speculative fashion.[3] The justification for this speculative argument lies in the fact of Catholics with high public profile claiming to be DBs in 'good faith'.[4] I do not question their subjective 'good faith'

---

[3]   Joseph S. O'Leary, 'oward a Buddhist Interpretation of Christian Truth', in Cornille, *Many Mansions*, 29–44, examines some magisterial teachings on this question, but his method and conclusions are very different to mine.

[4]   Drew, *Buddhist and Christian?* contains the best materials to track this claim as she is interested in fully fledged DBs, what I will call Z types below, see 12. However, I am unconvinced by Drew's 'testing' of this form of DB. When dealing with the three Catholics in her study, the ecclesial magisterium is not mentioned at all. She bypasses all ecclesial obligations with the assumption that it is to ultimate reality that absolute adherence must be given, not religious traditions. This entirely begs the question. Further, the theological authorities she summons are mainly liberal theologians. This is also true in her chapter in this collection.

for a moment, but I am exploring the objective nature of what that 'good faith' might have to be if they were DBs in 'good faith'. The reason for reaching for the magisterium is precisely because in much of the multi-disciplinary debate and in some of the theological debate, there seem to be no apparent agreed or recognisable authorities for judgement upon the legitimacy or otherwise of DB or of what actually defines being Christian. Talking about the 'legitimacy' of such an infant phenomenon may be premature, but there is a cultural urgency to provide some theological analysis. Finally, in justification of this speculative exercise, the benefit of attempting to answer this question theologically from within a single Christian tradition in relation to its authority sources is to throw further analytical light on the general phenomenon of DB as well as in respect of Catholic DB specifically.

The Roman Catholic Church puts its followers under an obligation to be answerable to Christ. This accountability is finally a matter of conscience, but only a conscience properly formed. One source of formation is accountability to the community's recognised authorities regarding practices and beliefs. The level of this obligation and the scrutiny regarding its practice obviously varies according to circumstance. If the DB is a priest, religious or lay person teaching in an official pontifical institution, their views and attitudes shape Catholic minds and they have a duty of accountability to the magisterium regarding the nature of the 'Catholicity' that they have been entrusted to pass on. This was the case, although DB was not the main issue, with Fr's Anthony De Mello, Tissa Balasuriya and Jacques Dupuis. They were all subject to investigation by the Congregation for the Doctrine of the Faith. There are lots of different situations. I suspect many of the Catholics in my parish Church could be DBs (most likely with civic secularism, understood as a religion), but no one knows and they rarely play a high-profile representative role. I am not interested in the 'policing' operation aspect of this question, but only in what might be achieved with theological clarity regarding DB.

Here then is the question: Can a Roman Catholic be a dual belonger and at the same time satisfy the requirements for 'belonging' as defined by the Roman Catholic magisterium?

Definition of the Terms Involved in the Theological Question

What precisely is 'DB'? There is a growing literature on this complex phenomenon which is sometimes referred to as 'dual belonging', 'multiple belonging', 'hyphenated belonging' and so on.[5] For conceptual clarity I will draw on the excellent literature cited, coin my terms and use them consistently. This is not to suggest an inadequate categorisation in the literature. The opposite is the case. Rather, because there is no single standard adopted set of terms, it will be helpful to set out my definitions employing them consistently. I will set out three distinct categories, within which there can be variations and degrees. While I restrict myself to the basic paradigm of 'dual'/'two' 'religions', the categories can be extended to include three or more religious traditions (multiple belonging). For the sake of simplicity, I will stick to two religions, one of which must be Roman Catholicism (Christianity) and the other, any form of Buddhism. Christian Buddhist DB is the focus of this book. [6]

The first type is *interior DB*. Here Jane is let us say a *DGe lugs* Tibetan Buddhist and Roman Catholic interiorly, but does not wish to gain recognition of her status from the actual communities of those names. Jane may be self-consciously highly selective about elements of incorporation from these traditions into her own spirituality. Call this condition 'A'. Or she may be conscientious in trying to accept and practice all that a Catholic and all that a *DGe lugs* Buddhist may be required to believe and practice, even while not belonging to any of those communities as a regular practitioner. Pretend Jane is stranded on a deserted island. There are no Roman Catholic or *DGe lugs* Buddhists, so that her desire to accept beliefs and practices that entail communal belonging cannot be satisfied through no fault of her own. Call this position 'Z'. Jane may have a number of stopping points in between these A and Z positions. In the A position, Jane approximates towards New Age religiosity which can sometimes have a tendency towards individualism.[7] All the different types I shall look at have one thing in common: a conscience; but their differences may lie in the formation of conscience and the levels of external accountability. When Jane is in the Z position she is still, through no fault of her own, the authoritative voice regarding the extent to which she has successfully achieved her goals as she is not in an accountable community. By definition, interior DB does not entail accepting an exterior magisterium or being open to correction about one's

---

[5]   See Cornille, *Many Mansions*; Gideon Gooshen, *Hyphenated Christians: Toward a Better Understanding of Dual Religious Belonging* (Oxford: Peter Lang, 2011); Rose Drew, *Christian and Buddhist?*; Perry Schmidt-Leukel, *Transformation by Integration* (London: SCM Press, 2009); and Peter Phan, *Being Religious Interreligiously: Asian Perspectives on Interfaith Dialogue* (Maryknoll, NY: Orbis Books, 2004).

[6]   This typology overlaps and is compatible with Vélez de Cea's typology, although I contest his findings regarding Catholic DB on theological, not phenomenological, grounds. Cornille's argument, when applied to Catholicism, is buttressed by my arguments, but logically my arguments cannot be applied beyond the Catholic DB sphere.

[7]   See Moyaert's arguments related to the New Age in this collection.

A Roman Catholic Approach to Buddhist-Catholic 'Dual Belonging'   111

understanding by an exterior magisterium. Usually, in interior DB, the person is their own magisterium. In the literature it is difficult to find Jane's of the Z position (not least because she is stranded on a desert island); but lots in the A position – some might say, stranded in modernity.

The second type is *single community exterior dual belonging*. Here, Malik is a Roman Catholic who practices in a Roman Catholic Church, but also draws upon his learning and practices which he receives from a *DGe lugs* teacher. Malik is not active within any *DGe lugs* community and his teacher is not concerned about his Roman Catholic affiliation. While there is thus a level of interior belonging in terms of his Buddhist practices, his exterior allegiance is to the Catholic community. Malik may be utterly selective about elements of incorporation from these two traditions into his own spirituality and practices. Call this the A position. Alternatively, Malik may be very conscientious in trying to accept all that a Roman Catholic or *DGe lugs* Buddhist may normally accept, although he only belongs practically to one of these communities. Call this the Z position. Here too there are a number of stopping points in between A to Z. When Malik is being highly selective about what he believes, through choice or circumstances, he may not be concerned or may not know about tensions that exist with formal magisterial teachings. When Malik is in Z mode, trying to accept both traditions on their own terms, he may well have difficulties balancing the tensions created by magisterial teaching and his *DGe lugs* practices and beliefs – and he may not. But Malik is at least taking seriously these possible tensions. I am interested in the single community exterior dual belonger of the Z type. I will assume that only this type is being referred to in the subsequent discussion, along with another Z type to be found in the third category.

The third type is *double community exterior dual belonging*. Here, Emi is a Roman Catholic who practices in a Roman Catholic community as well as a *DGe lugs* community who practices in a *DGe lugs* community. She has a lama who teaches her. She attends Ignatian retreats whenever possible and frequents the sacraments. Her exterior allegiance is to two communities to which she belongs and wishes to be accountable to. Emi is a Z type. She could be an A type in belonging to both but not wishing to follow both fully or/and be accountable to both. In many a congregation she may be a sort of celebrity and in some other congregations she may suffer hostile suspicion. On record, Anglican Vicar, Rev David Hart, was also a practising Hindu priest. The *Church Times* conducted a poll in which 53 per cent of Anglicans felt he should not be allowed to practice as an Anglican priest.[8] Paul Knitter reported verbally that he has been asked to take dual belonging retreats by some Catholics in his parish. I am interested in the double community exterior, dual belonging Z types. They, along with the previous Z type, will be the sole referent of my use of DB in what follows.

One more qualification: the forms of accountability to the non-Catholic tradition in DBs are not my business; and they vary greatly. But to up the stakes and attain clarity for the Christian theological question, let us assume that the DBs' accountability to the non-Catholic tradition is achieved. The *DGe lugs* community and its authoritative teachers are satisfied that the conditions of full belonging to the non-Catholic community are met by Malik/Emi, or that such a question is inappropriate or unanswerable.

Here then is our precise question: can Malik and Emi continue their DB in good faith in the light of magisterial teachings? To my surprise, the answer is both yes and no, and a lot of don't knows.

Some Magisterial Teachings to Help Theologically Analyse the Question

I cannot provide adequate textual exegesis for the select magisterial teachings outlined all too briefly, but I refer readers to a full book-length study where these teachings are textually grounded and explicated.[9] I have also conflated the three magisterial levels outlined above: (a) the Second Vatican Council; (b) popes subsequent to the Council at encyclical level; (c) the dicasteries of the Vatican that are entrusted with teaching and safeguarding doctrine. In the notes, I will give the sources for these three levels when mentioning any teaching. Catholic scholars may find my claims contentious and of course, intra-traditional argument is the order of the day. There are many other magisterial teachings that bear of the topic that I shall not be drawing on.[10]

The key magisterial *de fide* teaching that I will begin with is that there is no salvation outside the Church (*extra ecclesiam nulla salus*), which is taught with three qualifications.[11] *De fide* status indicates its theological status as a

---

[8]   See http://www.christiantoday.com/article/priest.converts.to.hinduism.still.claims. to.be.priest/7634.htm (checked July 2014).

[9]   See my *Vatican II. Catholic Doctrines on Jews and Muslims* (Oxford University Press, 2014), 59–113.

[10]   For example: that the non-Christian religions are at best *praeparatio evangelica*; that the beatific vision consists of the face to face enjoyment of the triune God.

[11]   See Johann Finisterhölzl, 'Theological Notes', in Karl Rahner, ed., *Encyclopedia of Theology. The Concise Sacramentum Mundi* (London: Burns & Oates, 1981 [1975]), 1678–85.

precondition of authentic and full Catholic faith. Denial of this while being a Catholic indicates heresy. I will draw on two further teachings later. This first teaching has been reiterated by the Second Vatican Council and taught over nearly 1,900 years in differing contexts.[12] It has been reiterated since Vatican II at all levels.[13]

In a positive sense the teaching indicates two interrelated claims. First, that salvation comes through Christ's atoning death (understood through a variety of models) and that without Christ, original sin and the devil have power over fallen humans. In his death, Christ overcomes sin, death and the devil. This means that salvation cannot be other than from Christ both causally and historically. Second, the Church is understood as the sacramental presence of Christ in the world (understood through a variety of models). So while the Church is not Christ as a matter of numerical identity, the 'traditional' developed claim has drawn on the model that the Church is Christ's body, of which Christ is its head. Aquinas is key here and is employed by Vatican II in *Lumen Gentium* 16 (note 18) – in the article dealing with non-Christian religions. The teaching thus means: Christ and his Church are the necessary means of salvation. It has not been defined whether this is a conditional or absolute necessity, but at the Council, the *relatio* on the matter indicates it is a necessity of means and not of precept.[14] The *relatio* has no formal teaching status, but at least frames the intention when a teaching is delivered.[15] Hence, Christ and the Church are the means of salvation.

Less this be misunderstood, there are some important interpretative rules. First, this sacramental salvific role of the Church does not mean that the Church is full of saints. It is full of sinners (including buggering bishops, paedophile priests and licentious laity, just to name some alliterating sins). It does mean that the objective means of salvation in the sacraments are found in the Catholic Church (and in varying degrees in other non-Catholic Christian churches) and that Christ's teachings are safeguarded and passed on by the hierarchical ecclesial

---

[12]   The history of this teaching is traced in Francis Sullivan, *Salvation Outside the Church? Tracing the History of the Catholic Response* (London: Geoffrey Chapman, 1992). I think some of Sullivan's interpretations contestable and discuss these in *Vatican II*, 62n, 63n, 65n, 68, 76n, 105n, 155, 156n, 182n.

[13]   For example Pope John Paul II, *Redemptor Hominis* (1969); CDF, *Dominus Iesus* (2000); *Catholic Catechism* (1994), 846–8.

[14]   See Aloys Grillmeier, 'Commentary on the Dogmatic Constitution on the Church', in Herbert Vorgrimler, ed., *Commentary on the Documents of Vatican II*, Volume 1 (London: Burns & Oates, 1967), 153–85, 175.

[15]   The *relatio* is the formal commentary on the draft document presented to the Council Fathers and is meant to help them understand the text they are voting on.

114 *Buddhist-Christian Dual Belonging*

teaching office. Second, the positive nature of the teaching is emphasised in Vatican II through applying *extra ecclesiam nulla salus* only to those who know the truth of Christ and his Church. It is not applied to those who 'do not know' this truth, the 'invincibly ignorant'.[16] It should be clear that 'no salvation outside the Church', while held as a matter of faith, *de fide*, is not a damnation of all non-Catholics in the world. This leads us to the three qualifications that have been found in formal magisterial teaching since 1854. They qualify rather than contradict the *extra ecclesiam nulla salus* teaching.

The three qualifications are as follows: (a) those Christian churches that are trinitarian and carry out baptism are now included in the phrase 'Church' in regards to salvation, not in regard to their equal ontological ecclesial status;[17] (b) those non-Christians who are in invincible ignorance cannot be said to be 'lost' or 'damned' by virtue of their explicit separation from Christ;[18] and (c) that if such non-Christians as in (b) are eventually saved, this salvation it is not given *de iure* through their religions.[19] The distinction here indicates that a *de iure* religion is willed by God and obviously used by God, but a *de facto* religion is used by God, but not willed by God. This last teaching has arisen because since the Second Vatican Council some theologians have seen the Council as granting salvific legitimacy to the world religions. Cornille points out that the ecclesial magisterium delivered this teaching in *Dominus Iesus*, 'as a reactionary document

---

[16]   See Stephen Bullivant, 'Sine Culpa. Vatican II and Inculpable Ignorance', *Theological Studies* 72 (2011): 70–86 for texts and discussion.

[17]   Herein lies the debate about the meaning of the crucial phrase in *Lumen* 8, 14 that the true Church of Christ 'subsists in' the Catholic Church *(subsistit in Ecclesia catholica)* and that other Christian churches or ecclesial bodies share elements of that gift of subsistence. See Karl Josef Becker, 'An Examination of *Subsistit in*: A Profound Theological Perspective', *L'Osservatore Romano*, English, 14 (December, 2005): 11; and Francis Sullivan's reply: 'A Response to Karl Becker, S.J., on the Meaning of *Subsistit In*', *Theological Studies* 67 (2006): 395–409.

[18]   See also D'Costa, *Vatican II*, 62–80. Invincible ignorance refers to one who is ignorant through no fault of their own and cannot thus be blamed. If, for example, we are speaking about supernatural truths only known through revelation, without revelation, they cannot be blamed for rejecting the trinity.

[19]   Catherine Cornille, 'Religious Pluralism and Christian Faith: A Case for Soteriological Agnosticism', *Actualidade Telogica* 40–41 (2012): 50–71, has read this as teaching a 'soteriological agnosticism' in so much as *Dominus Iesus (DI)* is 'vague and ambiguous' on this matter. I agree with her basic argument: no one knows who is saved and it is not always fruitful to pursue this question. I am not sure about the resulting moratorium on soteriology that she proposes to promote the truth questions, precisely because questions of truth are related to soteriology (which she acknowledges). I read *Dominus Iesus* differently – see my exchanges with Terrence Tilley and Perry Schmidt-Leukel in *Modern Theology* 23:3 (2007), and 24:2 (2008).

A Roman Catholic Approach to Buddhist-Catholic 'Dual Belonging'

which takes issue with theological positions which seem to go too far in admitting the salvific efficacy of all religions, and which thus threaten to lead to relativism'. Admittedly the key phrase *de iure* has not been used since.[20] Furthermore, this *de iure* teaching occurred while, at the same time, the same teaching office reiterated that grace, truth and holiness can be found in the religious cultures of peoples, a teaching continuously emphasised by the magisterium since the Second Vatican Council.[21] Nevertheless, the magisterial teachings still regard these cultures and religions as finally *praeparatio evangelicae*, preparations for the fullness of the gospel. They are not, *per se*, as with the sacraments, the means of salvation.[22]

The first teaching that there is no salvation outside the Church is a *de fide* teaching (to be held by all Catholics) and the three qualifications arise from the Church discerning in the modern period how to relate that *de fide* teaching to different and complex situations: of ecumenism, and other religions respectively. What, if anything, does this tell us about DB? In some ways very little, but it helps tease out some issues.

The 'very little' is because the claims generated from full belonging to the non-Catholic religion cannot be *a priori* incompatible with the *de fide* teaching outlined above. One has to make a case by case judgement and this is an *a posteriori* matter. The literature suggests Catholic DBs often do end up as denying this *de fide* teaching (or already denied the teaching prior to their DB).[23] I would argue this is the case with the later works of Abhishiktananda, Aloysius Pieris and Paul Knitter. All three, in the end or prior to DB, abandon this *de fide* teaching. All three become, or already were, 'pluralists' or what is technically termed 'indifferentism' or 'relativism' in magisterial statements. Pluralists hold that different religions, with reasonable qualifications, are equally soteriological in their own right, *de iure*. Please note, I am not questioning the experience or integrity of any of these three figures. Other thinkers like Scott Steinkercnher and Robert Magliola seem to

---

[20]   It arose with John Paul and was then was used again in *DI*, 4.

[21]   *Redemptoris Missio*, 21–7, 28–9.

[22]   See relevant magisterial texts in D'Costa, *Vatican II*, 99–107; and Carola, Joseph, 'Apendix: Vatican II's Use of Patristic Themes Regarding Non-Christians', in Karl J. Becker and Ilaria Morali, eds, *Catholic Engagement with World Religions A Comprehensive Study* (Maryknoll, NY: Orbis Books, 2010), 143–53.

[23]   Dupuis, 'Christianity and Religions. Complementarity and Convergence', in Cornille, *Many Mansions?*, 61–76, 72–3 is 'charitable' towards Pieris' claims about his dual belonging in Buddhism and Catholicism, even if Premawardhana, 'The Unremarkable Hybrid' claims that Pieris' never makes that claim. I say charitable, because Dupuis himself is clear that Christ's revelation cannot be in need of anything else for its fullness and completion (66) and this is certainly not Pieris' claim – see Dupuis quoting Pieris: 75, note 16.

provide more interesting cases where they have learnt deeply from Buddhism and Buddhist meditation over many years but they are not DBs.[24]

These and other cases prove nothing. In principle, another religion may well allow full adherence to it without generating contradictory truth or soteriological claims to orthodox magisterial Catholic Christianity. For example, using a thought experiment, take the religion of the 'Sunday newspaper and walk', followed by millions in Bristol and London. I speak experientially. The religion is called the 'Sunday middle-classes' religion. It requires one must always read a newspaper on Sunday and then take a walk in a green space. I use this trivial example as it is *prima facie* clear that belonging to these two 'religions' does not generate incompatible truth claims to followers of Christ, but a series of practices that are believed to attain well-being. Some authors argue that some religions are like this fictitious religion: they enjoin practices and do not entail cosmological or metaphysical beliefs. This is often said about forms of Buddhism.

It follows that if dual belonging to any non-Christian religious community requires that this *de fide* teaching is compromised, then full belonging to the Catholic Church is compromised. If Emi taught that 'salvation' comes through Buddhism as well as Catholicism and this is understood *de iure* in regard to Buddhism, as well as having nothing to do with Christ when such salvation happens in Buddhism, these beliefs clearly contravene what the magisterium teaches. This would mean that Emi would fail to be a Z type Catholic, which is purportedly what she wants to be. In fact, if Emi held this view she would be subscribing to 'pluralism'. The magisterium has repeatedly condemned 'indifferentism' or 'relativism', or in effect 'pluralism'. This is not to deny that there are different forms of 'pluralism' or 'relativism', but given what Emi holds, this would come under a form of relativism as defined by the magisterium.[25] Since Emi has not written any texts, I think that Paul Knitter's texts might suffice as exemplary illustration of pluralism or relativism.[26]

Now, let us consider a slightly different scenario. Could Emi argue that Buddhism has been for her a means of salvation *de facto*, and that Christ's grace, in

---

[24] Steinkercnher, *Beyond Agreement. Interreligious Dialogue Amidst Persistent Differences* (Lanham, MD: Rowman & Littlefield, 2010) and Magliola, *Facing Up to Real Doctrinal Difference: How Some Derridean Thought-Motifs Can Nourish the Catholic-Buddhist Encounter* (forthcoming).

[25] For the magisterial texts (and my assessment of Catholic theologians who are pluralist) see 'Pluralist Arguments: Prominent Tendencies and Methods', in Becker and Morali, *Catholic Engagement*, 329–44.

[26] See his *Without Buddha I Could not be a Christian* (Oxford: Oneworld, 2009) and my analysis of Knitter's in the article cited in note 24 above.

her own experience, operates within Buddhism in this *de facto* salvific manner, but not in a *de iure* manner? Could Emi also argue that for her Buddhism has helped her become a better Catholic? Let us leave aside whether 'salvific manner' means justification or a preparation for justification. Let us assume it means the latter as the former solution is more contentious. If Emi wanted to make these claims, at first sight it 'seems' possible that they could fit within the speculative boundaries of legitimate magisterial teaching. This would be because she is claiming that her own experience of Buddhism has led her to find Christ's grace which has helped her become a better Catholic. If she argued that Buddhists could find the fullness of Christ's grace without Christ or the Church, or that becoming a better Catholic through Buddhism is a logically necessary pre-requisite for all Catholics to become more fully Catholics, then Emi would be stepping over the line. She would be holding to a *de iure* status for Buddhism and also claiming the insufficiency of Christ's revelation for salvation. The latter claim about being a better Catholic, as long as it does not question the sufficiency of Christ's revelation for salvation or have a logical necessity about it, can have a lot of mileage.

We come upon an interesting paradox at this stage of the analysis, for that which Emi is claiming can only be claimed, according to the magisterium, by one who does not know the truth of the Gospel through no fault of their own.[27] That is, Buddhism could only be viewed in this manner for an invincibly ignorant Buddhist. The magisterium, I suspect, would rightly resist any particular prudential judgement. Their job in a teaching capacity is trying to clarify a principle. In their scrutinising capacity, the prudential judgement becomes important, but that is not of interest to me here. However, in my scenario Emi does know the truth of the Gospel and that it is the *de iure* means of salvation so the question becomes, why is she turning to another religion at all? She has apparently given her answer: because it has helped her follow Christ. I find this credible, especially after talking to DBs.

In trying to analyse this further, a number of new questions arise. Is Buddhism actually another religion in Emi's case or has it been so incorporated into Emi's Catholicism that it has become an inculturated form of Christianity, received by her as part of the fullness of Catholic faith? Is Buddhism as Emi understands and practices it the same religion as practiced and understood by Emi's community? Is Emi slowly moving away from a Z type belonging to Buddhism towards an A type belonging by making these claims? I think this takes us to the heart of one of the most complicated and vexing questions raised by DB. Can both traditions accept the DB as being in total good faith as a full adherent of each religion?

---

[27]   *Lumen*, 16 is framed entirely within this invincible ignorance clause.

Remember, for the sake of argument I have proposed that Emi's Buddhist community and authorities within that community say: 'yes, Emi, you are a Buddhist as far as we are concerned'. They add: 'even if you understand everything in terms of Christic causality, for practices alone matter'. This then leaves the ball firmly in the Catholic court. One could then analyse Emi's situation in a number of ways.

Emi could be an underground or explicit missionary who has discovered the true, good and holy within another religion and sees that it comes from and leads towards Christ, who is found within her Catholic faith. Jacques Dupuis has rightly noted that DB is predicated upon the possibility of complementarity, although he allows complementarity to not challenge the other religion or require mission towards it. Complementarity then is in danger of moving towards pluralism. He does call his position 'inclusivist pluralism' and I think his position was in this danger.[28] Returning to Emi, she may be embodying, within her own life, a proleptic sign of what Buddhists should become so that their *de facto* practices can be transformed into *de iure* practices, by their becoming communicant Catholics. Her Buddhist community may indeed be persuaded by Emi, or they may think she is mad or be entirely indifferent or a range of other things, but let us imagine they still think Emi's views and practices are fully compatible with full membership of the Buddhist community. This then becomes a case of successful dual community DB of a Z type. You will recall I said that DB may be possible in full faithfulness to the magisterium.

A good reason to think this scenario meets the highest Z condition is because Emi would also be embracing two further magisterial teachings: the necessity of mission to all those who do not believe in Christ; and the importance of inculturation for the full Catholicity of the Church. Together with the first *de fide* teaching regarding the necessity of Christ and the Church for salvation, I now use these two to further develop my case. The teaching on mission is, I would argue, equivalent to a *de fide* teaching, but has not been formally pronounced as such. I think this is simply because it has never been disputed, but clearly the modern period is calling the universal necessity of mission into question and in recent magisterial statements the universal necessity of mission

---

[28]   His Christological safeguard (in Dupuis, 'Christianity', 66) is clear, but its ecclesial and revelatory implications are not. I think this is because he thinks of fulfilment in terms of purely abrogation and supersession (67, giving Israel as his example) and thus destroying another religion. He develops the term 'pluralist inclusivism' in his ground-breaking, *Towards a Christian Theology of Religious Pluralism* (Maryknoll, NY: Orbis Books, 1977).

A Roman Catholic Approach to Buddhist-Catholic 'Dual Belonging'   119

is constantly reiterated.[29] It is certainly central to the teachings of Vatican II and the subsequent post-conciliar magisterium. Vatican II held that all trinitarian Christians are not to be 'objects' of 'mission', even if full communion with the See of Peter was still required for these Churches to properly and fully *subsist* in Christ. *Lumen Gentium* 16–7 is clear that mission must be carried out to all those who do not know Christ, regardless of the impressive, good and truthful religious (or non-religious) traditions they may inhabit. So it does seem possible to be a DB, as illustrated in the case of Emi, and a Roman Catholic.

Regarding mission, I am not denying the many evils and problems that have gone hand in hand with missionary work: the denigration of religious cultures; imperialism and arrogance; socio-political exploitation of those who are deemed as rejecting the gospel; and a failure to respect religious freedoms. The list could be longer. Nevertheless, missionary theology has to work out strategies where these and other evils are avoided, but it cannot give up on the central task: sharing Christ, the gospel and the triune God in non-coercive ways.

On the other teaching, inculturation, it has taken a slight back seat since the Council. This is in part because of the crisis of the inculturation of secularism and other religions that have so often led to relativism.[30] I think there is a lot of truth in the concern, but it can be overplayed at the cost of inculturation. Nevertheless, inculturation has returned more forcefully to the agenda in the pontificate of Pope Francis, although technically it has remained the continuous teaching of the magisterium since the Council.[31] For my purpose, inculturation involves two key elements – the recognition that: (a) there is truth, goodness and holiness outside the Church within non-Christian cultures, and (b) but these elements are ennobled, healed and purified, through their baptism and regeneration in Christ.[32] Daniel Strange's notion of 'subversive fulfilment' is helpful here to bring out the force of the change and transformation of (b) when it meets with (a).[33] There is no clear straight line of continuity between (a) and (b), for being converted to Christ generates serious and profound discontinuity. Recalling Emi, one might see that her appropriation of Buddhism (b) may not

---

[29]   See the necessity of mission taught in Paul VI, *Evangelii Nuntiandi* (1975); John Paul II, *Redemptoris Missio* (1990); and prior to that in *Lumen Gentium* 17; *Ad Gentes*, 3, 7.

[30]   See Tracey Rowland, *Culture and the Thomist Tradition: After Vatican II* (London: Routledge, 2003) for an excellent analysis of this crisis.

[31]   Pope Francis, *Evangelii Gaudium* (2013), 68–70.

[32]   I use the terms of *Lumen Gentium*, 16–17; *Ad Gentes*, 3, 8, 9; *Nostra Aetate*, 2.

[33]   See Strange, *For Their Rock is not as Our Rock: An Evangelical Theology of Religions* (Leicester: Apollos, 2014).

bear much resemblance to what her Buddhist community hold (a). That they live with this dissonance is beyond the remit of this chapter.

Pioneers who actually enter into the life of a religious tradition other than Christianity while trying to maintain full and complete adherence to the Catholic faith should be listened to with care, courtesy and genuine openness to the way the Holy Spirit may work in them and the religious traditions they encounter. If they are maturely formed Catholics who seek adherence to the teachings of the magisterium, then Catholics should be grateful to them for their explorations which may well bear great fruit. To say relativism is a danger is to say precisely that: it is a danger, but not a logically necessary outcome of intimate encounter with other religions.

Emi, for instance, may genuinely help her fellow Catholics through teaching them silent breathing meditation. Many may learn how to pray more deeply and to prepare for the Eucharist in a more fruitful manner. The use of such a technique of stilling the mind may be a helpful tool in Christian discipleship. A cursory reading of John Henry Newman's work on the development of Christianity makes it clear that there was never a pre-existing culture 'Christianity', but rather something was formed out of pre-existing non-Christian cultures in a Christic shape. But whether the pre-existing shapes Christianity or vice versa is the question of the difference between syncretism and genuine inculturation. Hence Emi's teaching meditation at church raises the question whether this practice comes with a bigger package that must buy into the Buddhist cosmology underlying the techniques of meditation. The Congregation for the Doctrine of Faith's *Letter to the Bishops of the Catholic Church on some Aspects of Christian Meditation* (1989) was nuanced about the matter and far from negative as has often been portrayed.[34] It shows that there can be very positive forms of integration and learning from 'eastern methods of meditation' and of the three methods listed, only the third is subject to serious questioning:

> 12. With the present diffusion of eastern methods of meditation in the Christian world and in ecclesial communities, we find ourselves faced with a pointed renewal of an attempt, which is not free from dangers and errors, 'to fuse Christian meditation with that which is non-Christian'. Proposals in this direction are numerous and radical to a greater or lesser extent. Some use eastern methods solely as a psycho-

---

[34] See for instance the comments of Joseph O'Leary, 'Towards a Buddhist Interpretation of Christian Truth', who suggests quite unfairly, and with little evidence, that the CDF/Vatican authorities lack any sense of hermeneutics and that they work with an *a priori* theological method (30, 39, 40). The only evidence of a generalisation is from a newspaper interview with Ratzinger that has no ecclesial authority (40).

A Roman Catholic Approach to Buddhist-Catholic 'Dual Belonging' 121

physical preparation for a truly Christian contemplation; others go further and, using different techniques, try to generate spiritual experiences similar to those described in the writings of certain Catholic mystics. Still others do not hesitate to place that absolute without image or concepts, which is proper to Buddhist theory, on the same level as the majesty of God revealed in Christ, which towers above finite reality. To this end, they make use of a 'negative theology', which transcends every affirmation seeking to express what God is, and denies that the things of this world can offer traces of the infinity of God. Thus they propose abandoning not only meditation on the salvific works accomplished in history by the God of the Old and New Covenant, but also the very idea of the One and Triune God, who is Love, in favor of an immersion 'in the indeterminate abyss of the divinity'. These and similar proposals to harmonize Christian meditation with eastern techniques need to have their contents and methods ever subjected to a thorough-going examination so as to avoid the danger of falling into syncretism.[35]

To return to the main argument, in the entire literature of DB, it is difficult to find Emi's, for if they are Z type Catholics they normally tend to an A type Buddhist adherence. However, if the Buddhist community accept Emi's Buddhist beliefs and practices as I have just outlined above and declare her a Z type, then we have the case of a Catholic-Buddhist DB Z type with double community adherence in good faith. One corollary of this, given the arguments above, is that Emi's Buddhist community should logically consider becoming practicing Catholics. If Catholics accept Emi as being a Z type Catholic, they should seriously consider the wonderful truths, goodness and practices that have helped Emi become a better Catholic and they should seek to integrate the great wisdom and truth they find into their own Catholic practices whenever appropriate. They should also learn from this close knowledge how to develop mission more thoughtfully. They should also rejoice that in Buddhism there is so much light and truth.

Conclusions

My conclusions are twofold.

First, DB is not possible if magisterial teachings are contradicted related to the necessity of Christ/Church for salvation, the necessity of mission and the

---

[35] Some of this argument would probably apply to J.P. William's contribution in this piece.

importance of inculturation. In the literature, most DBs who want to be Z type DB Catholics fail on these first two criteria. They do not fail on the third, but indeed bring refreshingly challenging questions into view.

Second, I have also shown that it is possible to be a DB Z type Catholic-*Dge lugs* Buddhist in good faith, if and only if such a person would inevitably see their DB as a missionary presence to Buddhism and that they hold that Buddhism reaches its *telos* through conversion to Christ.[36] Furthermore, if and only if, from the Buddhist side the above type of belonging was acceptable, then DB of the Z type is possible. In the literature I have found no such sentient beings, but that does not mean they do not exist. And if they did, we may learn greatly from them.

I cannot of course say anything from the Buddhist side about this Z type Catholic-*Dge lugs* Buddhist. That is a task for others.

---

[36] If I had time, I would develop this in terms of *praeparatio evangelica* (another magisterial teaching from the Council and reiterated with frequency since the Council).

Chapter 7

Dual Belonging, Ritual and the Spiritual Revolution

Marianne Moyaert

Dual belongers claim to be deeply *rooted* in more than one tradition and therefore capable of moving back and forth with relative ease between two communities. These 'flexible believers'[1] are intent on doing justice to the self-understanding of both traditions. I am intrigued by this relatively novel phenomenon, and the general question that occupies me especially is *how do dual belongers* construct their dual commitment.[2] Usually, when this question is being raised in the relevant literature, the focus is on the problem of *incompatible truth* claims, or as Rose Drew asks in her contribution to this volume: 'how [do] the insights of ... two traditions fit into a single coherent picture'.[3] This focus on the question of truth follows from a *belief-oriented approach to religion*, according to which the core of religion is centred upon certain propositions that require assent. I approach religion from a different angle; I regard religion as a symbolic practice revolving around strongly incarnated meanings.[4] Rituality is at the core of religion, and takes precedence over belief. From this perspective, I am interested more specifically in the role symbolic practices play in the construction of dual commitments. Because rituals often function as outstanding boundary markers of ritual communities, ritual boundaries tend to be the most difficult to transgress. Traditionally understood, rituals are not flexible. Hence, I ponder

---

[1]   Chris Doude van Troostwijk et al. (eds), *Buigzame gelovigen: Essays over Religieuze flexibiliteit* (Nijmegen: Boom, 2008).

[2]   While in other parts of the world the whole idea that one should restrict oneself to one religious tradition makes no sense, in the Western world dual belonging is still a relatively new phenomenon.

[3]   Rose Drew, 'Chasing two Rabbits? Dual Belonging and the Question of Salvation/ Liberation?' in this volume.

[4]   See Marianne Moyaert, 'Inappropriate Behavior? On the Ritual Core of Religion and its Challenges to Interreligious Hospitality', *Journal for the Academic Study of Religion* 27 (2014): 1–21; Marianne Moyaert, 'Christianity as the Measure of Religion?', in *Thirty Years of Theology of Religions*, ed. Paul Hedges (Leiden: Brill, 2015 forthcoming).

over what enables the ritual flexibility of dual belongers? What theory of ritual undergirds the phenomenon of dual belonging?

I propose the hypothesis that dual belonging presupposes a *weak theory* of symbolic practices (a mystical-experiential theory of religion), which is different from a *strong theory* of symbolic practices (revolving around the notion of meaning incarnation). I further elaborate on this hypothesis by arguing that dual belonging may be regarded as a specific expression of what has been called the *spiritualisation of religion*. I understand this *spiritualisation* in line with insights from sociologists of religion, Paul Heelas and Linda Woodhead.[5] Religion turns inward at the cost of more traditional expressions of religion that tend to be outward-oriented, materialistic and ritualistic. Though some will argue that dual belonging is the future of religion, I am concerned that it may contribute to a weakening of religions as they traditionally understand themselves.

Structure of My Argument

I want to develop my argument in three stages: (1) I begin by elaborating on some of the assumptions that underlie my understanding of religion and link it up with a *strong theory of symbolic practices*; (2) I explain what is meant by the *spiritualisation of religion* and how it is connected to a weak theory of ritual in particular; (3) I examine to what extent the phenomenon of dual belonging relates to the so-called 'spiritual revolution' and how this impacts on the way dual belongers perceive of the ritual dimension of their complex religious life. I conclude by formulating some concerns and questions with regard to the phenomenon of dual belonging.

Part 1: On Religion

How one assesses the phenomenon of dual belonging depends to a great extent on how one defines religion. I will therefore begin this exposition by elaborating on some of the assumptions that underlie how I understand religion in relation to ritual in particular.

---

[5]   Paul Heelas and Linda Woodhead, *The Spiritual Revolution: Why Religion is Giving Way to Spirituality* (Malden, MA: Blackwell, 2005).

Understanding Religion

I uphold an approach to religion, according to which religious adherence implies a willingness to respond to a heteronomous appeal that not only transcends us but also precedes us (anteriority), exceeds us (superiority) and is before us (exteriority).[6] In short, to be religious is to open oneself up to a call that comes from elsewhere, from beyond and higher than oneself.[7] This call is an invitation addressed to the religious imagination; it is not an imposition.[8] On this point, I find myself in basic agreement with the French philosopher Paul Ricoeur. He calls the religious self a *summoned* self who takes part in an economy of superabundance, excess and generosity; its condition is one of receptive dependence. From this perspective, religious identity springs from 'being chosen', rather than from being the result of (unlimited) choice. Though religious commitment builds on *assent*, it also includes an *involuntary dimension*.

In addition, the response of the religious self is always located in a 'chain of responses, a tradition kept alive in a community'. Ricoeur explains this chain of responses as follows:

> Other people are understood, first of all, as the transmitters of religious messages; behind them stand the founders of religions, who are men [sic] of their own word – of their acts, really, but these acts are meaningful. Finally, still further back, or higher up, there is recourse to a word that these founders declare to have been received, a fundamental word of last resort.[9]

The religious person responds to this 'earlier word' as it is transmitted by a particular religious tradition that revolves around particular symbolic practices and texts accepted as 'authoritative'. Together, they constitute the basis for the identity of a concrete religious community, establishing some sort of permanence over time.[10] The relationship between tradition and community is

---

[6]   See also Marianne Moyaert, *In Response to the Religious Other: Ricoeur and the Fragility of Interreligious Encounters* (Lanham, MD: Lexington, 2014), chapter 2.

[7]   Paul Ricoeur, *Critique and Conviction: Conversations with François Azouvi and Marc de Launay* (New York: Columbia University Press, 1998), 144.

[8]   Paul Ricoeur, *Essays on Biblical Interpretation* (Philadelphia, PA: Fortress Press, 1980), 117.

[9]   Jean-Pierre Changeux and Paul Ricoeur, *What Makes Us Think? A Neuroscientist and a Philosopher Argue about Ethics, Human Nature, and the Brain*, trans. Paul DeBevoise (Princeton, NJ: Princeton University Press, 2002), 267–8.

[10]   Richard Topping, *Revelation, Scripture and Church: Theological Hermeneutic Thought of James Barr, Paul Ricoeur, and Hans Frei* (Aldershot: Ashgate, 2007), 118.

analogous to that between master and disciple: there is a difference in altitude – the community accepts being instructed and formed by these symbolic practices and authoritative texts. Believers accept that they are being interpreted by the tradition they assent to while, at the same time, they reinterpret this tradition in view of novel challenges. Hence, no matter the shape one gives to one's own religious biography, it seems important to at least maintain a conversation with the religious tradition and religious community one claims to belong to and to recognise its authority.

To continue with this approach, religious identity can never be merely a subjective matter, there is also an 'objective' dimension to it. Religious identity also always rests on communal recognition. It would simply make no sense to call oneself a Buddhist or Christian (or both), if one is not *formally recognised as such*. Here I agree with Catherine Cornille who also questions a merely subjective understanding of religious commitment. She rightly explains that 'a religion cannot claim an individual as its member unless he or she consents to membership, just as an individual cannot claim membership unless that tradition confirms or grants it'.[11] For novel adherents, this usually implies that they have to meet certain requirements to be allowed full access to religious life. Personal commitment or assent to the truth conveyed by a tradition is often marked by entrance rituals that involve the larger community (either present or represented by a religious leader). These rituals demarcate the transition between standing outside and belonging to and participating in a community. Thus the distinction between 'insiders and outsiders' is reinforced.

On the Ritual Core of Religion

A religious adherence is the result of a long process of socialisation, in which a person learns to speak a particular religious language and becomes acquainted with the religious knowledge transmitted by that tradition. One has to listen before one can speak as a believer. Clearly, religious believers are not 'oversocialised automatons' – innovation and change are part and parcel of lived religion.[12] The more fluently one speaks a particular religious language, the more creative that person will be in reinterpreting the tradition with respect to novel challenges.

---

[11] Catherine Cornille, 'Strategies of Negotiation in Buddhist-Christian Dual Belonging', paper presented in Bristol, 26–28 June 2014.

[12] Meredith McGuire, *Lived Religion* (Oxford: Oxford University Press, 2008), 98.

Symbolic practices play a central role in this process of socialisation and in the process of acquiring a *primary religious language*, that is, tacit bodily religious language. This primary religious language, which points to *a* knowing how takes priority over *knowing that*, that is, explicit and codified in scripture, doctrine and commentaries. From this perspective, belief is what people know with their body.[13] Believers learn to master this primary religious language through practice: they are introduced to a 'tempo-spatial continuum' of concrete religious objects, festivities, ritual gestures, religious formula, customs and values central to the tradition. Symbolic practices stir the imagination in such a way that the religious object becomes vivid, real and present, they have the power to stimulate a deep understanding, elicit assent and induce the experience evoked by the ritual. As the cultural anthropologist David Morgan puts it: 'Handling objects, dressing in a particular way, buying, displaying and making gifts of particular commodities, attending certain events are all activities that engage people in the social relations and forms of the sacred imagination that structure their relation to the divine. Each of these activities and countless others, whether performed by Christians or Hindus or Wiccans, construct particular bodies of belief'.[14] Gradually, ritualists come to share the experience associated with the rite (for example chanting the mantra of the Lotus Sutra) and they become deeply permeated by the truths conveyed in that tradition.

Rituality is formal, repetitive and stable; it harks back to conventional practices established by fixed traditional rules handed down from one generation to another in a particular community and its meaning transcends both momentary concerns and mere subjective personal sentiments. Rituals tend to resist change, even though rituals, like all cultural elements, do undergo change. As cultural anthropologist Valeer Neckebrouck explains:

> The combination of the formal nature of rituals and their reference to tradition – in other words, their transindividual and transmomentary anchoring – guarantees, as it were, their stability. This is a feature of rituals that, in the classical view, is experienced as so essential that it is often seen as a primordial feature of ritual ... . What is meant [by stability] is that rituals succeed better than all other cultural elements in pretending they immune to the ravages of time and manage to

---

[13] David Morgan, 'Introduction: The Matter of Belief', in *Religion and Material Culture: The Matter of Belief*, ed. David Morgan (London: Routledge, 2010), 1–17, 9.

[14] Ibid., 12.

withstand more easily the influence of individual creativity and other contingent and time-bound components of the context in which they are performed.[15]

Different from other human activities, novelty or expressing one's deep personal feelings does not receive pride of place in the ritual domain; the ritualist rather acts in accordance with the prescriptions of the faith community. Instead of creativity, ritual performance implies conformity to traditional rules of stipulated patterns of behaviour, clearly implying a resistance to innovation. The ritualist executes a fixed, pre-determined, pre-existing mode of action as prescribed by the community. Right performance – doing things *they way they should be done according to tradition* – is an important dimension of ritual. This focus on a fixed sequence of actions (potentially) frees the ritualist of being overly preoccupied with him- or herself, thereby enabling her to become connected both to that community and to become part of a greater narrative. The meaning conveyed in ritual is not subjective, but rather collective: rituality provides individuals with meaning (not the other way around) and binds them together into one religious community that shares a single destiny and a collective memory.

A Strong Theory of Symbol and Ritual

Ritual performance is a very physical activity often revolving around particular things, whether they are concrete texts, symbols, sacred spaces, clothes, images food or other particular things. ... What is religiously meaningful is profoundly interwoven with particular words, standard formulas connected to particular rhythms and verses or objects, certain places or moments, specific sounds, chords and so on. The latter are an inextricable part of the symbolic practices that help shape the concrete religious experiences, feelings and beliefs of a religion. It is important to note that there exists a connection of *intertwinement* between what is tangible and elusive; material and spiritual; immanent and transcendent. Both dimensions are interwoven. The point is not simply to discover or uncover deep religious meanings about the Ultimate that lie beneath or beyond their material expressions; at stake is rather that we learn to grasp how these material expressions make the Ultimate present in this world.[16] Indeed, William Keenan and Elisabeth Arweck are right when they state that, in the religious realm, matter *matters*:

---

[15]   Valeer Neckebrouck, Mythen, riten en hun toekomst (Antwerp: Garant, 2008), 41.

[16]   See Marianne Moyaert, Materializing Theologies of Religions, in Theologies of Religions, ed. Paul Hedges, E. Harris, and S. Hettiarachchi (Amsterdam and New York: Brill publication in 2016)

> Without their material expressions, religions float in theological ether, and
> spiritualities enter the void, lifeless and deracinated. The human mind and hand,
> be they refined and delicate or rude and horny, are turned doggedly down the
> generations to the creation of countless material modes of expressing religious
> sensibility, identity and belonging. When dealing with the things of the spirit,
> matter matters inordinately.[17]

Drawing attention to the concrete and tangible dimension of religion is not
to the detriment of any interest in the spiritual dimension of religion. On the
contrary, according to a *strong theory of ritual* the 'outer' elements or better still
'the material coordinates or forms of religious practice' help 'shape the feelings,
spaces, and performances of belief'.[18] They are not merely expressive of but also
constitutive for religious meaning, that is why it is more appropriate to speak of
meaning embodiment, for all religious meaning is mediated by and incarnated
(as opposed to expressed) in concrete symbolic practices. From this perspective,
religions are irreducibly particular, and though there may certainly be overlaps
and commonalities between religions, it is highly unlikely that they all point in
one direction. It is more likely that the religious object embodied in different
symbols and vividly imagined in various ritual practices of various religious
traditions is really different. The diversity of religious objects corresponds with
the diversity of ritual traditions.

The notion of meaning incarnation clearly evokes the age-old idea of the
presentia realis, which points to the power of symbols to make present what is
holy; as a consequence, the symbols themselves acquire holiness. This notion
also explains why religious people may have the greatest regard and even
reverence for material things: they are seen as carriers of what is holy. Think of
the Eucharistic practice of 'eating the body of Christ and drinking his blood', the
fact that by entering a Hindu Temple one is already seen by the gods, the idea
that the torah is a holy object, therefore it must be set aside (in 'geniza'), it is
moreover considered as a token of great respect to bury the torah next to a great
torah scholar.

Symbols and symbolic practices bring the ritualist and the community
to which he or she belongs in the presence of the divine. However, precisely
the power of symbols (as carriers of holiness) simultaneously points to their
weakness and vulnerability: the particularity of symbols as embodiments of

---

[17]   William Keenan and Elisabeth Arwick, 'Introduction: Material Varieties of Religious
Expression', in *Materializing Religion: Expression, Performance and Ritual*, eds William
Keenan and Elisabeth Arwick (London: Ashgate, 2006), 1.

[18]   David Morgan, 'Introduction: The Matter of Belief', 2–3.

religious meaning, as carriers of holiness, as incarnations of the transcendent implies that matter matters in religion, even to the extent that when a symbol is contaminated, lost or destroyed *something holy is lost*. Strongly incarnated meanings are vulnerable. When the external/the form/the material in which the meaning is embodied changes, its meaning alters and something may be lost. Believers with a strong symbolic sensibility know that they have to tread carefully when entering the symbolic realm. From this perspective, we may also understand why most religious communities maintain certain strictures with regard to the participation of outsiders in their religious ceremonies, certainly when they are connected to the heart of their tradition. The fact that there are ritual boundaries that 'protect' certain mysteries of faith belongs to the particularity of religious traditions and seems to be imperative for the survival of religious communities.

Part 2: Spiritualising Religion

This understanding of religion as a symbolic practice revolving around strongly incarnated meanings is not popular among religious scholars and theologians. It often elicits sharp resistance: the charge is that it would amount to a form of idolatry, lead to undue exclusivism, often attachment to concrete symbolic practices and their material components is regarded as an expression of immature childish faith, tribalism or a desire for power. The strong resistance and the idea of an 'immature expression of faith' especially resonates with the *genealogies of religion* as developed since the 19th century mainly by liberal protestant religious scholars. The more a religion stresses the importance of ritual, symbol, space and matter, the more likely it would be depicted as less developed; the more a religious tradition relativises the importance of such particular meaning incarnations, the more likely it would be presented as elevated, developed and cultivated. In such genealogies of religion, the 'uncivilised' tribal religions were fixated on their *fetishes*, Hindus on their idolatrous statues and Catholics only one level up on a misconception of the Eucharist and a highly problematic cult of Saints. Religious scholar Birgit Meyer puts it as follows:

> Hierarchies of religious development, from 'fetishism' and 'animism' to 'monotheism', share a view of 'inward'-centred religiosity as forming the highest level of religion; it is posited as intellectually and morally ahead of and superior to religions that still rely on 'outward' forms. The pivot of these evolutionary models

is the idea that the human mind can do increasingly better without the baggage of 'outward' forms.[19]

This 'modern, Enlightened' understanding of religion does not exist solely in the heads of religious scholars and theologians; it is an understanding that has become current in many Western countries. As sociologists of religion show, there is a move away from 'institutionalised religion' with all its external manifestations and a move towards understanding religion as an inward phenomenon and faith as a personal relationship with a *higher, spiritual or transcendent* realm. Faith is gradually seen as an inner state, rather than a relationship made possible, expressed and enhanced by concrete religious practices.[20] Communal ritual practices are declining, private devotional practices, such as prayer and meditation are retained. The material dimension of religion is connected with the risk of idolatry and fetishism and symbolic practices with the possibility of empty ritualism. Sociologists of religions call this sociological *trend* the spiritualisation of religion.

The Spiritual Revolution and the Turn to the Subject

In the past, traditions were simply passed on from one generation to another without further ado, whereas today the transfer of symbolic practices, habits and beliefs is hampered.[21] This process of detraditionalisation contributes to a much more reflective dealing with tradition, commitment and identity, even to the extent that sociologists and religious scholars nowadays speak of flexible believers and their fluid affiliations. Since the transmission of tradition no longer happens naturally, identity is no longer given but has to be constructed. From this perspective, detraditionalisation goes hand in hand with individualisation: identity is not a given but a task and project. Identity is being formed continuously, and the believer is involved in that process in a productive way. As a consequence, the emphasis is less on the objective pole of

---

[19] Birgit Meyer, Inaugural Lecture: *Mediation and the Genesis of Presence: Towards a Material Approach to Religion*, Utrecht, 19 October 2012: http://www2.hum.uu.nl/onderzoek/lezingenreeks/pdf/Meyer_Birgit_oratie.pdf (accessed 2 December 2014).

[20] Talal Asad, 'Reading a Modern Classic: W.C. Smith's The Meaning and End of Religion', in *History of Religions* 40 (2001): 205–22.

[21] Paul Heelas (ed.), *Detraditionalization: Critical Reflections on Authority and Identity* (Oxford: Blackwell, 1996).

religious belonging (the authority of tradition) than on its subjective pole.[22] The formation of religious identity is increasingly freed from the rule of conformity. Sociologists call this the *subjective turn*.

In their analysis, Linda Woodhead and Paul Heelas explain that 'this turn is shorthand for a major cultural shift of which we all have some experience. It is a turn away from life lived in terms of external or 'objective' roles, duties, and obligations, and a turn towards life lived by reference to one's own subjective experiences'.[23] This turn to the subject often goes together with a modern critical attitude *vis-à-vis* institutions that embody claims to authority. Indeed, what seems to be primarily important is: '[n]ot to follow established paths but to forge one's own inner-directed, as subjective, life. Not to become what others want one to be, but to "become who I truly am". Not to rely on the wisdom of others ... but to live out the Delphic "Know thyself" and the Shakespearian "To thine own self be true".'[24] The subject is called to exercise authority in the face of the great existential questions and this opens up to the possibility of experimentation, questioning and exploring, also across religious boundaries.

The 'turn to the subject' not only explains the decline of religion, it also shows how religion in a Western context has undergone transformation in recent decades. Religious practice is not simply disappearing; rather, it seems to be the case that over time religion is being turned inward.[25] This transformation is captured in what Heelas and Woodhead call the spiritualisation of religion. If 'to be religious conveys an institutional connotation, prescribed rituals and established ways of believing [then] to be spiritual is more personal and experiential, and has to do with the deepest motivations of life for meaning and wholeness. The first is "official" religion, standardised and handed down by religious authorities; the second is "unofficial", highly individualistic, religion, à la carte'.[26] More and more people dissociate themselves from official religion as traditionally understood and rebel against its formal structures; its ritual patterns and doctrinal boundaries. The whole idea of bounded traditions under the guidance of some heteronomous authority is being questioned. What is of

---

[22] Catherine Cornille, 'Multiple Religious Belonging', in *Understanding Inter-Religious Relations*, eds David Thomas, David Cheetham and Douglas Pratt (Oxford: Oxford University Press, 2012), 328.

[23] Linda Woodhead and Paul Heelas, *The Spiritual Revolution. Why Religion Is Giving Way to Spirituality* (Oxford: Blackwell Publishing, 2005), 2.

[24] Ibid., 4.

[25] Mark C. Taylor, 'Introduction'. in *Critical Terms for the Study of Religion*, ed. Mark C. Taylor (Chicago, IL: Chicago University Press, 1998), 1–20.

[26] Roof Wade Clarke and Lyn Gesch, *Boomers and the Culture of Choice: Changing Patterns of Work, Family and Religion* (London: Routledge, 1995), 72.

primordial importance is rather if a religion and its practices satisfy one's deep yearnings and nourishes authentic religious experiences that are beyond compare. One seeks wholeness, but without being limited by the traditional religious frames. The symbolic realm, as embodying the 'divine', is losing its appeal, at best symbols are regarded as expressing religious emotions or experiences, but their meaning lies beyond themselves. There is no need to become 'overly attached' to them.

A Weak Theory of Symbol

Often the spiritualisation of religion goes together with what has been called an a mystical-experiential understanding of religion, according to which the singularity of religions should be sought not only in their religious and cultural differences but also in what transcends these differences. What really *matters in religion* is what remains elusive, lies beyond our ordinary, tangible world and resists any conceptualisation.[27] Faith is nourished by depth experiences (the religious 'inside') that are only secondarily coloured by all sorts of cultural and religious practices, rituals, doctrines and narratives (the religious 'outside'). In line with this view of religion, the concrete religious symbols, practices, rites and narratives are seen pointers to the ultimate. They help religious people with their orientation towards the ultimate, but once this ultimate has actually been obtained, these tools may be left behind. Since they are mere vehicles or transporters, they are not to be cherished too much.[28] It would be a token of undue reverence to regard them as carriers of what is holy. They are penultimate, hence the appropriate religious attitude is one of detachment. To miss that point is to run the risk of idolatry.

If a strong theory of symbolic practices revolves around the notion of meaning incarnation (the symbol understood as a carrier of what is holy), a weak theory of symbol departs from a polarised scheme that 'privileges spirit above matter, belief above ritual, content above form, mind above body, and inward contemplation above 'mere' outward action, producing an understanding if religion in terms, basically, of an interior spiritual exercise.'[29] In any case the relation between

---

[27]   Birgit Meyer and Dirk Houtman, 'Introduction: Material Religion – How Things Matter', in *Things: Religion and the Question of Materiality*, eds Dick Houtman and Birgit Meyer (New York, Fordham University Press, 2012), 1–23, 3.

[28]   Harold Coward, 'Religious Pluralism and the Future of Religions', in *Religious Pluralism and Truth: Essays on Cross-Cultural Philosophy of Religion*, ed. Thomas Dean (New York: SUNY, 1995), 45–86, 47.

[29]   Birgit Meyer and Dick Houtman, 'Introduction', 1.

symbol and symbolised is weaker. The weaker the connection between the symbol and what it symbolises, the more plausible the idea of reaching 'the Ultimate' via various religious trajectories. Some would regard the latter as interchangeable, others rather point to their complementarity, illuminating various aspects of what is Ultimate. In any case, the particular *symbolic expressions* ought to be relativised in light of the Ultimate that lies beyond. This does not necessarily mean that people *should* pursue different religious trajectories at the same time, it does mean this becomes a worthwhile possibility.

Part 3: Dual Belonging as Spiritualisation?

Mature faith is increasingly regarded as private and interior, not public; it is mystical rather than ritualistic; it is, moreover, an expression of (personal) choice and commitment rather than one of being immersed in a long-standing tradition.[30] Once the authority of religious traditions has been abandoned, one may also move beyond the particular and concrete religious formula, rituals and rhythms, and then the way is open to individual religious explorations beyond religious boundaries. To limit oneself to one religious tradition and its symbolic practices may even be seen as unduly limiting.

My hypothesis is that dual belonging is an epiphenomenon of the spiritualisation of religion. I expect to find evidence of (1) the 'turn to the subject' (detraditionalisation and individualisation), (2) of a mystical-experiential understanding of religion; (3) and of a weak theory of symbols. Those elements together may explain the relative flexibility with which dual belongers move between various religious traditions and communities. I will explore the viability of this hypothesis. Rose Drew's empirical inquiry into the nature of dual belonging and the testimonies of her interviewees are an important resource.[31] As will become clear shortly, the outcome of this exploration is ambiguous, as is the phenomenon under scrutiny. This is not a black or white story; the signals are mixed, as will be my final judgement.

---

[30] Robert Orsi, 'Lived Religion', in *Lived Religion in America: Towards a History of Practice*, ed. David Hall (Princeton, NJ: Princeton University Press, 1997), 3–21.

[31] Rose Drew, *Christian and Buddhist: An Exploration of Dual Belonging* (London: Routledge, 2011).

Dual Belonging, the Subjective Turn and Religious Flexibility

Dual belongers are *border-crossers*; they challenge traditional authorities, religious boundaries, conservative tendencies or exclusivist claims to truth. The very idea that one should restrict oneself to one religious tradition makes no sense to them, thus they challenge the boundaries of belonging. Tradition holds no self-evident authority over them; no doctrine is critically off limits. From a sense that religions have tended to overvalue dogmatic issues, dual belongers welcome the possibility of rethinking, transforming or even rejecting doctrines. They are seekers rather than conformists. Autonomy is important to them. Sallie King for example is recorded saying 'Forget this "incarnation of God" thing ... and make ... [Jesus] a great teacher and Buddha a great teacher'.[32] In any case, we are dealing with persons, who as comparative theologian John Thatamanil would depict, 'are no longer under the constraining power of Christian traditions, characterized by strong exclusivist impulses [and thus] are far more likely to be open to modes of religious life that are marked by fluid multiplicity'.[33]

As such, there can be no doubt that dual belonging is an epiphenomenon of the subjective turn; a key aspect of the spiritualisation of religion. Processes of detraditionalisation and deinstitutionalisation enable dual belongers to take charge of their own religious biography, and they do so in a very active way. They are free agents composing their own religious identity with flexibility. As Michael Amaladoss explains, they create for themselves an identity without accepting the limits laid down by the structures of tradition.[34] What compels them is a sense of exuberance and superabundance (as surplus of meaning that cannot be exhausted by one tradition), pointing to what I have called earlier a mystical-experiential understanding of religion. That is why they embark on a journey in 'search for something deeper'.[35] Dual belongers strongly believe that truth may be found beyond the boundaries of their own traditions, and regard it even as their responsibility to deeply engage other traditions in their search for wisdom. Dual belonger Paul Knitter explains that 'the two traditions (Catholic Christianity and Buddhism) have helped to point him toward the one "holy Mystery" even if the

---

[32] Sallie King in Rose Drew, *Christian and Buddhist: An Exploration of Dual Belonging* (London: Routledge, 2011), 87.

[33] John Thatamanil, 'Eucharist Upstairs, Yoga Downstairs'. Paper delivered at the Third Cohort of the Luce Summer Seminar on Theologies of Religious Pluralism and Comparative Theology, Atlanta, June 2013.

[34] Michael Amaladoss, 'Religious Identity and Mobility', http://sedosmission.org/old/eng/amaladoss_7.htm (accessed 14 December 2014).

[35] Cf. Ruth Furneaux in Rose Drew, *Buddhist and Christian?*, 23.

two faiths understand that mystery differently.[36] He exhibits the possibility of being are oriented to the Ultimate Reality that underlies all religious traditions, through two traditions: Buddhism and Christianity.[37] Appreciative of this phenomenon, Manuela Kalsky depicts the religious traditions as travel guides assisting dual belongers on their spiritual pilgrimages. According to her:

> The individual subjects have the final say in the assessment of what can be and what cannot be religiously accountable. Religious traditions become the open heritage of multiple meanings and values from which the individual chooses in all freedom to give her own life content, form, and direction, possibly as Christian, Hindu, and Muslim at the same time.[38]

A First Qualification: Dual Belongers and their Process of Identity Formation

Based on the testimonies of dual belongers, it is important to further qualify the above reflections. Dual belonging may be a product of the subjective turn, nevertheless it would be overstated to depict this phenomenon as an expression of sheer individualism. One still finds traces of a more 'classical' understanding of religion amongst dual belonging. Even though the subject is in charge of her own religious identity and they clearly exercise personal choice in the construction of their religious biography, thereby challenging traditional authorities, at the same time many dual belongers show an outspoken desire to be recognised and accepted by the religious communities to which they claim to adhere. They want to be part of a greater narrative as it is celebrated communally.

All of this shows itself primarily in their willingness to undergo a formative process of immersion in which they learn to appropriate their *second* religious language under the guidance of a master to whom they obey. As most novices, Drew's interviewees learned to speak their 'second first language' by imitation, accepting the authority of someone else, who 'represents' the tradition and community in which they want to enter. Following the example of their master

---

[36] Paul Knitter quoted in Amy Frykholm, 'Double Belonging: One Person, Two Faiths', *Christian Century*, 25 January 2011, 20–23, 21.

[37] Rose Drew, 'Christian and Hindu, Jewish and Buddhist. Can You Have Multiple Religious Identities?', in Paul Hedges (ed.), *Controversies in Contemporary Religion: Education, Law, Politics, Society and Spirituality (Santa Barbara and Oxford: Praeger, 2014)*, 247–72, 257.

[38] Manuela Kalsky, Het flexibele geloof van Pi. Meervoudige religieuze identiteiten als toekomstvisioen', in C. Doude van Troostwijk, Evert van den Berg, Leo Oosterveen (eds), Buigzame gelovigen. Essays over religieuze flexibiliteit (Amsterdam: Boom, 2008), 64–73, 71.

(and the community), they are gradually initiated into some of the mysteries of faith, interiorise certain values, ideals and norms and most importantly learn proper ritual comportment. The words of prayer, meditation, and confession, the rhythm of the chants, the actions of the ritual all have to be appropriated. This immersion in tradition transforms their religious imagination and enables a deepening of the existential grasp of the 'religious object'.[39] Learning by example, little by little they become convinced of the truths conveyed in that 'other tradition', to such an extent that they are unable to 'return' home. Ritual practice has shaped and complicated their faith, and as a consequence they cannot but claim for their own religious identity a form of dual belonging: Christian-Buddhist; Buddhist-Christian.

Exemplary in this regard is the testimony of Ruben Habito, who took up the practice of Zen Buddhism under the guidance of Zen master Yamada Koun Roshi, and relates that he has experienced *kenshō*:

> [W]ithin a few weeks, ... came the Big Bang. ... In the flash of an instant, I *understood*, in a rather direct and immediate way, that is *from within*, what was behind the intriguing half-smile of the Buddha figures, we see in sculptures and paintings.[40]

But sr Ruth Furneaux also makes mention of her training:

> Initially her teacher was a senior student of John Garrie Roshi, followed by Garrie Roshi himself (until his death in 1998); he confirmed that experiences of hers had been authentic insights. Once the relationship was established, frequent contact with her teacher was maintained, with several meetings a day for the period during which she lived at the Sat Society centre in Wales. There she was trained 'in all aspects of sati in everyday life – true spiritual training not just sitting mediation. In 1991 Furneaux was granted permission by John Garrie Roshi to teach in the Zen and Satipatthana traditions.[41]

It is, moreover, not uncommon that dual belongers undergo a 'rite de passage', by which they mark their commitment formally and affirm their affiliation to a new community (baptism, taking refuge in the Buddha, the dharma and

---

[39] Terrence Merrigan, "Imagination and Religious Commitment," Louvain Studies 27 (2002), 197–217, 210.

[40] Testimony taken from Rose Drew, *Christian and Buddhist: An Exploration of Dual Belonging* (London: Routledge, 2011), 26.

[41] Rose Drew, *Christian and Buddhist*, 23.

the Sangha) and vice versa, it would seem that they think it important that their membership is also formally recognised by the community. As any novel religious identification, this personal decision is transformative and deeply affects one's mind and body. From this perspective, dual belonging shows clear resemblances with (interreligious) conversion, albeit that multiple belongers claim not to leave behind their primary faith community of which they continue to be active participants.

Second Qualification: Dual Belonging, Pluralism and a Weak Theory of Symbol

The religious trajectory of dual belongers shows (1) a desire to be accepted to the community to which they claim to belong and (2) the importance of ritual in their religious formation. Indeed, their testimonies seem to affirm the efficacy of rituals, and illustrates that rituals do something with people; they enable profound religious knowledge and experience.[42] The fact that dual belongers appreciate the ritual dimension of religion, however, does not contradict my hypothesis that dual belonging is an epiphenomenon of the spiritualisation of religion. To explain this claim, I need to return to the distinction I introduced earlier between a strong and a weak theory of symbols. Above I explained that the first revolves around the notion of meaning incarnation, whereas the second is expressivist and 'weakens' the connection between the symbol and what is symbolised. I also explained that the weak theory of symbols is often undergirded by a mystical-experiential understanding of religion.

Looking at the testimonies recorded by Rose Drew, it seems clear most of them uphold a mystical-experiential understanding of religion, which Drew terms *monocentric pluralism* (and is regarded as an outstanding example of the spiritual revolution). According to this view, which draws on the work of pluralist philosopher John Hick, none of our human categories or interpretations can be made to apply to the Ultimate. The nature of the Ultimate is elevated beyond personal and impersonal descriptions, and is thus transcategorical. Human descriptions cannot be applied literally nor can they claim absoluteness. The different religious traditions are historically and culturally determined interpretations of the one Ultimate Reality. The great world faiths embody different perceptions and conceptions of, and correspondingly different responses to, the Real. These different responses constitute the various ways in

---

[42]   Robert E. Innis, 'The Tacit Logic of Ritual Embodiments', *Social Analysis: The International Journal of Social and Cultural* 48 (2004): 197–212.

which ultimate Reality has impinged upon human life.[43] From this perspective it becomes possible that

> God-talk and *nirvana*-talk concern a single ultimate reality, i.e., a reality which his *uniquely* greatest, supreme, most fundamental and most worthy of commitment (greater than everything, rather than merely not lesser than anything). ... Different religions are seen as equally valid responses to this one ultimate reality.[44]

The ineffable nature of the ultimate Mystery is emphasised especially. Most of dual belongers *are oriented to what lies beyond what is concrete, material and tangible*. Rose Drew explains that for 'dual belongers the idea that Buddhism and Christianity point beyond themselves provides and implicit integrative framework which allows them to relativise both Buddhism and Christianity with respect to Mystery with a capital "M"'.[45] Thus the symbolic practices (and religious teachings) are regarded as relative to the Ultimate Reality that lies beyond these particularities. As a consequence the tensions that may exist between different rituals – tensions that spring from the fact that different symbols embody different 'religious objects' and that different symbolic practices orient the body in quite diverging directions – are dissolved. The relation between the Ultimate and its material components is loosened, thereby downplaying the way in which religion is embodied in particular symbolic practices. As a consequence one can be oriented to the Ultimate through different traditions and their practices. As Drew explains: 'as long as both traditions are experienced as beneficial and as orienting them in a single direction for the time being, what is to prevent dual belongers form committing fully to the practice of both in the here and now'.[46] The fact that several of Drew's interviewees come to see Christian prayer and Zen mediation as overlapping to a great extent seem to affirm the relative importance of 'the form' of ritual. Though these practices may, *at first glance*, seem very different, if one moves beyond their formal distinctions, it becomes clear, according to Drew's interviewees, that one can develop in both Christian and Buddhist practices 'an awareness of one's non-seperateness from ultimate reality'. As Reis Habito suggests that over time Buddhist and spiritual practice become integrated:

---

[43] John Hick, *An Interpretation of Religion* (New Haven, CT: Yale University, 1989), 313.

[44] Rose Drew, *Christian and Buddhist*, 53.

[45] Rose Drew, *Buddhist and Christian*, 192.

[46] Rose Drew, 'Christian and Hindu, Jewish and Buddhist'. 261.

It's not god or you, it's not God and you together, it's not all is one ... The question simply doesn't arise and, so, at that point you have fully integrated all the opposites of appearance and reality; conventional and absolute have come so close together that there's not a jot of difference anymore ... so while we're saying ' ... this is Buddhist practice and this is Christian practice', ...hopefully, we'll be going, at some point, to the acceptance of 'eventually, it *simply doesn't matter*'.[47]

Conclusion

In this chapter I asked how do dual belongers negotiate their dual commitment and I hypothesised that this negotiation is made possible by means of a spiritualisation of religion. This spiritualisation of religion is often regarded in terms of 'liberation': it liberates believers from the constraints of traditions and opens up a whole new world of possibilities. Closed traditions with fixed boundaries are being replaced by open traditions, with messy contours and flexible believers. The shift to the subject offers more opportunities to exercise choice in matters of religion. According to some religious scholars and theologians the spiritualisation of religion is to be embraced, as is the phenomenon of dual belonging.[48] It would open up the possibility of a spiritual transformation that is profoundly enriching and existentially decisive.[49] Moreover, rather than weakening faith commitments, it would enhance them. As Paul Knitter puts it, 'without the Buddha I would not be a Christian'.[50] Dual belonging is an expression of openness and interreligious transformation, it may even be regarded as the future of religion. I do not share this enthusiasm, because I am concerned about the spiritualisation of religion. Departing from an understanding of religion that revolves around symbols and symbolic practices—rituals, artefacts, sacred places I am concerned that as the primary locales for the perpetuation of religious life – I am concerned about the spiritualisation of religion which also underlies the phenomenon of dual belonging, and will further

---

[47]   Rose Drew, *Buddhist and Christian*, 173.

[48]   For example Manuela Kalsky, 'Embracing diversity: Reflections on the Transformation of Christian Identity', *Studies in Interreligious Dialogue* 17 (2007): 2, 221–31.

[49]   Perry Schmidt-Leukel, *Gott ohne Grenzen. Eine christliche und pluralistische Theologie der Religionen* (Gütersloh: Gütersloher Verlagshaus, 2005), 495.

[50]   Paul Knitter, *Without the Buddha I Could not be a Christian* (London: Oneworld, 2009).

add to the weakening of religious communities.[51] The fact that the 'spiritual turn' is the left hand of the decline of religion as traditionally understood should at least be food for thought. I cannot help but wonder whether it is not necessary for religious communities to give some counterweight to the spiritualisation of religion, which seems to undergird the phenomenon of dual belonging. My concern is that dual belongers, knowingly or unknowingly contribute to the dematerialisation of the traditions to which they belong. Even though, they rightly draw attention to the apophatic dimension of both Christianity and Buddhism, they seem the underestimate that matter matters in religion.

---

[51] Julian Droogan, *Religion, Material Culture and Archeology* (London: Bloomsbury, 2013), x.

Chapter 8

Strategies of Negotiation in Buddhist-Christian Dual Belonging

Catherine Cornille

The claim to belong to different religious traditions has become more prevalent as individuals are increasingly exposed to the reality of religious diversity and choice. The phenomenon of multiple religious belonging is certainly not new in many parts of the world. Until the cultural revolution, the religious identity of the Chinese was defined by a combination of Confucian, Taoist and Buddhist teachings and practices, while Japanese religiosity since the 7th century has been configured through a mixture of Shinto, Buddhist, Confucian and later also Christian elements, at times based on individual choice and at other times on religious theories (*Shinbutsu-shūgō*).[1] Indeed, throughout history individuals have sought mental, physical and spiritual solace from any religious source or power promising to address and solve a particular need or problem. However, what characterises the current phenomenon of multiple belonging is its highly deliberate and selective nature. Whereas in the past, multiple belonging was often a matter of belonging to a culture defined by many different religions, or of temporarily seeking help from certain powerful gods belonging to another religion, the present phenomenon of multiple belonging expresses itself often in a personal choice to identify with (elements of) different religious traditions.[2] In that respect, the current phenomenon of multiple religious belonging may be regarded as a continuation of what in the late 20th century was called 'New Age', with the obvious difference that while the latter rejected all established religious traditions and identities, the former embrace many.

---

[1]   Jan Van Bragt, 'Multiple Religious Belonging of the Japanese People', in *Many Mansions? Multiple Religious Belonging and Christian Identity*, ed. Catherine Cornille (Eugene, OR: Wipf and Stock, 2010, 2002), 7–19.

[2]   I have elsewhere elaborated on the distinction between involuntary and voluntary, and temporary and permanent forms of belonging to different religions. See Catherine Cornille, 'Multiple Religious Belonging', in *Understanding Interreligious Relations*, eds David Cheetham, Douglas Pratt and David Thomas (Oxford: Oxford University Press, 2013), 324–40.

Among the many possibilities for multiple belonging, the most prevalent expression of this phenomenon in the West involves cradle Christians who also claim to be Buddhists. There is little consistency in terms of which traditions of Buddhism and Christianity are combined. Whereas Zen Buddhism used to be a popular draw for Christians interested in meditation, some dual belongers have come to adopt Tibetan Buddhist teachings and practices, while others focus on the Theravāda tradition. The particular combination of traditions is often based on which particular teacher or temple happens to come into one's purview, though most Buddhist-Christian dual belongers tend to be well versed in the Buddhist tradition as a whole.

The category of multiple religious belonging has also come to cover a variety or continuum of degrees of belonging to more than one religion. It may be used for individuals who identify primarily with one tradition but are drawn to selective elements of another, all the way to those who claim to belong fully and equally to the two traditions. Since the former may be seen to include all forms of religious openness and generosity in interreligious dialogue, we will focus here only on the second, strong understanding of multiple belonging where neither of the two traditions is consistently normative or dominant in the experience of the individual.

This raises numerous questions regarding the category of religious belonging. It is first of all interesting to note that, in contrast with the second half of the 20th century, there seems to be again a desire to 'belong'. This may have to do with an attempt to avoid the sense of superficiality and self-centeredness often associated with New Age religiosity. But it may also have to do with a desire to be part of a religious community, with its rich history and tradition. The claim to belong to particular religious traditions, however, also raises questions regarding the criteria of belonging set by the traditions themselves, and whether these traditions allow for the possibility of multiple belonging. As in all cases of institutional identity, religious belonging involves an interplay between subjective and objective assent or recognition. An institution thus cannot count an individual as a member without his or her assent, while an individual cannot claim to belong to a religion without some degree of institutional or communal recognition, usually marked by certain formal or informal rites of initiation. While the phenomenon is usually approached from the perspective of the subject who claims to belong to more than one tradition,[3] we will here also

---

[3] A good example of this is Rose Drew's *Buddhist and Christian? An Exploration of Dual Belonging* (London: Routledge, 2011). The book deals exclusively with the experience of individuals who claim to belong to Christianity and Buddhism.

reflect on it from the perspective of the traditions to which he or she claims to belong. In his chapter, Gavin D'Costa approaches this question with particular reference to the Roman Catholic tradition. I will here offer some more general and phenomenological reflections, based on the logic of religious identity and belonging.

Every religion may have different criteria for belonging and may admit to various degrees of belonging. But the claim to belong to a particular religion only makes sense if that religion recognises the individual as a member, and his or her beliefs and practices as consistent with its own self-understanding.[4] Belonging to a particular religion involves a combination of assent to a particular worldview and beliefs, participation in rituals and communal life and the orientation of one's life around certain values and spiritual goals. It is clear that the goal for most religions involves a complete commitment to that tradition and a transformation of the individual according to the highest ideals set out in its teachings. This is reflected in the life of monks, priests or the religious elite who embody the ideal of their respective religions. From this perspective, the very idea of multiple religious belonging may be regarded as an oxymoron. One can only give oneself fully to one religion at a time, just as one can only commit oneself to one marriage at the time. Abraham Vélez de Cea states in this book that he does not find the marriage metaphor for religious belonging particularly illuminating, and proposes rather to compare religious commitment to one's relationship with each of one's parents or each of one's children. While his alternative metaphor may work from the perspective of the subject, who may indeed be fully committed to both parents or love both children equally unconditionally, it fails when understood from the perspective of the object of one's love and commitment: the religions themselves. Whereas each parent may recognise the existence of another parent, and each child the reality and needs of other children, religions do not readily acknowledge the equal right of other religions to one's time and commitment. This of course has much to do with the incompatibility of the religious claims of different religions and with the non-compossibility[5] of the religious demands placed on the individual. But the exclusive commitment required from its members may also have something to do with the pervasive idea that spiritual growth requires a complete surrender

---

[4]   This, of course, does not mean that the institutional assessment of who does or does not belong is always reflective of who lives according to the highest ideals of a religion, whether they do or do not actually claim to belong.

[5]   See Paul Griffiths, *Problems of Religious Diversity* (Oxford: Blackwell, 2001), 32–6.

146   *Buddhist-Christian Dual Belonging*

of self, and that such surrender can only take place with regard to one particular master or religious path.[6]

It would thus seem that for both Buddhism and Christianity, the idea of dual belonging would be undesirable, if not impossible. Though the two religions undoubtedly share a good number of beliefs and values, and though the teachings and practices that differ from one another may be often regarded as complementary rather than contradictory, the two traditions are still based on certain beliefs which are fundamentally incompatible (such as belief in versus denial of a personal Creator God)[7] and place demands on the individual that are irreconcilable (such as participation in a liturgical cycle based on the saving events of Jesus Christ's death and resurrection, versus rejection of the final or eschatological efficacy of such unique historical event). While there are any number of particular examples that may be given of doctrinal incompatibility or practical non-compossibility, the very basic demand of complete surrender placed upon adherents involves undivided commitment. As such, it would seem that fully belonging to Christianity logically precludes simultaneously belonging fully to Buddhism.

In spite of this, some individuals still adamantly claim to belong fully to both Buddhism and Christianity. Realising that such dual belonging is less than evident, they tend to develop various strategies to counter or overcome some of the objections raised. I will sketch four strategies which seem to emerge in the literature and which also represent logical options: (1) a shift from multiple religious belonging to multiple religious participation, (2) a focus on the transcendent and apophatic unity of religions, (3) a reinterpretation of one religion in terms of another and, finally, (4) the development of a personal synthesis.[8]

---

[6]   For more on this, see my article, 'Mehrere Meister? Multiple Religionszugehörigkeit in Praxis und Theorie', in *Multiple religiöse Identität*, eds, Reinhod Bernhardt and Perry Schmidt-Leukel (Zurich: Theologischer Verlag Zurich, 2008), 15–35.

[7]   See the articles by Strange and Tilakaratne which deal more extensively with conflicting conceptions of God or ultimate reality.

[8]   Some of these strategies are also corroborated by other articles in this volume, both in defense of and as critique of multiple belonging. While Rose Drew and J.P. Williams provide examples of the second strategy (focus on the transcendent and apophatic unity of religions), Marianne Moyaert offers a more detailed and thorough critique of this same strategy. I believe that this list of strategies captures the actual and potential ways in which the problems facing dual or multiple belonging may be addressed. However, as with all phenomenological work, the typology is open for correction and amending.

1) Shift from Multiple Religious Belonging to Multiple Religious Participation

One of the strategies for engaging different religions simultaneously has been to focus on praxis, rather than on theoretical or theological questions. While the latter tends to lead to the impasse of conflicting truth claims, the former is thought to facilitate greater compatibility. Some therefore propose to change the nomenclature from multiple religious belonging to multiple religious participation.

One of the most common expressions of religious hybridity in history is indeed that of individuals participating in the ritual practices of various religions. This usually involves visiting miraculous shrines, places of pilgrimage or religious healers, regardless of their religious affiliation, in hopes of deriving certain this-worldly benefits. In India, Christians may thus visit Hindu shrines,[9] and Hindus Christian shrines, whereas African Christians often continue to visit traditional African healers, and many Brazilian Christians admit to also participating in and belonging to the healing religions of Santeria and Candomblé. Here, identification with particular traditions or practices usually lasts as long as a particular problem exists, though the effectiveness of particular practice may lead to more enduring loyalty or identification.[10] Multiple religious belonging is thus often based on this-worldly needs and benefits, congruent with a more vitalistic approach to religion, which is often also associated with the religious life of East Asia. In China and Japan, religions are indeed often judged less according to their theological consistency, but rather according to their practical efficacy or aesthetic appeal. The desire of many Japanese to marry in a Christian Church, for example, has little to do with belief in Jesus Christ or in the Christian understanding of marriage, but rather with the beauty of the ritual, and in some cases also with the efficacy of the sacrament. Japanese may thus effortlessly combine a Christian wedding with Buddhist funeral rituals and Shinto rites of passage.

But the focus on praxis may also arise from more purely spiritual pursuits in which the practices of another religion are thought to deepen, enhance or expand the set of religious and spiritual practices offered in one's own tradition. This is particularly the case in experiences of Buddhist-Christian dual belonging, where

---

[9]   For numerous examples of this, see Selva Raj and Corinne Dempsey, *Popular Christianity in India: Riting Between the Lines* (Albany, NY: SUNY Press, 2002).

[10]   For numerous examples of this type of popular mixing, see Devaka Premawardhana, 'The Unremarkable Hybrid: Aloysius Pieris and the Redundancy of Multiple Religious Belonging', *Journal of Ecumenical Studies* 46:1 (2011): 100.

Christians tend to turn to Buddhist forms of meditation to develop mindfulness and to pursue other spiritual goals. Since the threshold for participation in Buddhist practices is relatively low, and its fruits largely reconcilable with Christian teachings, Christians have often approached Buddhist practice as an unproblematic form of multiple belonging.

Though less frequently, Buddhists have also occasionally participated in Christian liturgies. Here, however, the challenges of multiple religious participation become more evident. While Buddhists are welcome to participate in the Catholic celebration of the mass, they are not allowed to partake in the eucharistic meal, that which for Catholics is regarded as the apex of the ritual. Many religions indeed contain ritual elements which are reserved for members only, and participation in the ritual life of another religion often leads to difficulties and embarrassments, both for insiders and for outsiders.[11] For individuals steeped in a particular religion, ritual life becomes part of a way of being, a second nature, which is not easily assumed or appropriated by individuals who do not fully participate in the life of a tradition.

While certain religious practices may be universally accessible and effective beyond the strictly defined boundaries of religious identity and belonging, the shift from doctrine to praxis does not solve the problems or challenges related to multiple religious belonging. For those who approach religion primarily in terms of its ability to provide this-worldly benefits, multiple religious participation may be unproblematic. However, as soon as questions regarding the deeper meaning of rituals and the truth of their underlying beliefs are raised, the impossibility of fully participating in the ritual life of two or more traditions becomes clear. Though logical coherence may not be a priority for some practitioners, it is certainly so from the perspective of the religion which supplies the rituals. Whereas these religions may be lenient with regard to average practitioners, they do demand a more thoughtful and coherent engagement with the religion on the part of their more serious practitioners, scholars, leaders or monks. From the point of view of the religions, the ideal remains thus one in which teachings and practices form a coherent and integrated whole.

Moreover, even when focusing only on the practices prescribed by particular religions, multiple religious participation presents a problem. As Paul Griffiths also points out, the demands placed upon individuals by two different religions

---

[11] For more on this, see Catherine Cornille, 'Interreligious Hospitality and its Limits', in *Hosting the Stranger Between Religions*, eds, Richard Kearney and James Taylor (New York: Continuum, 2011), 35–45.

Strategies of Negotiation in Buddhist-Christian Dual Belonging   149

are such that 'it would be impossible for a single person to perform both'.[12] He gives the example of the admonition to 'give all your surplus resources to the Church and give all your surplus resources to the Buddhist monastic community' which would of course be impossible to achieve. From this type of 'non-compossibility' Griffiths draws the general conclusion that 'no one can inhabit more than one form of religious life at a time' and that 'being religious, while it lasts, is a monogamous affair'.[13]

To be sure, certain types of rituals allow for easier cross-religious access than others, insofar as they are less imbued with explicit religious meaning, or may be readily reinterpreted to accord with various religious meanings. As such, Buddhist forms of meditation may be practiced by Christians who view it as a means to cultivate mindfulness or contemplative prayer. In most cases, however, this practice becomes part of the broader Christian spiritual life and goals. As William Johnston, Roger Corless and Winston King have observed, Christians practicing Zen meditation tend to practice a 'Christian Zen', understanding the meaning and the goal of the practice as part of a Christian worldview.[14] Or conversely, Buddhists participating in Christian rituals might interpret the ritual acts and contents in Buddhist terms. This form of borrowing and reinterpretation, however, is a far cry from fully belonging to two traditions or fully participating in the ritual life of two religions.

2) Focus on the Transcendent Unity of Religions

One of the most common ways to argue theologically for the possibility of multiple religious belonging is to view religions as derived from and oriented toward the same ultimate and ineffable reality. Throughout his book, *Without Buddha I Could not be a Christian*, Paul Knitter uses the famous Zen image of religious teachings as 'fingers pointing to the moon', and in her article in this volume, J.P. Williams also grounds the possibility of Buddhist-Christian dual

---

[12]   Paul Griffiths, *Problems of Religious Diversity* (Oxford: Blackwell Publishers, 2001), 34.

[13]   Ibid., 34 and 35.

[14]   William Johnston, *The Still Point: Reflections on Zen and Christian Mysticism* (New York: Fordham University Press, 1970), 77; Roger Corless, 'The Mutual Fulfillment of Buddhism and Christianity in Co-inherent Superconsciousness', in *Buddhist-Christian Dialogue: Mutual Renewal and Transformation*, eds, Paul Ingram and Frederick Streng (Honolulu: University of Hawaii Press, 1986), 133; Winston King, 'Buddhist-Christian Dialogue Reconsidered', *Buddhist-Christian Studies* 2 (1982): 8–9. This is also the case with Christian Insight Meditation, pioneered by Mary Jo Meadow.

belonging in a radically apophatic approach to ultimate reality. Rose Drew notes that all the individuals she studied in her research on Buddhist-Christian dual belonging started from what she calls a 'monocentric pluralist perspective'.[15] She points out that individuals who claim to belong to both traditions 'are logically obliged to accept it [the monocentric hypothesis]' since 'one is required to endorse both the Buddhist and the Christian claim that there is no more than one ultimate reality' and since one cannot 'endorse both the Buddhist and the Christian claim to be concerned with that which is uniquely ultimate unless one takes these religions to be concerned with the same ultimate'.[16] In order to function as the unifying ultimate reality, multiple belongers also have to accentuate the discontinuity between particular Buddhist and Christian conceptions of the ultimate, and that ultimate reality itself, since each religion maintains significantly different, and in some respects mutually exclusive views. Conflicting truth claims are then minimalised by relegating them to the different historical, cultural and linguistic contexts in which they emerged, rather than to irreconcilable religious differences. Drew also observes that there is a tendency among dual belongers toward 'treating certain pivotal points of disagreement between the Buddhist and Christian worldviews as "bracketed questions" rather than siding firmly with one tradition or the other'.[17] These questions are regarded as secondary in relation to the deeper unity between religions.

Against the critique that pluralists and dual belongers tend to dismiss the particularities of religions, Paul Knitter counters that for him differences between religions really do matter. He argues that though 'we might say that although the different fingers are pointing to the same moon, each, as it were, points to a different part of the moon. Without the Buddhist fingers, there are parts of the moon that Christians would never see. But the same is true of what Christian fingers might mean for Buddhists'.[18] From this perspective, multiple religious belonging may be regarded as not only possible, but also necessary, or highly desirable.

The idea of a transcendent and mystical unity of religions is of course not new or unique to theological pluralists or multiple belongers. It has its modern roots in the tradition of Perennial Philosophy (Huxley, Coomaraswamy,

---

[15] Rose Drew, *Buddhist and Christian?* 53. The 'monocentric' approach to pluralism stands over against a 'polycentric' approach which sees different religions as reflective of and oriented toward a different goal.

[16] Rose Drew, *Buddhist and Christian?* 83.

[17] Rose Drew, *Buddhist and Christian?* 210. Drew bases her analysis largely on interviews with Christians who claim Buddhist-Christian dual belonging, primarily Ruben Habito, Maria Ries-Habito, Sallie King and Roger Corless.

[18] Paul Knitter, *Without Buddha I Could not be a Christian* (London: Oneworld), 72.

Schuon) and Theosophy (Blavatsky, Olcott, Krishnamurti). It draws support from the essentialist approach to mystical traditions as various expressions of the same fundamental religious experience (James, Stace, Forman), as well as from the fact that a good number of religious and monks have either explicitly professed dual belonging or else have been profoundly inspired and shaped by two traditions (Henri Le Saux, Kevin Hunt, Robert Kennedy, Aloysius Pieris, Raimon Panikkar, Shigeto Oshida, Hugo Enomiya-Lassalle, Michael Amaladoss, Elaine MacInnes and so on). In his theological reflection on dual belonging, the French theologian Claude Geffré states that while 'It would be absurd to affirm that one can be both Christian and Hindu or Buddhist from the perspective of these traditions as religious systems', nevertheless, 'if religion is understood as an interior experience and as the total surrender of oneself to a transcendent and Absolute reality, it would be possible to affirm a continuity between my Christian experience and my previous spiritual experience'.[19] Dual religious belonging thus presupposes a clear distinction between religious experiences and their expression in religious teachings and practices, and a privileging of those experiences, or, as Marianne Moyaert puts it, a spiritualising of religion.

While the pluralist idea of the transcendent and apophatic unity of religions is indeed a necessary philosophical or theological basis for multiple belonging, it is far from uncontested. Against the view of a mystical unity of religions, constructivists have argued that every ultimate experience is fundamentally shaped by the texts, rituals and categories leading to that experience so that the mystical experiences generated from within different religions are as diverse as their respective teachings and practices.[20] And the position of theological pluralism has itself been subject to widespread critique in the course of the past decades. Many have pointed to the religious incongruency of drawing a sharp distinction between religious teachings and practices and the ultimate reality or deepest experiences to which they refer. While most religions do recognise the radical transcendence of ultimate reality itself, they also affirm their own teachings and practices as a faithful and efficient reflection of that reality. When seen from within particular religions, there is thus continuity between experience and expression, or between the ultimate reality and the symbols and categories used

---

[19] Claude Geffré, 'Double Belonging and the Originality of Christianity as a Religion', in *Many Mansions? Multiple Religious Belonging and Christian Identity*, ed. Catherine Cornille (Maryknoll, NY: Orbis Books, 2002), 99.

[20] See the volumes edited by Steven Katz, *Mysticism and Philosophical Analysis* (Oxford: Oxford University Press, 1978), *Mysticism and Religious Traditions* (Oxford: Oxford University Press, 1983), *Mysticism and Language* (Oxford: Oxford University Press, 1993) and *Mysticism and Sacred Scripture* (Oxford: Oxford University Press, 2000).

within that tradition to express this reality. The apophatic strands of religious traditions are not meant to discount the contents of religious representations, but rather to purify them. If religions refer to a reality and experience beyond concepts, it is still the beyond of particular categories, and through those particular categories and practices that one may attain to the highest reality and truth. It is certainly true that some traditions, such as Mahayana Buddhism, place greater emphasis on the finite and fallible nature of doctrinal expressions. But even here, a hierarchy of truths is maintained, and certain teachings are regarded as more reflective of the ultimate truth than others. Both Buddhism and Christianity presuppose some continuity between their teachings and the ultimate reality itself and some sense that access to that reality occurs through its own particular teachings. As such, the tendency to relativise religious teachings or to 'bracket' difficult or conflicting claims of the different religions clashes with their self-understanding and sense of inner coherence. Moreover, the idea that different religions would represent differing and complementary dimensions of the same ultimate reality would also contradict the sense of self-sufficiency and comprehensiveness prevalent in the self-understanding of religions.

On a practical level, such discontinuity would also threaten to weaken one's commitment to particular religious observances, since they inevitably become relativised in relation to the transcendent religious goal. Marianne Moyaert rightly points to an inevitable devaluation of the ritual dimensions of religions. While individuals engaged in multiple belonging may continue to be engaged in the practices of both traditions, these rituals no longer contain the sense of necessity derived from traditional beliefs in the continuity between particular teachings and practices and their transcendent referent. And the calculation and choice involved in combining two ritual systems already implies a certain reticence to surrender to either.

3) Interpretation of One Religion in Light of Another

A third strategy to resolve the tensions or contradictions involved in dual belonging involves the reinterpretation of the teachings and practices of one tradition in terms of the other.[21] This takes place in all forms of interreligious dialogue, where one tends to understand the teachings and practices of another religion in terms of one's own religious tradition. And it forms an integral part

---

[21] See also the article by Ross Thompson for an example of and further elaboration of this strategy.

of religious borrowing or learning, where elements from one religion become absorbed in another, thus acquiring new connotations and meanings. As pointed out above, Christians practicing Buddhist meditation usually infuse the practice with Christian meaning, while Buddhists integrating Christian social teachings tend to ground the impulse or motivation for social change in Buddhist teachings. This is part of the hermeneutical negotiation that occurs in all forms of interreligious exchange.

In the case of dual belonging, however, the attempt to reconcile two traditions often leads to a complete reinterpretation of one tradition in light of the other. Most often, this involves a reinterpretation of the fundamental teachings of Christianity in Hindu or Buddhist philosophical terms. As such, Henri Le Saux (Abhishiktananda) and Raimon Panikkar have attempted to express their identification with both Hinduism and Christianity through a reinterpretation of Christian faith through the categories of *Advaita Vedanta*, and John Keenan and Joseph O'Leary have used Madhyamika teachings to give new meaning to some of the fundamental tenets of Christian faith. Paul Knitter uses the Buddhist category of 'inter-being'[22] to reinterpret the Christian notion of God, and both Reis Habito and King interpret Christian salvation and eschatology purely in terms of the Buddhist emphasis on being fully present in the moment.[23] While some regard this as part of their experience of dual belonging, others view it simply as an answer to the call to make sense of Christianity in different cultural contexts, and to enrich Christian self-understanding through the use of different philosophical frameworks. Just as early Christianity came to be interpreted in Hellenistic terms, they argue that other philosophical systems may provide new insight into the fundamental tenets of Christian revelation.

In so far as much of the experience of Buddhist-Christian dual belonging tends to involve the reinterpretation of Christianity in Buddhist philosophical terms, reflection on the possibility and limits of such exercise seems to be at the heart of the discussion of multiple belonging. If, as some suggest, Christianity should be able to express itself anew through a Madhyamika philosophical framework, then Buddhist-Christian dual belonging would be unproblematic, and one would not even speak of dual belonging, since it would merely involve a new interpretation of Christianity. However, if such reinterpretation presents certain fundamental challenges for traditional Christian faith, then one is confronted with the reality and the problems of dual belonging.

---

[22]   He states: 'the God whom both my head and heart can relate to – this God or my Gos bears a much greater resemblance to *Sunyata* and InterBeing than to the prevalent Christian image of God as the transcendent Other', *Without Buddha I Could not be a Christian*, 17.

[23]   See Rose Drew, *Buddhist and Christian?* 135.

Since the theological reflection on this question is ongoing, I wish to merely point here to some of the elements or questions that are to be taken into consideration. At the heart of the discussion lies the question whether or not religions are indissolubly linked to or determined by the philosophical framework in which they were originally expressed, and whether philosophical frameworks are themselves religiously neutral. While it is certainly true that the fact that Christian doctrines came to be formulated within a Greek or Hellenistic philosophical context is largely accidental, it has become difficult, if not impossible to distil the essential message of Christianity from its earliest layers of interpretation. The New Testament (in particular the letters of Paul and the gospel of John) is itself already profoundly shaped by Hellenistic categories. On the other hand, Mahayana Buddhism did not merely adopt a Madhyamika philosophical system, but played an important role in shaping it. Nagarjuna indeed regarded his philosophy as a development of the Buddhist teaching of dependent origination. If this is true, the reinterpretation of Christianity in Mahayana philosophical terms would amount to a Buddhicisation of Christianity, and the claims to Buddhist-Christian dual belonging to a primary belonging to Buddhism.

To be sure, the experience of multiple religious belonging often involves a going back and forth between two different hermeneutical frameworks in which neither is consistently dominant. And the experiences of theological dialogue involve a more nuanced and qualified engagement with the philosophical framework of another tradition.

However, in so far as dual belonging consistently involves the reinterpretation of Christian symbols in Buddhist terms, one must wonder whether it still makes sense to speak of *dual* belonging.

4) Development of a Personal Synthesis

While individuals claiming dual belonging often seek to justify their claim by seeking recourse in the teachings of one or both traditions, some come to develop their own personal synthesis of elements of the two traditions. This may be based on a realisation of the impossibility of reconciling the two traditions in their own terms, or else on an attitude of indifference toward the self-understanding of religions. As pointed out above, for many involved in multiple belonging, identification with different religions has less to do with theoretical truth and consistency than with practical efficacy. However, some still attempt to make some synthesis out of the elements they have appropriated from the different religions. This was the case, for example, with Roger Corless, one of the first scholars in the United States to claim to be both Buddhist and Christian. After long, in-depth study and practice of the two religions, he declared that 'A person cannot be authentically a Buddhist and a Christian at the same time, since the systems are complete in themselves and at several important points (such as the existence of God) contradictory. One can only be a "Buddhist-Christian" if one either ignores the differences between the systems or blends them in a transcendental unity'.[24] Corless resolved the dilemma of adhering to two irreconcilable traditions by suggesting the reality of a *polyverse* in which the different absolutes exist in different worlds. Parallel to this, he suggested that these different worlds also inhere in different selves so that the different religions or worldviews well up in our being as 'semi-autonomous realities'.[25] This was his attempt to preserve the self-understanding of Christianity and Buddhism while integrating them in his own life and practice.

There are of course as many forms of personal syntheses as there are individuals involved in dual belonging. The attempt to theologise from a perspective in between two or more religious or theological systems has been called 'interstitial theology' which Tinu Ruparell defines as 'a mode or methodology for the comparative philosophy of religion which exploits the structure of metaphor and aims at the construction of liminal, hybrid perspectives or standpoints for continuing the conversation of religions in a creative and open-ended way'.[26] He envisions the emergence of 'newly formed recombinant traditions',[27] the truth of which lies not so much in their propositions but in their pragmatic value:

> If sufficient people settle the liminal land, the newly formed recombinant tradition will have been found to be viable. Interstitial theology thus asks pragmatic questions: does the new tradition 'speak' to people, does it fill their needs, reflect their unique place between traditions? A viable tradition will retain ties to its parents yet exhibit the openendedness and novelty which will be its hallmarks,

---

[24] Roger Corless, 'The Coming of the Dialogian: A Transpersonal Approach to Interreligious Dialogue', *Dialogue & Alliance* 7:2 (1993): 13.

[25] Roger Corless, 'Many Selves, Many Realities: The Implications of Heteronomy and the pLurality of Worlds Theory for Multiple Religious Belonging', *Pacific Coast Theological Society Journal*, 6 October 2002.

[26] Tinu Ruparell, 'Inter-Religious Dialogue and Interstitial Theology', in *The Wiley-Blackwell Companion to Inter-Religious Dialogue*, ed. Catherine Cornille (Oxford: Wiley-Blackwell, 2013), 121.

[27] 'The Dialogue Party: Dialogue, Hybridity and the Reluctant Other', in *Theology and the Religions: A Dialogue*, ed. Vigo Mortensen (Grand Rapids, IN: Eerdmans, 2003), 235–48.

156   *Buddhist-Christian Dual Belonging*

but being pragmatically justified, the viability of a recombinant tradition can only be ascertained after the fact.[28]

While such interstitial theology may be reflective of a trend among dual or multiple belongers, it remains difficult to imagine how it may lead to a new tradition or community, since it is based not on a revealed text or event, but on the subjective judgements and insights of individuals. To be sure, certain books, such as *Without Buddha I Could Not Be a Christian* may inspire other individuals who find themselves in between two traditions.

The strategy of developing a personal synthesis is a reminder of the fact that multiple religious belonging is not in essence very different from the New Age religiosity of the past. It involves a selection of elements from two or more religious traditions which are brought together largely on the basis on one's own taste and judgement. To be sure, multiple belongers have more respect for the traditions from which they borrow, and they attempt to develop a synthesis which gives the greatest possible allowance for the self-understanding of the two traditions. But in the end, neither of the traditions can be done full justice, and one ends up with a compromise which works mainly for oneself, and possibly for those who adhere to one's new, recombinant tradition.

Conclusion

The desire to belong to different religions, combined with the awareness that such dual or multiple belonging does not always obey the laws of non-contradiction has led to various strategies of negotiating the fault lines between religions. One of the oldest and most common strategies is to shift the attention from the theoretical or theological to the ritual or practical dimension of the religions, and to focus on ritual efficacy, rather than logical coherence. More recently, scholars and individuals have come to resort to the idea of a transcendent or mystical unity of religions to justify the possibility of belonging to several religions simultaneously. Another strategy involves interpreting one religion in light of the other. This raises the crucial question of the hermeneutical adaptability of religions and of the relative importance of texts and symbols versus interpretation of these in defining the definition of a particular religion and the contours of belonging. If, as some claim, Christianity should and could be reinterpreted in Madhyamika terms, then such exercise does not constitute

---

[28]   Ibid., 129.

multiple belonging. If, however, it proves to be impossible, practically and/or theologically, then the question may be raised whether one's religious identity is determined primarily through symbolic or through hermeneutical identification, or both. In the first case, Christianity might still be considered dominant, in the second case Buddhism, and in the third case both, or neither. In the absence of such dominant or normative tradition, individuals tend to develop their personal synthesis, which may or may not rejoin that of others.

The various strategies of negotiation of dual or multiple belonging have their own logic and efficacy and provide meaning for those who inhabit them. The question is whether they are also meaningful or coherent for the religions to which they claim to belong. The latter question may not be relevant if religious belonging is regarded as purely a matter of individual choice or subjective inclination. But if religious belonging also involves recognition on the part of the religion, then the strategies of negotiation should also accord with the self-understanding of the religions. Different religions may have different levels of tolerance of multiple belonging. However, when considering Buddhism and Christianity, neither the exclusive focus on practice, nor the shift to a mystical unity of religions, the reinterpretation in categories belonging to the other tradition or the idea of an autonomous synthesis of religions accords neatly with current religious self-understanding. One might argue that the strategies are somewhat more compatible with Buddhism than with Christianity. The emphasis on practice as well as on the ineffability of the ultimate reality and the conventionality of all teachings are indeed an integral part of the Buddhist teaching. And the reinterpretation of one tradition in light of the other tends to take the form of interpreting Christianity in Buddhist philosophical terms. But that in itself may suggest that Buddhist-Christian dual belongers in actual fact identify more readily (though not always consciously) with Buddhism, while remaining attached to their Christian religion of origin.

The phenomenon referred to as dual or multiple religious belonging is undoubtedly here to stay. The very availability of choice in matters of religion will lead to different combinations of teachings and practices. In many cases, one or the other religion may remain dominant. Paul Knitter, for example, still writes primarily for his fellow Christians, for 'those Christians who like me are struggling, often painfully, with trying to hold together what they believe personally and intellectually as Christians'.[29] Moreover, he states explicitly that 'the "orthodox question" I'm asking ... is directed to the Christian community,

---

[29] Paul Knitter, *Without Buddha I Would Not Be a Christian*, p. xiv.

not the Buddhist'. As such, he clearly seeks to be Christian, evidently realising that such decision does not depend solely on his own claim or expectation.

While the claim to fully belong to more than one religion may not be entirely coherent, the continued desire to belong, and the struggle to come to terms with multiple loyalties might motivate religions to engage in a more systematic dialogue with the religion or religions to which many of their members seem to be drawn. In so far as most Buddhist-Christian dual belongers are cradle Christians who have also come to identify with Buddhism, they may point to certain unmet needs and desires in Christian religious life, as well as hint at ways in which these might be addressed, either through advanced dialogue with Buddhism and/or through internal Christian reflection and resourcement. Their strategies of negotiation also form a challenge for religious thinkers to further explore the flexibility and limits of religious belonging.

PART III
Explorations

Chapter 9

An Alternative Conception of Multiple Religious Belonging: A Buddhist-Catholic Perspective

Abraham Vélez de Cea

This chapter proposes an alternative conception of multiple religious belonging called 'interreligious belonging'. Instead of using the metaphor of monogamous marriage to understand dual belonging, the chapter advocates the metaphor of love for one's parents and one's children. The chapter also suggests that interreligious belonging is best understood as having two distinct yet interrelated dimensions: affiliative and incremental. Full belonging in the affiliative sense depends on whether someone fulfils the requirements for membership established by specific traditions and communities within religions (objective factor), and on whether someone experiences a sense of belonging (subjective factor). Full belonging in the incremental sense is a logical impossibility because nobody can embrace at the same time all the different theological frameworks or all the vocations of a religion. The distinction between affiliative and incremental dimensions of religious belonging allows us to overcome the reservations of some scholars about the impossibility of interreligious belonging.

1. Understanding Multiple Religious Belonging from Inside

I find the expression 'multiple religious belonging' problematic because the term 'multiple' is highly misleading. At least for some people, the word 'multiple' conveys the idea of personality disorder, division or fragmentation. However, those who claim to belong to more than one religious tradition do not see themselves as having a personality disorder and a divided or fragmented religious identity. Rather, they see themselves as having a single yet complex religious identity that has been expanded by the contribution of other religions. For instance, I have expanded my Catholic identity with the contribution of

Buddhism. More specifically, my Spanish Catholicism has been expanded by Sri Lankan, Thai, Burmese, Tibetan and Chinese Buddhism. My commitment to Catholicism has not been diluted but rather enhanced by my encounter with Buddhism. Likewise, my commitment to the Buddha's path is reinforced rather than undermined by my commitment to the Catholic tradition. My sense of belonging is interreligious rather than multireligious, and that is why I prefer to use the expression 'interreligious belonging' rather than 'multiple religious belonging'. My sense of belonging is broader in scope than the sense of belonging of those who remain within the confines of one religion, but that does not mean that it is fragmented or divided, which is what the term 'multiple' seems to suggest.

I fail to recognise myself and fellow interreligious belongers in descriptions that characterise the phenomenon of belonging to more than one religion as presupposing a fragmented religious identity with constant unresolved tensions and a lukewarm commitment. For instance, according to Catherine Cornille:

> The experience of multiple religious belonging also often arises from, or can lead to, a somewhat tentative or lukewarm commitment to any one particular religion ... This means that those who experience multiple belonging do not fully embrace either religion on its own terms, but rather choose to live in the tension between irreconcilable or competing worldviews. In relinquishing full commitment or belonging to any one tradition, they thus also abandon the willingness or ability to speak from or for either tradition. [1]

The implication is clear, if multiple religious belongers relinquish full commitment or belonging to any one tradition, it follows that their commitment and sense of belonging must be divided or fragmented, that is, less than full.

I do not deny that interreligious belongers may experience at some point in their lives theological and spiritual tensions that may make them question their identity and commitment to certain aspects of the religions they claim to belong. However, I would describe such tensions as provisional in most cases, and as a healthy sign of spiritual and theological growth. Besides, such tensions and subsequent questioning of one's identity and commitment to certain aspects of religions are also common among mono-religious belongers. Given that mono-

---

[1] 'Multiple Religious Belonging and Interreligious Dialogue', in eds David Thoms, David Cheetham and Douglas Pratt, *Understanding Inter-Religious Relations* (Oxford: Oxford University Press, 2013), 334. I would like to express my gratitude to Catherine Cornille for kindly sharing with me her ideas and having encouraged me to think harder about the im/possibility of interreligious belonging.

religious belongers may also experience theological and spiritual tensions, as well as less than full commitment to their religions, it does not seem fair to associate only interreligious belonging with a troubled religious identity and a less than full sense of belonging.

I also prefer the expression 'interreligious belonging' rather than 'multiple religious belonging' because the term 'interreligious' facilitates a quick connection between 'interreligious belonging' and interreligious dialogue. This is important because people who expand their identity and sense of belonging with the contribution of other religions do so as a result of practicing advanced forms of interreligious dialogue. In a way, interreligious belonging represents the culmination of interreligious dialogue, at least for some individuals.

Far from being a challenge and an obstacle for interreligious dialogue,[2] people who claim to fully belong to more than one religion are uniquely qualified to facilitate interreligious dialogue. Interreligious belongers are exceptionally competent to build bridges of understanding and cooperation among the religions they belong precisely because they have a broader perspective and can see things from both sides of the bridge. Given their liminal, in-between location, interreligious belongers are not the best candidates to represent the official position of religious institutions, but they are ideal facilitators for dialogue among people from different religions including their official representatives. Interreligious belongers are indispensable to foster advanced forms of interreligious dialogue, not only because they can provide expert guidance, but also because, given their unique interreligious perspective, they can prevent many misunderstandings and the conflicts that may derive from them.

Although the main causes of interreligious belonging are the advanced forms of theological and spiritual interreligious dialogue, it would be a mistake to think that interreligious belonging is a necessary outcome of interreligious dialogue. Not everyone who participates in advanced forms of dialogue expands their religious identity, deepening and broadening their sense of belonging. Negative experiences while practicing interreligious dialogue may lead some people to contract and stiffen up their identity and sense of belonging.

Why does interreligious belonging occur as the consequence of advanced interreligious dialogue in some cases, but not in all of them? Why do some people who practice interreligious dialogue fail to develop interreligious identities? Perhaps a quote by Raimundo Panikkar will provide a plausible answer: 'we are somewhat chosen by the religion we accept to belong to. Acceptance, and free acceptance is here paramount ... My religious identity

---

[2] Ibid., 324, 334, 336.

comes as a sort of gift, a kind of grace which comes to me and that I am free to accept, reject, or modify'.[3] That is, there is always an element of grace in the experience of interreligious belonging that escapes our control. The element of free choice comes only afterwards, as a deliberate response to such experience of interreligious belonging.

Two things can be inferred from Panikkar's quote. First, people do not choose to experience a sense of belonging to one religion, even less so to more than one. Experiencing a sense of religious/interreligious belonging is a gift, a grace, something that happens to us, never produced at will. For instance, I have not decided to feel a profound sense of belonging to both Buddhism and Catholicism. I have been 'chosen' by the two religions, or rather, I have received the gift of experiencing a sense of belonging toward Buddhism and Catholicism. I know it is a gift or a grace because I cannot replicate a similar sense of belonging toward other religions that I respect and admire deeply, including Judaism, Islam, Jainism and Hinduism. I have been enriched by my dialogue with such religions but never to the point of experiencing a sense of belonging toward them. I only experience a sense of belonging toward Buddhism and Catholicism, and this is not my choice, I cannot help it.

Second, people may choose to do different things with the gift/grace of interreligious belonging. For instance, I have chosen to accept both Catholicism and Buddhism with humility, utmost respect and endless gratitude for their contribution not only to my life, but also to the lives of many people past and present. I love Buddhism and Catholicism fully and equally, in a way similar to the way I love my two parents and two daughters. I cannot choose not to love them or to love one more than the other. Besides, it would not be right to choose one religion over the other, just as it would not be right to love one of my daughters more than the other, or to love my mother more than my deceased father and vice versa.

The metaphor of love for one's parents works very well with dual belonging and the metaphor of love for one's children works even better with religious belonging involving more than two traditions. Personally, I do not find comparisons of religious belonging to monogamous marriage particularly illuminating.[4] Obviously, if we assume that interreligious belonging is analogous to polygamy and ideal religious belonging to monogamy, then it follows that

---

[3]   Raimundo Panikkar, 'Religious Identity and Pluralism', in eds, Arving Sharma and Kathleen M. Dugan, *A Dome of Many Colors* (Harrisburg, PA: Trinity Press International, 1999), 42.

[4]   Catherine Cornille, 'Double Religious Belonging: Aspects and Questions', *Buddhist Christian Studies* 23 (2003): 43–9.

there is something wrong with belonging to more than one religion. But I do not experience my Buddhist-Catholic belonging as being unfaithful to either Buddhism or Catholicism. Quite the contrary, I see myself as being a better Catholic when I endorse the elements of truth and holiness that I encounter in Buddhist traditions and a better Buddhist when I embrace the elements of the Dharma that I find in Catholicism. To not be a Catholic would make me a worse Buddhist, and to not be a Buddhist would make me a worse Catholic.

Comparing religious belonging to monogamous marriage is also unhelpful because religions are not similar to partners with whom people choose to have sexual intercourse. I have not chosen to have a sense of belonging with two religions just as I have not chosen my parents or my daughters. I am aware of mystical literature comparing the relationship between the soul and God to erotic, romantic and marital love. However, I doubt that such types of love correspond to the kind of love that people experience toward their religions. Besides, an intimate loving relationship with God is qualitatively different from the relationship that people establish with religious teachers, religious communities and religious institutions. Even the image of the Church as the bride of Christ cannot be understood literally in terms of monogamous marriage because Christ also has a loving relationship with people outside the Church. Would it not be ridiculous to accuse Christ of being unfaithful to his bride for loving people outside the Church?

If ideal belonging is akin to monogamous marriage, it follows that multiple religious belonging is somewhat similar to sleeping around with other partners, but that degrades one's spouse as well as the people used for frivolous extra-marital affairs. Rather than likening religious belonging to monogamous relationships, somehow broken by sleeping around and having extra-marital affairs, I prefer to view the religions to which I belong as parents who give me life, guidance and protection, or as children to whom I serve with patience, unconditional love and undivided commitment. For instance, I feel a profound love, respect, gratitude and sense of loyalty towards both Catholicism and Buddhism in a way similar to the love, respect, gratitude and loyalty I feel toward my parents at all times in my life. Likewise, I serve and love both of my children unconditionally and with undivided commitment just as I serve and love both Buddhism and Catholicism. I am ready to give my life for my children and in case of conflict, that is, when my children fight, I seek peace among them: listening to what they have to say, trying to reconcile them and reaching a just solution. Similarly, I offer my life to Buddhism and Catholicism, I pay close attention to the similarities and differences that exist among them, and I seek to reconcile them whenever possible, though not at any price. Just as I do my best to find a solution fair to my children whenever they are in conflict, I try to find a solution that is fair to Buddhism and Catholicism whenever their doctrines or practices are in tension. I am not as naïve as to think that my theological and spiritual solutions will always be perfect and agreeable to all Buddhists and Catholics, but I am not as pessimistic as to assume that no satisfactory solution will ever be reached.

People may choose to respond differently to the gift/grace of interreligious belonging. Some people may choose to reject both traditions and adopt a secular standpoint in a way similar to those who have a difficult relationship with their parents or their children, preferring to discontinue the relationship altogether for the sake of their mental health or everybody's well-being. Still others may choose to follow only Buddhism or only Christianity, again, in a way similar to those who decide to have a relationship only with one parent or only with one child, perhaps because they cannot forgive the other parent or the other children for something that they did or failed to do. But I have chosen to accept the gift/grace of interreligious belonging and seek a harmonious relationship with both Buddhism and Catholicism despite their shortcomings and incompatibilities, as I have accepted my parents and children, who are also far from being perfect or in full agreement.

Even if I wanted to, I would not be able to blur the differences that exist between Buddhism and Christianity or to ignore the dark chapters of their history. Similarly, my parents and my children are distinct human beings with their respective identities and idiosyncrasies, which sometimes leave much to be desired. Although I do not comprehend all the riches of Buddhism and Catholicism, I respect them both deeply even when my conscience does not let me agree with some of their teachings. These disagreements might be painful and disheartening, but they are never strong enough to make me question my belonging to Buddhism and Catholicism. Similarly, I do not understand and I do not agree with everything that my parents or children say and do. When I disagree with them and even suffer for their choices and ways of thinking, I do not question my service and belonging within the family. I have never thought for a second about discontinuing my love and commitment to my parents and children. Whether I like it or not I belong to my parents and my children in the same way that I fully belong to both Buddhism and Catholicism. I cannot do otherwise because I am intrinsically related to them, that is, we are family and they constitute my identity.

I may attempt to modify the two religions that constitute my religious identity and develop a creative synthesis that remains faithful to the core insights and values of both religions, or I may decide to accept the two religions as they are with all their strengths and weaknesses without attempting any artificial synthesis. Similarly, I may attempt to change the ways of my parents and children, or perhaps know better and embrace them as they are without attempting any forceful transformation of them.

I could not agree more with Catherine Cornille when she states, following Panikkar, that religious belonging is more than a subjective experience.[5] In order to determine whether someone fully belongs to a religion, we need to take into account not only subjective factors but also objective ones. By objective factors I mean fulfilling the requirements for membership established by traditions and communities. Without fulfilling the objective requirements for membership, traditions and communities would not recognise anybody as one of their members, and without such recognition there would not be religious belonging proper.

I wish to extrapolate the same criterion to interreligious belonging. I can only be recognised as a Buddhist and a Catholic because I fulfil the objective requirements for membership established by specific traditions and communities within these two religions. More specifically, if I wish to be recognised as a Roman Catholic, I need to comply with the requirements for membership established by the Roman Catholic Church, for instance in *Lumen Gentium* 14. That is, profession of faith, partaking in the sacraments, accepting ecclesiastical government and being in communion with such government.[6] Similarly, if I wish to be recognised as a Theravāda Buddhist, I need to take refuge in the three Jewels, observe at least the five precepts and hold the fundamental teachings attributed to the Buddha in the Pali Canon in high regard.[7]

However, in order to fully belong to more than one religion, besides fulfilling the objective requirements for membership established by specific traditions and communities within religions, it is also necessary to experience a sense of belonging (subjective factor). This means that genuine belonging is irreducible to membership or mere external affiliation to a religious organisation. It is the combination of objective and subjective factors what allows us to speak about

---

[5]   *Many Mansions? Multiple Religious Belonging and Christian Identity* (Maryknoll, NY: Orbis Books, 2002), 123.

[6]   Interestingly, LG, 14 also talks about perseverance in charity as necessary to attain salvation even for those belonging to the Church: 'The bonds which bind men to the Church in a visible way are profession of faith, the sacraments, and ecclesiastical government and communion. He is not saved, however, who, though part of the body of the Church, does not persevere in charity'.

[7]   Personally I consider fundamental teaching of the historical Buddha the doctrines of non-self, dependent origination and the four noble truths.

full belonging to more than one religion or interreligious belonging in the full sense.

By 'a sense of belonging' I mean a cluster of emotions toward a religion including love, gratitude, loyalty and a diffuse feeling of being at home in some communities and traditions. For instance, I claim to be a Buddhist and a Catholic because I experience love, gratitude and loyalty toward both religions, as well as a feeling of being at home in at least some Buddhist and Catholic communities and traditions. Please note that I do not claim to love, be grateful and loyal to each and every aspect of Buddhism and Catholicism, which would be theoretically contradictory and practically impossible. Similarly, please notice that I do not claim to feel at home in each and every Buddhist and Catholic community or tradition. Yet, I fully belong to both Buddhism and Catholicism. How is this possible?

The key that renders interreligious belonging possible is a distinction between two dimensions of religious belonging: affiliative and incremental.[8] People belong to a religion in the affiliative sense if they fulfil the requirements for membership established by particular communities and traditions within the religions they claim to belong (objective factor), and if they experience a subjective sense of belonging (subjective factor). The affiliative dimension of religious belonging can be understood in black or white, all or nothing terms: people either fulfil the objective requirements for membership or they do not; people either experience a subjective sense of belonging or they do not.

The incremental dimension of religious belonging, however, can increase or decrease over time. People belong in lesser or greater degrees to a religion depending on their level of identification and commitment to diverse elements of that religion. People and religions disagree about what elements are most fundamental. In some religions, the fundamental elements are understood primarily in terms of beliefs, while in others they are understood mostly in terms of practices and lifestyles. The more identification and commitment there is to the elements that a religion deems most fundamental, the stronger the belonging to that religion will be in the incremental sense.

For instance, I may identify with a greater or smaller number of fundamental Buddhist and Catholic doctrines and practices, and I may be more or less committed to them. Thus, my level of identification and commitment will make me a better or worse Buddhist/Catholic, but not necessarily less Buddhist or less Catholic. In other words, the incremental dimension of religious belonging, that is, my level of identification and commitment to the fundamentals of a

---

[8]   I am indebted to Caroline Brazier for this terminology.

religion, does not necessarily modify the affiliative fullness of my belonging. I say 'necessarily' because there might be extreme cases in which doing certain things or holding certain views may entail excommunication or expulsion from a religion. In those cases, the specific number of doctrines and practices someone embraces or fail to embrace might modify one's religious identity and affect the affiliative dimension of religious belonging. However, in most cases, moral imperfections and intellectual dissent do not imply a lessening of one's religious identity and sense of belonging, even less the losing of that identity and belonging. For instance, when I sin or when I perform an unwholesome action, I do not become less Catholic or less Buddhist because of that. My identity and sense of belonging do not change, that is, I remain fully Catholic and fully Buddhist in the affiliative sense of the term. What I become is a worse Catholic or a worse Buddhist (the incremental dimension of religious belonging changes, but not the affiliative one). Likewise, when I disagree with a particular interpretation of a Buddhist or a Catholic teaching, I do not become less Catholic or less Buddhist because of that, at least not necessarily. That is, whether dissenting with a religion on intellectual or moral grounds renders someone a reformer or a heretic cannot be determined *a priori*. Religions evolve and the heretics of the past may well become the reformers of the present and vice versa. Besides, religions are constituted by many traditions and different traditions within the same religion may evaluate someone in contradictory ways. For instance, someone might be considered a reformer in some Christian traditions and a heretic in others, for example, Martin Luther, John Calvin.

Needless to say, different traditions and communities within religions have diverse criteria for recognising someone as one of their members. For instance, some Catholic communities and traditions may think that unless I accept teaching X as it is interpreted by Y, I cannot claim to fully belong to Catholicism, but other Catholic communities and traditions may think otherwise and allow for belonging to Catholicism even when somebody rejects teaching X as interpreted by Y. This is a complex theological issue and this is not the place to discuss which teachings and whose interpretations are indispensable to fully belong to such and such religion. Suffice to say that there are many interpretations of the fundamental elements of religions, and that it is in principle possible to develop compatible understandings of those elements and be accepted as a member by at least some communities and traditions within those religions.

The affiliative and the incremental dimensions of religious belonging are intertwined. It does not make sense to speak about degrees of affiliative belonging: either there is full belonging in the affiliative sense or not. However, some of the specific requirements for membership may admit of degrees. For instance, in the case of Catholicism, profession of faith and partaking in the sacraments clearly admit of degrees (incremental dimension), but there is a minimum without which it is no longer possible to speak about fulfilment of the requirements for membership (affiliative dimension). Similarly, in the case of Buddhism, the faith (*saddhā*) necessary to take refuge in the Triple Gem admits of degrees (incremental dimension), but without a minimum of faith in the Buddha, the Dharma and the Sangha, it does not make sense to call somebody a Buddhist (affiliative dimension).

Full religious belonging depends on the affiliative dimension. As we will see in the next section, full belonging in the incremental sense does not exist in reality, except perhaps as an ideal that can be approached but never reached. Unless the requirements for membership include the acceptance of a fixed and univocally interpreted number of elements, for example doctrines, practices, and vocations, it is in principle possible to fully belong to more than one religion without having to be a saint, and without having to suspend one's critical thinking skills in order to submit to what one's conscience finds objectionable on intellectual and moral grounds. In other words, unless we essentialise religions once and for all, and unless we conflate the affiliative and incremental dimensions of religious belonging, full belonging to more than one religion is in principle possible.

People who experience an interreligious identity and sense of belonging might be a minority that dwells on the margins of religions, but they are never outsiders. For instance, I may not be the most typical Buddhist or Catholic, but that does not make me any less Buddhist or any less Catholic than anybody else. As long as I experience an interreligious sense of belonging, and as long as I fulfil the requirements for Buddhist and Catholic membership, I fully belong to both religions.

2. The Possibility of Multiple Religious Belonging

Some scholars object to the possibility of multiple religious belonging. For instance, according to Catherine Cornille, the expression 'multiple religious belonging' is something of a misnomer because it 'suggests a measure of equal belonging to two or more religious traditions. However, such "equal" belonging is both theoretically impossible and concretely impracticable, at least when belonging is understood in terms of the self-understanding of particular religions'.[9] Cornille also finds the expression problematic because

---

[9] 'Multiple Religious Belonging and Interreligious Dialogue', 328.

the term 'belonging' 'would presuppose at least a desire to fully belong to more than one tradition and to live up to its requirements for membership'.[10] That is, full and equal belonging to more than one religion is impossible both in theory and in practice.

However, the distinction between affiliative and incremental dimensions of religious belonging allows us to overcome Cornille's reservations about the possibility of multiple religious belonging. I am not sure the term 'belonging' in the expression 'multiple religious belonging' connotes the desire or the idea of full/equal belonging to more than one religion. But even if that were the case, once we accept that there are degrees of religious belonging and that full religious belonging in the affiliative sense may take place without having to be accompanied by full religious belonging in the incremental sense, the possibility of multiple religious belonging becomes unproblematic.

It is uncontroversial to assume that there are degrees of belonging. In fact, Cornille herself admits that there are degrees of belonging, from nominal membership to full and active participation.[11] If it is the case that there are degrees of belonging, then multiple religious belonging is in principle possible. Using full belonging in the incremental sense as the standard to judge the possibility of multiple religious belonging is questionable. First, there are people who fully belong to more than one religion because they fulfil the requirements for membership established by traditions and communities (affiliative belonging). Second, among those who fully belong to more than one religion in the affiliative sense, not all of them embrace the same elements of religions or understand them in exactly the same way (incremental belonging).

It is precisely because there are different degrees of belonging in the incremental sense that it is in principle possible to think about people who belong to one religion more than others, as well as people who belong to two or more traditions with a similar sense of belonging or, using Rose Drew's expression, with a 'roughly equal'[12] identification to more than one tradition. For instance, some Buddhist-Catholics may belong primarily to Buddhism, others may belong primarily to Catholicism and still others may belong to both Buddhism and Catholicism with a similar sense of belonging. It is important to point out that in the three aforementioned cases of different degrees of belonging

---

[10] Ibid., 339.

[11] Ibid., 324, 329. See also Catherine Cornille, 'Mehrere Meister? Multiple Religionszugehörigkeit in Praxis und Theorie', in eds Reinhold Bernhardt and Perry Schmidt-Leukel, *Multiple religiöse Identität* (Zurich: Theologischer Verlag Zurich, 2008), 16–35.

[12] Rose Drew, *Buddhist and Christian? An Exploration of Dual Belonging* (New York: Routledge, 2011), 5.

to Buddhism and Christianity, there must be full belonging in the affiliative sense, that is, fulfilment of the requirements for membership (objective factor) and experiencing a sense of belonging (subjective factor).

Cornille may object that she does not deny the possibility of partial multiple religious belonging, but rather the adequacy of using the term 'belonging' to denote a partial identification with other religions or a limited participation in their rituals and spiritual practices. Thus, from this perspective, would not it more appropriate to speak about multiple religious participation/identification rather than multiple religious belonging? My response is that multiple religious belonging is irreducible to multiple religious identification/participation. In fact, many people may identify with elements from other religions and would be happy to participate in some of their rituals without experiencing a subjective sense of belonging and without fulfilling the objective requirements for membership established by religions. I would also respond that religious belonging does not have to be full in the incremental sense in order to presuppose full belonging in the affiliative sense. Someone may fully belong to a religion in the affiliative sense simply because s/he fulfils the minimum requirements for membership and experiences a sense of belonging.

Although Cornille rejects the possibility of multiple religious belonging in the full and equal sense, she nevertheless acknowledges that such a form of multiple religious belonging actually exists in reality, although she qualifies that it is a radical,[13] rare[14] and extreme[15] form of multiple religious belonging.[16] But this idea is problematic. That is, if it is the case that multiple religious belonging in the full sense of the term is theoretically and practically impossible, then Cornille cannot claim at the same time that such a form of multiple belonging is a rare, extreme and radical form of such phenomenon. Either multiple religious belonging in the full sense of the term is possible or impossible. And if it is possible, yet rare, radical and extreme, then the expression 'multiple religious belonging' cannot be either a misnomer or an oxymoron.

Assuming that someone can belong only to one religion because genuine religious belonging always involves the desire to fully belong, and such full belonging cannot take place more than once, is questionable on empirical grounds too. The empirical data that we currently possess indicate that there

---

[13] 'Multiple Religious Belonging and Interreligious Dialogue', 335.
[14] Ibid., 329.
[15] Ibid., 334.
[16] Ibid., 329.

are people who claim to fully and equally belong to more than one religion, and such people seem to succeed in doing so both in theory and practice.[17]

Given that there is empirical evidence in favour of the possibility of full multiple religious belonging, and given that Cornille herself admits the existence of different degrees of belonging as well as the existence of a rare, radical and extreme variety of multiple religious belonging in the full sense, Cornille's reservations seem unfounded.

Perhaps Cornille may object that the aforementioned empirical evidence about the existence of multiple religious belonging in the full sense fails to demonstrate that full multiple belonging in the incremental sense is possible in practice. Cornille quotes Paul Griffiths, who also denies the possibility of multiple religious belonging on practical grounds. According to Griffiths, 'it is reasonable to say that Greek Orthodox Christianity and Gelug Tibetan Buddhism are different religions just because it is performatively impossible to belong to both at once – in much the same way that it's performatively impossible simultaneously to be a sumo wrestler and a balance-beam gymnast.'[18] Griffiths' logic is very clear, that is, we cannot live simultaneously two types of life that are performatively incompatible. Thus, if what Griffiths says is correct, and that seems to be what Cornille thinks because she quotes him in support of her view, those who claim to fully belong to more than one religion are somewhat deceiving themselves because full multiple religious belonging is performatively impossible.

Again, the impossibility of multiple religious belonging depends on questionable assumptions. One of these assumptions is that people must practice a religion fully in order to fully belong. But this conflates full practice with full belonging, and ignores that there are degrees not only of religious belonging, but also of religious practice. We cannot have it both ways. Either we assume that there are different degrees of practice and religious belonging, or we assume that religious belonging and practice must be full in order to qualify as genuine belonging and practice.

Obviously, if religious belonging is understood as having only an incremental dimension, anybody who claims to be a full member of more than one religion is necessarily talking nonsense. Nobody can seriously claim to be fully Buddhist and Christian if the term 'fully' is understood in an incremental sense. Similarly, it would be logically impossible to claim to be 100 per cent

---

[17]   Rose Drew, *Buddhist and Christian? An Exploration of Dual Belonging.*

[18]   Paul Griffiths, *Problems of Religious Diversity* (Hoboken, NJ: Wiley-Blackwell, 2001), 13.

Buddhist and 100 per cent Christian if the percentage '100' is understood in an incremental sense.

The problem with such incremental understanding of 'fullness' and '100 per cent' is that it does not apply to multiple religious belonging. Those who claim to fully belong to more than one religion or be 100 per cent members of one religion and 100 per cent members of a different religion at the same time, do not seem to understand the term 'full' and the percentage '100' in an incremental way. For instance, when I claim to be 100 per cent Buddhist and 100 per cent Catholic, or when I say that I fully belong to Buddhism and Christianity, I am not making an incremental or merely quantitative statement. That is, I am not suggesting that I identify with each and every Buddhist/Christian theological framework that exists, or that I practice each and every ethical guideline and spiritual exercise that Buddhist and Catholic traditions contain. A purely incremental conception of belonging is unhelpful to understand the experience of interreligious belongers. What I mean when I claim that I am 100 per cent Buddhist and 100 per cent Catholic or fully Buddhist and fully Catholic is two things: first, I claim that I fulfil all the requirements for membership established by Buddhist and Catholic traditions and communities; second, I claim that I experience a sense of interreligious belonging, which presupposes profound love, gratitude and loyalty toward Buddhism and Catholicism, as well as a diffuse feeling of being at home in at least some of their traditions and communities.

Cornille would be right if religious belonging had to be full in the incremental sense in order to qualify as genuine belonging. The problem is that multiple religious belonging in the full incremental sense of the term does not exist in reality, so she can be accused of targeting a straw man. Personally, I have never encountered anyone who claims to fully belong to multiple religions in an incremental sense, that is, embracing all the doctrines of religions including contradictory ones, or engaging in all the practices of multiple religions including those that are performatively incompatible.

I asked the late Raimundo Panikkar about how to best understand his sense of belonging to Catholicism, Hinduism and Buddhism at the same time and without contradiction. He compared incremental approaches to religious belonging to those who try to understand in quantitative terms the Trinity (one and three) or the nature of Jesus Christ (fully, 100 per cent divine and fully, 100 per cent human). He explained that certain realities cannot be properly understood in incremental, quantitative terms.

The type of reality underlying interreligious belonging, like the Trinity and the dual nature of Christ, cannot be understood with a simplistic binary either/or logic. We are before an interreligious identity that is one and many at the same time, but without contradiction, or *a pluribus unum* if you like. An interreligious identity is neither a monolithic whole nor a fragmented multiplicity. I like to think about my single yet complex Buddhist-Catholic identity as conceptually analogous to the single yet complex identity of the Trinity and Christ. Needless to say, I am not suggesting that my interreligious identity is similar to the identity of Christ and the Trinity. In the same way that I do not subordinate nor reduce any of the persons of the Trinity to others, nor any of the two natures of Christ to the other, I do not attempt to reduce one religion to the other or to subordinate Buddhism to Catholicism and vice versa. Both religions are intrinsically and dynamically interrelated to constitute one single yet complex identity, which is interreligious rather than multireligious.

If the word 'full' had to be understood always in incremental terms, then even full belonging to a single religion would be theoretically and practically impossible. For instance, if we restrict ourselves to just one religion, let us say, Catholicism, it is impossible to endorse all the conceptual frameworks that theologians have formulated throughout history and to live all possible vocations that the Church permits their followers to have.

The same argument that Griffiths applies to multiple religious belonging could be applied to single religious belonging. Paraphrasing Grifftiths, it is reasonable to say that the Franciscan order and Opus Dei are different Catholic institutions just because it is performatively impossible to belong to both of them at once. Likewise, it is performatively impossible to fully endorse the theological systems of Thomas Aquinas and Duns Scotus at the same time, or to fully live the religious life as an enclosed Carthusian nun and a Missionary of Charity in the streets of Calcutta. Strictly speaking, nobody can fully belong to one single religion in the incremental sense of the term and live at the same time all the possible vocations that a religion allows or believe in all the doctrines that their theologians have developed throughout history. Such full belonging in the incremental sense would be performatively impossible and theoretically contradictory. Griffiths and Cornille are right in rejecting the possibility of full multiple religious belonging in the incremental sense, but they forget that full mono-religious belonging in the incremental sense is also impossible. In other words, Griffiths' argument loses traction once we acknowledge that religious belonging has two dimensions: one dimension that admits of degrees (incremental dimension), and another dimension that is either full or inexistent (affiliative dimension).

Whether full belonging to more than one religion is possible depends on how we understand the term 'full'. A purely incremental understanding of the term 'full' renders full religious belonging, whether to one or many religions, impossible both in theory and practice. Religions are diverse and complex entities with numerous traditions, thinkers, texts and practices. Even if I wanted to, I would not be able to identify with all the traditions, thinkers, texts and practices of one religion, let alone more than one. Similarly, even if we decided to essentialise religions, for instance, reducing them to a limited number of beliefs and observances, we would have to admit that many of such beliefs and observances have been understood differently throughout history and that they may continue to evolve in the future. That is, what ultimately constitutes the 'essence' of a religion is a dynamic reality open to further interpretations. We all make hermeneutical choices, and we all select among a wide range of possibilities those that fit best the spirit of the times and our personal experience. For instance, it would be naïve to think that all Catholics today agree on the exact meaning of all the teachings of the Church. If this were the case, we would not need theologians any more and any further elaboration on the magisterium of the Church would be superfluous. Likewise, it would be naïve to think that Buddhists from different traditions and even from the same tradition agree on the exact meaning of the Buddha's teachings. If something can be inferred from the commentarial and scholastic literature of Buddhist traditions, it is precisely that Buddhism grows and that there is more than one possible reading of core Buddhist teachings, texts and terms. But the impossibility of multiple religious belonging in a full incremental sense does not render impossible multiple religious belonging in other senses.

Even if it were possible to reach full belonging in the incremental sense, we would have to admit that the fullness of religious belonging would be reached in many different ways. That is, incremental fullness could not be quantified in the same way as we quantify the number of millilitres in one litre. If full religious belonging were like one litre, then everybody who did not reach 1,000 ml would fall short of that fullness. However, this way of thinking cannot be extrapolated to religious belonging because religions are intrinsically diverse and religious followers are not like monolithic one-litre receptacles. There are many different types of receptacles, that is, vocations and charismas, and the fullness of the receptacles need not be understood monolithically, that is, as involving the exact amount of millilitres to reach fullness. For instance, some receptacles would reach fullness with 900 ml, others with 850 ml, and still others with 500 ml. Similarly, religious practitioners come in many forms, shapes and circumstances. What for some people would be the fullness of religious belonging in the incremental sense need not be identical to what fullness would be for others. And this diversity of ways to 'reach' the fullness of belonging in the incremental sense would only be possible with a non-incremental, that is, qualitative understanding of the term 'full'.

Assuming that all followers of a religion have to believe and practice exactly in the same way in order to reach exactly the same level of incremental fullness would be simplistic and would not do justice to the complexity of both religions and their followers.

It is in principle possible to think about certain types of religious practitioners who, given their vocation, charisma or personal circumstances, can only 'reach' the fullness of religious belonging in the incremental sense with the contribution of other religions. For instance, some people may keep growing spiritually and theologically only by practicing advanced forms of interreligious dialogue and eventually experiencing an interreligious sense of belonging. In other words, some people can only be religious interreligiously.[19] Asking whether such interreligious way of belonging is superior or inferior, greater or smaller than a mono-religious way of belonging misses the point, pretty much in the same way as asking whether the incremental fullness of receptacle X is superior or inferior, greater or smaller than the incremental fullness of receptacle Y.

Not all receptacles/practitioners are alike, and not all of them require exactly the same things in order to progress toward a fuller religious belonging in the incremental sense. In my case, rather than being an impediment for spiritual growth, being a Buddhist-Catholic is what allows me to keep growing spiritually. The same can be said about my theological development, practicing Buddhist-Christian dialogue continues to be essential to keep growing in faith and wisdom.

The incremental and the affiliative dimensions of my interreligious belonging are intertwined. Growing in Buddhist virtues makes me a better Catholic, not only enhancing the incremental dimension of my belonging to Catholicism, but also encouraging me to remain affiliated to the Catholic Church. In turn, growing in Catholic virtues makes me a better Buddhist. By loving more the truth and holiness I find in Buddhism, I cannot but deepen my Buddhist practice (incremental dimension of belonging) and fully belong to Buddhism as a religion (affiliative dimension).

Keeping in mind the distinction as well as the intrinsic connection between the affiliative and the incremental dimensions of religious belonging, I can say without contradiction that my interreligious identity fully belongs to Buddhism and Catholicism. More specifically, I would not be fully Catholic without being at

---

[19] Peter C. Phan, *Being Religious Interreligiously: Asian Perspectives on Interfaith Dialogue* (Maryknoll, NY: Orbis Books, 2004).

the same time fully Buddhist, and I would not be fully Buddhist without being at the same time fully Catholic. In other words, if I were not 100 per cent Buddhist, I could not be 100 per cent Catholic, and if I were not 100 per cent Catholic, I could not be 100 per cent Buddhist. Or, paraphrasing Paul Knitter, without the Buddha I could not be a Christian,[20] though I would add that without Jesus I could not be a Buddhist either.

In sum, I have suggested that the reservations of some scholars about the possibility of multiple religious belonging can be overcome with a distinction between the affiliative and the incremental dimensions of religious belonging. I have also contended that such reservations are based on questionable assumptions. It is only by assuming that genuine religious belonging requires full practice, or by understanding full belonging in a purely incremental way that multiple religious belonging becomes problematic. Once we accept the existence of different degrees of belonging and practice, and once we realise that there are two distinct yet interrelated dimensions of belonging, 'multiple religious belonging' is no longer a misnomer or a practical impossibility.

---

[20] Paul F. Knitter, *Without the Buddha I Could Not Be a Christian* (Oxford: Oneworld, 2009).

Chapter 10
The Buddhist Faith of Non-Buddhists: From Dual Belonging to Dual Attachment[1]

Rupert Gethin

I do not in the present context intend either to criticise or defend the notion of dual Buddhist-Christian belonging directly. Instead what I want to do is explore and articulate a way of thinking I find expressed in specific Buddhist texts that might be used at least to make *Buddhist* sense of certain kinds of dual Buddhist-Christian belonging. It is a way of thinking that ultimately sees in dual belonging a dual attachment, which like all attachments must ultimately be given up. While this way of thinking is clearly not the only response to issues of religious diversity found in the Buddhist tradition, it does seem to me a significant and important one. It is a way of thinking that I believe manifests in various places and in various forms in the history of Buddhist thought. Here I wish to focus on how it is articulated in Indian Buddhist systematic thought (Sanskrit *abhidharma*, Pali *abhidhamma*), especially in certain texts composed between the second century BCE and the seventh century CE belonging to the Theravāda school. This way of thinking starts from a universalist understanding of goodness and truth as the same wherever they are found; despite there being talk of insiders and outsiders in Buddhist texts, goodness and truth are not ultimately conceived as contingent on being a Buddhist or having faith in the Buddha, his teaching (Dharma) and his community (Sangha).[2] In short,

---

[1] Abbreviations of Pali texts: A = Aṅguttara Nikāya; Abhidh-av = Abhidhammāvatāra; As = Atthasālinī; Be = Burmese Sixth Council edition; D = Dīgha Nikāya; Dhp = Dhammapada; Dhs = Dhammasaṅgaṇi; M = Majjhima Nikāya; Nett = Nettippakaraṇa; Paṭṭh = Paṭṭhāna; Ps = Papañcasūdanī; S = Saṃyutta Nikāya; Sv = Sumaṅgalvilāsinī; Vin = Vinaya; Vism = Visuddhimagga (Warren-Kosambi edition); Vv = Vimānavatthu; -a = aṭṭhakathā; -anuṭ = anuṭīkā; -mṭ = mūlaṭīkā. Unless indicated editions are those of the Pali Text Society. English translations from Pali texts are my own.

[2] Given the Christian West's Platonist heritage, some might see my choice of the terms 'goodness' and 'truth' here as begging the question; while I would not wish to claim any simple correspondence between Platonist, Christian and Buddhist conceptions of goodness and truth, I am assuming a sufficient general correspondence with such Buddhist terms as Sanskrit *kuśala* (Pali *kusala*) and *satya* (Pali *sacca*) to make my universalist claim meaningful.

180   *Buddhist-Christian Dual Belonging*

this way of thinking can be characterised as inclusivist – at least loosely so – rather than exclusivist.[3]

A well-known story found in the earliest stratum of Buddhist literature – the Nikāyas or Āgamas (ca third century BCE) – tells of the Jain lay follower UPali's conversion to Buddhism. At the end of a conversation with the Buddha UPali is moved to declare that henceforth he will take as his refuge the Buddha, his teaching and his community. At this the Buddha reminds him that his family has long supported Jain monks and that it would be appropriate for him to continue offering them alms.[4] This might suggest an attitude sympathetic to dual belonging: it is possible to become a supporter of Buddhist monks, and hence a Buddhist, while continuing to offer support to Jain monks. Yet there is something of a twist at the end of this tale. UPali does indeed continue to offer Jain monks food when they come to his door, but he expressly excludes them from entering his home to eat; that privilege is granted only to Buddhist monks. Jain monks, it seems, are not deserving of quite the same respect as Buddhist.

That genuine 'faith' (Pali *saddhā*, Sanskrit *śraddhā*)) is understood in the earliest stratum of Buddhist literature as a characteristically Buddhist virtue might be inferred by the way it is described as having as its object the Buddha and his enlightenment.[5] The closely related term *prasāda*, which in Buddhist texts denotes the clarity and composure of complete 'trust' or 'confidence', is similarly presented as properly directed towards the Buddha, Dharma and Sangha.[6]

When, sometime before the beginning of the Common Era, the Ābhidharmika systematisers of Buddhist thought came to set out in detail their understanding of what constitutes and characterises a 'good', 'wholesome' or 'skilful' (*kuśala*) state of

---

[3]   For discussions of the various ways – inclusivist, exclusivist, pluralist – in which the Buddhist tradition's attitude to religious diversity might be interpreted see Richard Hayes, 'Gotama Buddha and Religious Pluralism', *Journal of Religious Pluralism* 1 (1991): 65–96; Kristin Beise Kiblinger, *Buddhist Inclusivism: Attitudes Towards Religious Others* (Aldershot: Ashgate, 2005); *Buddhist Attitudes to Other Religions*, ed. Perry Schmidt-Leukel (St Ottilien: EOS, 2008); J. Abraham Vélez de Cea, *The Buddha and Religious Diversity* (London: Routledge, 2013).

[4]   M I, 371–87 (379). For a discussion of the various parallel versions of this story see Anālayo, *A Comparative Study of the Majjhima-Nikāya*, 2 vols (Taipei: Dharma Drum, 2011), I 320–33. A similar tale of the conversion of the Jain Sīha is told at A IV 180–88 and Vin I 233–8.

[5]   D I 63; I 179; D II 237; M I 356; S V 197–8; A III 65.

[6]   M I 320; A II 34.

The Buddhist Faith of Non-Buddhists　　181

mind, both the Theravāda and Sarvāstivāda schools specified *śraddhā* as one of its necessary qualities.[7] Such a move would seem to cause problems.

According to the general Abhidharma approach to the Buddhist ethic of intention, good acts (*karman*) of body, speech and mind are acts done precisely when in a skilful state of mind (*kuśala-citta*); it is not possible to perform a good act when in an unskilful state of mind (*akuśala-citta*).[8] Yet if *śraddhā* is a necessary condition of a skilful state of mind, and *śraddhā* is understood as faith in the Buddha, Dharma and Sangha, that is, something characteristically and exclusively Buddhist, then it would seem that only Buddhists can have skilful states of mind, and hence that only Buddhists can do good deeds. But this seems to run directly counter to the Buddhist ethic of intention: what makes a deed good is *not* that it is done by a Buddhist, but that it is motivated by the opposites of greed (*lobha*), hatred (*dveṣa*) and delusion (*moha*), namely by non-attachment, friendliness and wisdom. Can it really be the case that non-Buddhists never have such selfless motivations? We might conclude that what we have discovered here is an egregious example of the unthinking manner in which the Buddhist scholastics re-envisioned what the Buddha taught, making of it a religion with absolute distinctions between insiders who have the opportunity to progress towards liberation and outsiders who are excluded from even the opportunity of performing the kind of good deed that would allow a better rebirth. Yet such a conclusion is certainly in tension, if not clear contradiction, with various explicit principles and statements in the extant Abhidharma literature.

The question of whether non-Buddhists can have what Buddhists call 'faith' is one that has been explicitly raised in the context of the modern exegesis of ancient Buddhist systematic thought by the Sri Lankan monk Nārada Thera (1898–1983) in the 1950s. Having suggested that faith is to be understood as 'well-established confidence in the Buddha, Dhamma, and the Sangha', he comments: 'One might question whether a non-Buddhist could also possess this *Saddhā*'.[9] He goes on to cite a passage from the *Atthasālinī*, a fifth-century CE commentary to the *Dhammasaṅgaṇi*, the first book of the Theravāda canonical Abhidhamma (ca second century BCE), in which its author (an associate of the

---

[7]　A mental constituent that is classed as *sobhanasādhāraṇa* by the Theravādins, and a *kuśalamahābhūmika* by the Vaibhāṣikas.

[8]　See Rupert Gethin, 'Can Killing a Living Being Ever be an Act of Compassion? The Analysis of the Act of Killing in the Abhidhamma and Pali Commentaries', *Journal of Buddhist Ethics* 11 (2004): 167–202.

[9]　Nārada Thera, *A Manual of Abhidhamma*, 2 vols (Colombo: Vajirarama, 1956–57), I 99–100.

182   *Buddhist-Christian Dual Belonging*

renowned commentator Buddhaghosa) comments on the absence of the mental quality of faith (*saddhā*) from all but skilful (*kusala*) types of consciousness:

> In this [unskilful] *citta* the qualities (*dhamma*) of faith, mindfulness, wisdom and the six pairs are not accepted. Why not? Because when the mind lacks faithfulness there is no real composure (*pasāda*). So in the first place there is no faith. Does that mean those who hold false views (*diṭṭhigatika*) do not have faith in their own teachers? They do, but it is not faith. It is mere approval of what their teachers say. In fact it is either a lack of investigation (*anupaparikkhā*) or [false] view (*diṭṭhi*).[10]

How are we to take this comment? We might take it as reiterating a form of simplistic Buddhist scholastic chauvinism: 'faith' means faith in the Buddha, Dhamma and Sangha; only Buddhists can have true faith in their teachers because only Buddhist teachers teach a proper view of things. Non-Buddhists, on the other hand, even though they are enthused by what their teachers say, cannot have true faith because what their teachers teach is a false view of things. This appears to be how Nārada himself understands the *Atthasālinī's* comment, though he is clearly somewhat troubled by it, suggesting that the *Atthasālinī's* answer to the question of whether or not non-Buddhists can have faith 'is rather unsatisfactory and inadequate':

> If Saddhā is limited only to Buddhists, what shall we say when a non-Buddhist places his faith or confidence in his teacher? Surely his mind also gets purified to some extent when he thinks of his particular religious teacher. Could it be *Diṭṭhi* – false view? Then it is immoral (*Akusala*). In such a case there is no occasion for a non-Buddhist to experience a moral consciousness. Would it not be more correct to say that *Saddhā* is mere confidence or faith, instead of restricting to the Triple Gem?[11]

As a solution to his problem, Nārada goes on to refer to the list or quasi-synonyms or alternative terms for *saddhā* given in the *Dhammasaṅgaṇi* by way of definition, namely 'having faith' (*saddahanā*), 'trusting' (*okappanā*), complete confidence (*abhippasādo*), faith (*saddhā*), the faculty of faith (*saddhindriya*), the power of faith (*saddhābala*), with the implication that such terms are indicative of a more general confidence or trust that need not be exclusively Buddhist – that is, need not be directed towards the Buddha, Dhamma and Saṅgha in the manner he thinks is

---

[10]   As 249–50.

[11]   Nārada, *Manual of Abhidhamma*, 99–100. This discussion is omitted in the revised and updated Bhikkhu Bodhi et al., *A Comprehensive Manual of Abhidhamma: The Abhidhammattha Saṅgaha of Ācariya Anuruddha* (Kandy: Buddhist Publication Society, 2007).

The Buddhist Faith of Non-Buddhists 183

assumed by the commentary's explanation. In fact I think Nārada is certainly right in his interpretation of 'faith' here. Where I think he is wrong, however, is in his interpretation of the commentary as saying something at odds with this.

There are a number of considerations that suggest that what we have in the *Atthasālinī's* comment should not be construed as plain religious chauvinism, but something rather more subtle and sophisticated. In itself the *Atthasālinī* comment does not explicitly restrict faith to the Buddha, Dharma and Sangha. Certainly it implies that it is only possible to have faith in those who teach what is good (*puñña, kusala*) and true (*sacca, dhamma*); faith in those who do not teach what is good and true cannot, by virtue of being directed towards what is untrue (*asacca, adhamma*) and what is not good or bad (*pāpa, akusala*), be faith. But to read this as an Abhidharma claim that faith and truth are exclusively Buddhist domains runs counter to certain general principles of early Indian Buddhist thought and also to some specific points of systematic Buddhist thought as expounded in the Theravāda Abhidhamma that express a universalist understanding of the nature of goodness and truth.

The Abhidharma was conceived as a comprehensive and universal account of the way the mind operates – the minds not just of Buddhists, but of beings more generally. The Theravāda Abhidhamma outlines the possibilities for consciousness universally: all possible states of mind, for all types of being, born in whatever realm of the cosmos are circumscribed by just 89 classes of consciousness; there is no possibility of consciousness apart from these. A section of the *Abhidhammāvatāra*,[12] a summary of systematic Buddhist thought composed probably in the fifth century by Buddhadatta, spells out in full precisely which classes of consciousness can occur to which types of being in which realms of existence. This makes explicit that beings born in the four descents (the realms of hell, animals, hungry ghosts and 'jealous gods') may experience skilful states of mind. This means that beings in hell, animals, hungry ghosts and jealous gods may all on occasion have faith. Should we then, according to the Abhidhamma vision of the world, think of the beings in these realms as in effect made up of Buddhist and non-Buddhist groups? A tendency to anthropomorphise animals' and other non-human beings' states of mind is perhaps evident in some Buddhist collections of tales such as the *Jātaka* and *Dhammapadaṭṭhakathā* (which those formulating the details of the Abhidhamma account of the world would have been familiar with), such that the possibility of Buddhist cats and dogs on the one hand and non-Buddhist cats and dogs on the other should not be dismissed

---

12   The *cittuppatti-niddesa*, Abhidh-av 36–42.

184   *Buddhist-Christian Dual Belonging*

as absurd.[13] And yet such naïve and unthinking anthropomorphism is perhaps not entirely in keeping with the character of the Abhidhamma.

Returning to the question raised by the author of the *Atthasālinī* about whether those who hold false views should be said to have faith in their own teachers, it is noteworthy that he does not in fact couch the question in terms of whether or not *non-Buddhists* can have faith in their teachers but in terms of whether those who hold *false views* can do so. To understand that the question is about Buddhists and non-Buddhists is thus to already assume not only what Abhidhamma texts must mean by faith but also what they mean by speaking of holding 'false views'. Yet neither the nature of faith nor that of false views is unproblematic in Abhidhamma texts. Does our commentator really mean to exclude not only the possibility that non-Buddhist teachers and their audience might ever get it right and touch on the truth, but also the possibility that Buddhist teachers and their audience might ever get it wrong and fall foul of false views? To argue that he does mean to exclude both these possibilities involves committing him to a very simplistic equation of Buddhism and the truth that, as I have already suggested, goes against statements found elsewhere in the Abhidhamma literature.

In fact, like the earlier *Dhammasaṅgaṇi*, the Abhidhamma exegetical tradition characteristically defines faith with only oblique reference to the Buddha, Dharma, and Sangha:

> Faith is that by means of which [mental qualities] have faith, or it itself is what has faith, or it is just having faith. Its characteristic is having faith or trusting; its function is to bring [mental] clarity (*pasādana*), like a water-clearing gem, or to leap forward, as when crossing a river in flood; it appears as the absence of impurities, or as commitment; its immediate cause is any ground for trust, or the constituents of stream-attainment, such as hearing the true Dharma. It should be seen as a hand, wealth and a seed.[14]

The reference to 'the true Dharma' and the constituents of 'stream attainment' here do in part key into a specifically Buddhist framework: faith is what arises

---

[13] Examples of stories of, as it were, 'Buddhist' animals include the frog who was inadvertently crushed when listening to the Dharma and as a result was reborn as god in the Heaven of the Thirty-Three (Vv-a 217), the bats who heard monks reciting the Abhidhamma and were reborn as pupils of Sāriputta (Dhp-a III 23) and the parrot who practiced meditation on bones in a nunnery (Sv III 742). These stories are discussed by Rita Langer, *Buddhist Rituals of Death and Rebirth: Contemporary Sri Lankan Practice and Its Origins* (London: Routledge, 2007), 45–7.

[14] Vism XIV 140.

The Buddhist Faith of Non-Buddhists   185

in response to the Buddha's teaching, and the constituents of stream attainment are sometimes explained with reference to faith in the Buddha, Dharma and Sangha. Yet the definition does not exclude the possibility of faith outside the Buddhist tradition.

Modern discussions of faith distinguish between its cognitive and affective dimensions. As I and others have argued, Buddhist thought understands faith primarily in affective terms. Buddhist texts understand faith in the Buddha, Dharma and Sangha not so much as a question of belief that certain propositions about the world are true, as a state of trust, confidence, affection and devotion inspired by the person of the Buddha, his teachings and followers – a confidence that there is indeed a path leading to the cessation of suffering which has been walked by the Buddha and at least some of his followers.[15]

But what does it mean to hold false views (*diṭṭhigatika*)? Is holding false views something restricted to non-Buddhists and holding right views something restricted to Buddhists? The most frequent general characterisation of mistaken views in early Buddhist texts is in the following terms:

> There is nothing in giving, sacrifice and offerings; good and bad deeds have no fruit or result; there is no this world and the next; one's mother and father are nothing; there are no beings born in heaven, no ascetics or brahmins who have reached perfection and live the perfect life, who gain for themselves a higher knowledge of this world and the next, and who, having experienced it directly, make it known.[16]

Holding right views, on the other hand, is presented in precisely opposite terms. But such opposite terms do not amount to something specifically Buddhist, but rather are in line with what many religious teachers in ancient India might have taught at the time of the Buddha: that there is something in giving, and religious observances; that good and bad deeds do have consequences; that there is a next world (whether heaven or hell); that there are higher beings in sublime realms of existence; that there are those who have reached moral perfection, and the highest wisdom, and teach an appropriate path. What we have here is in effect an expression of approval of an understanding that there is rebirth and how you behave in this life has consequences. As Steven Collins notes, to hold right view in this sense is not to do or believe anything that is specifically Buddhist: 'It is merely ... to have a general "pro-attitude" towards ideas of *karma* and *saṃsāra*, and to the services

---

[15] See Rupert Gethin, *The Buddhist Path to Awakening*, 2nd edition (Oxford: Oneworld, 2001), 106–16.

[16] See for example D III 264–5; M I 287, 401–2, 515, III 22; S III 206–7; Dhs 212.

186 Buddhist-Christian Dual Belonging

of those religious practitioners with whom the ideas are associated'.[17] In other contexts, however, 'right view' can be expressed in more overtly Buddhist doctrinal terms, that is, as involving an understanding of characteristically Buddhist ideas, such as the four noble truths, dependent arising and not-self.[18]

In the context of the present discussion, then, if we take the term used in the *Atthasālinī*, namely *diṭṭhigatikā* ('those who hold false views'), in its weaker and most general sense then it should refer to those who more generally deny that there is any point in giving and that deeds have consequences, *not* to those who reject or fail to adhere to a specifically Buddhist version of 'right view'. In which case, while certain non-Buddhists are excluded from the possibility of having faith, others – those who teach and accept that there is some point in giving and that deeds do have consequences – are not. In early Buddhist texts it is one in particular in the standard list of six teachers of non-Buddhist schools, the *titthiyas* or *tīrthikas*, who is typically given as the example of a teacher who directly denies the point in giving and that deeds have consequences, namely Ajita, who espouses a form of the ancient Indian materialist philosophy known as Lokāyata and associated with the name of Cārvāka.[19] Other teachers, including certainly the Jain teacher Mahāvīra and the wanderer Sanjaya, would seem to advocate doctrines that meet the criteria for basic 'right view'. We can speculate that Christians would too, in so far as they teach that how we behave in this life has consequences and that we will be reborn in some form after death.

If we turn to the early Abhidhamma treatment of false view in the *Dhammasaṅgaṇi*, we find various terms used to define false view or *micchā-diṭṭhi*, including the following: the bond of views (*diṭṭhi-saṃyojana*), holding (*gāha*), fixity (*patiṭṭhāha*), conviction (*abhinivesa*), clinging (*parāmāsa*), a bad path (*kummagga*), a false way (*micchāpatha*), falsity (*micchatta*), and the sphere of [non-Buddhist] religious systems (*titthāyatana*) and the grip of the perverted views (*vipariyesa-gāha*).[20]

The term *titthāyatana* clearly suggests non-Buddhist religious systems or schools as the sphere of false views. If we pursue the definition of some of the other terms within the *Dhammasaṅgaṇi*, the conclusion that we have primarily to do with non-Buddhists is perhaps reinforced. The bonds of view and of clinging to precepts and vows are defined using the same set of terms we have

---

[17] Steven Collins, *Selfless Persons: Imagery and Thought in Theravāda Buddhism* (Cambridge: Cambridge University Press, 1982), 89.

[18] See especially the *Sammādiṭṭhi-sutta* (M I 46–55). Cf. Collins, *Selfless Persons*, 87–95.

[19] D I 55.

[20] For example, Dhs 78 (§ 381), reading *patiṭṭhāho* with As.

The Buddhist Faith of Non-Buddhists

seen used for wrong view generally. But in addition the bond of clinging to precepts and vows is defined as the false view that 'purification' (*suddhi*) can be accomplished simply by adhering to moral precepts and vows, and such a view is explicitly attributed to certain 'outsiders' (*ito bahiddhā*) or non-Buddhist ascetics and brahmins.[21] The commentary is more specific. It suggests that the kind of non-Buddhist ascetics meant are those who reduce the religious life to mere conformity with a vow to live in basic simplicity, like a cow or a dog.[22]

Of particular significance for the present discussion, however, are a series of passages from the *Paṭṭhāna*, the final (and perhaps, by modern scholars, least studied) work of the Theravāda Abhidhamma. These passages make it explicit that false views are not the special preserve of non-Buddhists:

> A skilful quality may be a causal condition for an unskilful quality by way of the causal condition of being an object [of thought]: when having given a gift, undertaken the precepts, or fulfilled the religious observances of the full and new moon days, one is pleased and happy about those things and then, with reference to those things, greed arises, a [false] view arises, doubt arises, anxiety arises, unhappiness arises.[23]

In a similar way, we are told, unskilful qualities may arise where the object of thought is past good deeds, the attainment of meditation (*jhāna*) and the loss of meditation.[24] Later the same point is expressed with reference to 'the causal condition of dominance' and 'causal condition of immediate support'.[25]

Hitherto we have been considering the question of whether the Abhidhamma vision allows for the possibility of right view, and hence faith, outside the Buddhist fold. These passages from the *Paṭṭhāna* turn the tables. It is explained how Buddhist ideas and practices can also become the object of unskilful attachment in the form of false views. This means that in fact from the perspective of the *Paṭṭhāna*, those of false view mentioned in the *Atthasālinī* as having a quasi 'faith' in their teachers' words can on occasion include Buddhists. Being pleased and happy about one's Buddhist ideas and practices is not necessarily a mark of *true* faith according to the *Paṭṭhāna's* presentation of the types of consciousness set out in the *Dhammasaṅgaṇi*.

---

21   Dhs 198.

22   The kind described in the 'Dog-vow Discourse' (*Kukkuravatika-sutta*, M I 387–92).

23   Paṭṭh (Bᵉ) I 133.

24   Cf. also the warning that the kind of joy and happiness that arises by way of thinking '*our* Buddha, *our* Dharma, *our* Sangha' is connected with greed and so an obstacle to progress in meditation (Sv I 54).

25   Paṭṭh (Bᵉ) I 136 (*adhipatipaccaya*), I 146 (*upanissayapaccaya*).

188   *Buddhist-Christian Dual Belonging*

The kind of psychological approach indicated by these passages from the *Paṭṭhāna* is picked up, I think, elsewhere in the exegetical Abhidhamma literature. That faith is not completely unlike attachment, and so can drift towards and slip into a form of attachment to what is good and true, is brought out in the discussion of the different temperaments where faith is seen as having a close affinity with greed or attraction to things (*rāga*):

> In one of greed temperament, when skilful [consciousness] occurs, faith is strong because its quality is close to that of greed, therefore one of faith temperament has an affinity with one of greed temperament. For, just as greed is affectionate and not mean on the unskilful side, so is faith on the skilful; just as greed seeks out the objects of senses, so faith seeks out the qualities of virtue, and so on; just as greed does not give up what is unhelpful, so faith does not give up what is helpful.[26]

We can note in this context that the early post-canonical text, the *Nettippakaraṇa*, somewhat unexpectedly introduces the possibility of a skilful form of that most unskilful of qualities from the Buddhist perspective, namely craving (*taṇhā*). Alongside the familiar *unskilful* craving that motivates one to act in ways that take one further away from nirvana, perpetuating the round of birth and death (*saṃsāragāminī*), there is a *skilful* craving, a craving to abandon defilements, a craving that motivates behaviour that brings one closer to nirvana, leading eventually to the stopping of the round of rebirth (*apacayagāminī pahānataṇhā*).[27] The *Nettippakaraṇa* confronts here that most obvious of Buddhist dilemmas: if nirvana, the goal of the Buddhist path, is the cessation of all desire, what of the desire to reach nirvana? Surely that is a good craving. The ancient commentary explains that this 'skilful' craving is not, however, 'skilful' in the strictest and absolute sense, it is only relatively 'unskilful'. It suggests that craving can be called 'skilful' not because it is in itself skilful, but because it is directed towards something skilful, presumably as the *Paṭṭhāna* has it, Buddhist ideas and practices:

> Here 'skilful' means 'having skilful qualities as its object'. The word 'skilful' should be understood here in the sense of 'not reproachable' ... But why is craving specified here as something skilful? By specifying craving ... as the cause of distorted views, how it contributes to the defiling side of things is shown. However, by switching perspective, craving is specified as something skilful in

---

[26]   Vism III 75.

[27]   Nett 87.

order to show that in this case it is precisely craving that can also contribute to the purification side of things.[28]

What is being suggested here is that craving is always strictly 'unskilful' and deluded, yet some forms of craving are better than others, some forms of craving are not reproachable (*anavajja*). Thus craving for the objects of the senses or attachment to the view that actions have no consequences will only make matters worse, but craving for good deeds, the bliss of meditation or the peace of nirvana, while still ultimately just more craving, can motivate actions that make things better. Yet like all craving it has its dangers.

These dangers are highlighted in the *Paṭṭhāna* in its exposition of 'the causal condition of immediate support'. Here the *Paṭṭhāna* provides more details of how skilful qualities can condition the arising of unskilful qualities:

> Immediately dependent on faith, on virtue, on learning, on generosity, on wisdom one generates pride, one holds to a false view: by way of the causal condition of immediate support faith, virtue, learning, generosity, wisdom become a causal condition for greed, hatred, delusion, conceit, view, desire.[29]

The commentary explains further:

> Thinking, 'I am someone with faith and confidence', one produces pride. Not investigating (*anupaparikkhanto*) by wisdom the meaning of what one has reached by virtue of faith in some statement, one holds to a false view, such as 'a person exists'. Thinking, 'I am virtuous, learned, generous, wise', one generates pride. When, in a similar way to having conceit, one forms and clings to some view about virtue, learning, generosity, or wisdom, then one holds to a false view. In immediate dependence on one's accomplishment in faith, and the other [virtues], each one of these qualities [of faith, virtue, learning, generosity, and wisdom] becomes the causal condition for greed when one feels pleased with oneself, the causal condition for hatred when one feels contempt for others, the causal condition for the delusion that is associated with both these, and the causal condition for conceit and views in the manner stated; in immediate dependence on accomplishment in faith [each quality] becomes a condition of immediate support for the desire for existence and wealth. Only the ordinary skilful qualities are indicated here. The transcendent [skilful qualities], however – which are

---

[28] Nett-a (B^e) 147.
[29] Paṭṭh (B^e) I 147.

pure, sublime, ultimate, and destroy the unskilful, and therefore, like the moon in respect to the places of darkness, not a support for the unskilful – are not included here.[30]

What the commentary explains here is that the same lack of investigation (*anupaparikkhā*) that we have seen above attributed to those who hold false views is here attributed to Buddhists who take pride in and become attached to what in effect their Buddhist teachers teach. It is noteworthy that in the course of commenting on the *Atthasālinī's* question about the 'faith' of those of wrong view, the sixth and seventh century subcommentaries of Ānanda and Dhammapāla take 'lack of investigation' as meaning 'delusion' (*moha*), explaining that '[a kind of] reverential commitment to something undeserving (*avatthu*) can arise by way of delusion or by way of [false] view'.[31] In the present context, namely lack of investigation with regard to what *Buddhist* teachers teach, presumably what we have is a case of 'reverential commitment' – as distinct from true 'faith' – to something deserving.[32] Thus ordinary Buddhists are always in danger of becoming proud in their spiritual attainments, of thinking that such attainments make them better than others. It is only when they come to the very end of the spiritual path that they let go of such pride and attachment: the good qualities (including faith) associated with the transcendent (*lokuttara*) 'consciousness' that constitutes the moment of enlightenment cut off such pride and attachment.

I have been considering whether a statement in the *Atthasālinī* allows that non-Buddhists might have what the Abhidhamma understands as faith. So far I have concluded that it does. Moreover I have suggested that from the perspective of the *Paṭṭhāna* not every apparent instance of Buddhists having 'faith' should be understood as in reality faith proper, namely *saddhā*. That is, Buddhists are sometimes in precisely the same position as non-Buddhists: they hold a false view and what appears to be faith may in fact from a strict Abhidhamma perspective not be true faith, but rather a mere reverential commitment in the guise of faith.

---

[30] Paṭṭh-a (B^c) 443–4.

[31] Dhs-mṭ (B^c) 120.

[32] Dhammapāla's *Anuṭīkā* expands further: '*Lack of investigation is delusion*. But the delusion in this case should be understood as being disassociated from [false] views. But because a view is something that conforms to [the delusion] with which it is associated, it is precisely by holding to that [view] that people hold on. *Something inappropriate*: something that one should not have faith in. *Reverential commitment*: the commentator states how it seems like faith to those who are deluded or hold false views' (Dhs-anuṭ (B^c) 126).

The Buddhist Faith of Non-Buddhists 191

The suggestion that non-Buddhists may experience what Buddhist systematic thought understands as faith and are therefore in some sense unbeknown to themselves Buddhists may appear in part to be a Buddhist counterpart to Karl Rahner's (1904–84) notion of 'the anonymous Christian'. Here Rahner suggests that 'a non-Christian religion' may be considered also to contain 'supernatural elements arising out of the grace which is given to men as a gratuitous gift on account of Christ' and a 'member of an extra-Christian religion ... can and must already be regarded in this or that respect as an anonymous Christian' since God's grace, 'understood as the a priori horizon of all his spiritual acts, accompanies his consciousness subjectively, even though it is not known objectively'.[33]

Similarly, from the Abhidhamma perspective we have been considering, all beings, whether they know it or not, are when they perform an act motivated by generosity and kindness Buddhists in so far as they have faith in precisely what Buddhists have faith in. Yet it is important to note here the manner in which faith is conceived as primarily a mental episode, rather than an ongoing and stable dispositional attitude. In his classic study of Indian philosophical theories of knowledge B.K. Matilal wrote at some length on Indian philosophy's tendency to focus on knowledge as a momentary mental episode as opposed to a Western philosophical tendency to focus on knowledge as a more or less stable disposition in the form of justified true belief. Matilal notes how Indian philosophers 'constructed a world of a series of cognitive events rather than collected a mass of true propositions'.[34] Such thinking deeply informs Buddhist approaches to matters of 'faith' and 'wrong view'.

European traditions of thought may be used to thinking of emotions or affective conditions as short-lived passing mental states, yet seem disinclined to think of conditions that are conceived as cognitive in nature – such as views, opinions and faith – as existing in this manner.[35] Yet Buddhist Abhidharma wants to treat all mental states as similar in this respect: faith, wrong view, right view and so on are all equally and finally understood as short-lived mental episodes or events. Thus it is not so much a question of some non-Buddhists qualifying, as

---

[33] Karl Rahner, 'Christianity and the Non-Christian Religions', in *Theological Investigations: Volume V, Later Writings* (London: Darton, Longman and Todd, 1966), 115–34 (121, 131).

[34] Bimal Krishna Matilal, *Perception: An Essay on Classical Indian Theories of Knowledge* (Oxford: Clarendon Press, 1986), 105–6.

[35] For further consideration of 'faith' by way of the distinction between 'cognitive' and 'affective', see Gethin, *Buddhist Path to Awakening* 16; for a discussion of the Buddhist understanding of *diṭṭhi*; see Rupert Gethin, 'Wrong View (*micchā-diṭṭhi*) and Right View (*sammā-diṭṭhi*) in the Theravāda Abhidhamma', *Contemporary Buddhism* 5 (2004): 15–28.

it were, as 'anonymous Buddhists' while others do not, but of *all* non-Buddhists sometimes qualifying as 'anonymous Buddhists', and *all* Buddhists sometimes qualifying as 'anonymous non-Buddhists': sometimes Buddhists cannot help but be non-Buddhists and non-Buddhists camnot help but be Buddhists. Put another way, non-Buddhists sometimes have Buddhist mental episodes and Buddhists sometimes have non-Buddhist episodes. Put yet another way, being a Buddhist or not is not finally the question: the question is what sorts of mental episode occur, those motivated by greed, hatred and delusion or those motivated by generosity, kindness and understanding. It is not who or what we consciously like to think we are – Buddhist or non-Buddhist – that is important, but the underlying motivations of our acts, words and thoughts. In short, what matters is now what we believe, but how we behave.

Indian Buddhist systematic thought as expressed in the Abhidharma thus sees the world not so much as a domain of beings who are divided into Buddhists and non-Buddhists by way of those that have faith in the teaching of the Buddha and those that do not, as a domain where skilful and unskilful thoughts come and go and where the work of those who seek liberation for themselves and others is to cultivate and encourage the arising of skilful states. Being a Buddhist then is a way of – or a special kind of commitment to – increasing and enhancing the opportunities for the cultivation of skilful consciousness. From a Buddhist perspective, being a Buddhist may well be the best way of enhancing such opportunities, but it need not be the only way, and indeed, as we have seen, being a Buddhist can also create its own opportunities or occasions for the arising of unskilful states: pride in one's Buddhism and contempt for the failings of others, as well as wrong views based on misunderstandings of Buddhism.

At one point in his *A Treatise on Human Nature* (1739), David Hume discusses the inconsistency between what people say they believe and what they must in their heart of hearts truly believe:

> [A]nd 'tis with reason, that many eminent theologians have not scrupled to affirm, that tho' the vulgar have no formal principles of infidelity, yet they are really infidels in their hearts, and have nothing like what we can call a belief of the eternal duration of their souls. ... I ask, if these people really believe what is inculcated on them, and what they pretend to affirm; and the answer is obviously in the negative.[36]

---

[36]   David Hume, *A Treatise of Human Nature*, ed. by L.A. Selby-Bigge, 2nd ed. with text revised and variant readings, P.H. Nidditch (Oxford: Clarendon Press, 1978), 113–4.

The answer is obviously in the negative because, Hume observes, their behaviour in other respects reveals 'that they really do not believe what they affirm' (115). Hume's observations point towards the fact that we may not always *consciously* be aware of what we believe or do not believe. Hume's example concerns those who claim formally to hold certain beliefs but whose behaviour indicates otherwise. But we can turn this round. We may claim, for example, that we do not believe that there is any point in giving, or that deeds have consequences; or we may not be consciously concerned at all with whether we believe or do not believe in such things; and yet in both cases our behaviour might reveal that deep in our hearts we do.

For Buddhist systematic thought as expressed in the Theravāda Abhidhamma traditions, faith is one of a set of mental qualities whose combined presence or occurrence causes skilful (*kusala*) behaviour, causes skilful actions of body, speech and mind; and skilful actions are by definition actions that show – no matter what one *consciously thinks* one believes – that in one's heart of hearts one believes and trusts in truth, one of whose dimensions is that there is a point in giving, that actions have consequences.

For the Abhdhamma authors true faith is not a mere 'reverential commitment' (*sānunayo adhimokkho*) to the Buddha, Dharma and Sangha as institutional symbols. Nor is it the mere 'conviction' (*abhinivesa*) about the truth of Buddhist doctrine. Such reverential commitment, such conviction are in fact occasions for pride or opinionatedness. While it may look like reverential commitment or conviction and even be mistaken for them, true faith is nonetheless to be distinguished as a trust that arises in direct response to the goodness and truth that those symbols represent, to the truths expressed in the Buddha's teaching.

Faith is something that comes and goes, not something that is constantly there. It arises and passes with skilful states of mind (*citta*). Just as non-Buddhists are not excluded from skilful states of mind, so Buddhists are not excluded from unskilful states of mind. And when Buddhists have unskilful states of mind they have no faith. So just as non-Buddhists become Buddhists, so Buddhists become non-Buddhists.

Buddhists' faith in the Buddha, Dharma and Sangha can effectively turn into an unskilful (non-Buddhist) attachment that manifests as conceit and pride, and an opinionatedness about the Buddha, Dharma and Sangha which causes unskilful actions and words. Nonetheless such attachment may have a role to play in encouraging skilful acts and words. But ultimately, like all attachments, it is to be given up if the goal is the Buddhist goal of complete liberation. Christianity and other religions are not so different. From the Buddhist perspective outlined above, Christian faith need not be limited to conceit and

194   *Buddhist-Christian Dual Belonging*

pride in one's Christianity, or to an attachment to and opinionatedness about the articles of Christian faith; it too may also encourage skilful acts and words. But again it must be given up if the goal is final freedom.

From this perspective dual *belonging* becomes a kind of dual *attachment* – an attachment to the conventional religious forms and expressions of Buddhism and Christianity, which while offering a solution to our problems are at that same time part of the problem: part of what we need to be liberated from. As long as Christian faith constitutes at heart faith in the goodness and truth that the doctrines, symbols and institutions of Christianity stand for then it can be considered 'faith' in the sense found in Buddhist texts. Or to put it another way, as long as an attachment to Christianity encourages and motivates one to do good deeds, to do the kinds of things that lead one closer to nirvana, then it qualifies as what the *Nettippakaraṇa* would call 'skilful' craving: not absolutely skilful, but a helpful attachment that can be given up when the time comes.

In articulating a religious understanding of the problem of conceit and pride in one's religion, the Abhidharma traditions of Buddhist systematic thought are taking up a well-established Buddhist theme, one most famously expressed in the simile of the raft: 'I have taught you how the Dharma is like a raft – for the purpose of crossing over and not for the purpose of holding on to. When you understand how Dharma is taught as like a raft, you will let go of even good things, let alone bad things'.[37] That this is an understanding which privileges Buddhism's own position must, of course, be acknowledged and is made explicit in an early discourse, the *Cūḷasīhanāda-sutta*, in which the Buddha makes his 'lion's roar' (*sīhanāda*): realised and enlightened ascetics are to be found only in his religious tradition; other systems are empty of such realised ascetics.[38] The

---

[37]   M I 135.

[38]   M I 63–8. The traditions recorded by Buddhaghosa in his fifth-century commentary to this *sutta* explain how these non-Buddhist traditions do not lead to a final release from the round of rebirth, but at best only to a temporary respite from the woes of the round of rebirth in the form of rebirth in a relatively pleasant realm: non-Buddhist brahmins are born in the World of Brahmā, non-Buddhist ascetics among the gods of Streaming Radiance (ābhasssarā), non-Buddhist wanderers among the gods of Complete Beauty (subhakinhā), Ājīvikas among the Infinite Minded (*ānantamānasa*) or unconscious beings (Ps II 9–10). These are the cosmological equivalents of various meditation attainments which, apart from the last, are recommended for Buddhist ascetics too. But since these are rebirths *within* the round rebirth, they will eventually come to an end. Buddhaghosa explains that faith in a religious tradition that does not lead to release from the round of rebirth is inappropriate because both the teacher and his followers will continue to be reborn which will eventually have unfortunate consequences: 'In a religion that does not lead to release [from the round of rebirth], when the teacher dies he becomes a lion, a tiger, a bear, a leopard, a hyena, while his

The Buddhist Faith of Non-Buddhists

Buddha explains that there are four types of 'grasping' (*upādāna*): to sense-pleasures, views, precepts and vows and the doctrine of the self. Some non-Buddhist ascetics may understand the first, second and third types of grasping, but *never* (significantly) the fourth. In such a tradition confidence in the teacher is not appropriate (*sammaggata*): the teaching and way of practice are badly explained, and do not lead to release. The Buddha, on the other hand, understands all kinds of grasping, and in his teaching and way of practice confidence in the teacher is fully appropriate: the teaching and way of practice are well explained, and lead to release. While denying that complete realisation is found in other religious traditions, this *sutta* allows for a partial realisation in other traditions; non-Buddhist ascetics have real faith, but their faith is at least in part misplaced since it is directed towards a religious tradition that is wanting.

---

disciples become deer, boars and antelope. He does not then feel patience, kindness, or mercy for them out of consideration for the fact that they were once his attendants and supporters; rather he pounces on them and then drinks their blood and eats their fat and plump flesh. Or the teacher becomes a cat, and the disciples become chickens or mice, then exactly as stated, showing no pity, he eats them. Or the teacher becomes a guardian in hell and the disciples become inhabitants of hell. He does not feel pity for them remembering that they were once his attendants and supporters, but inflicts various punishments on them, tying them to a burning wheel, making them climb a mountain of hot coals, throwing them into a metal pot, putting them through many painful ordeals. Or perhaps when the disciples die they become the lions, and such like, and the teacher becomes a deer, or some other kind of animal. Then they do not feel patience, kindness, or mercy for him remembering that he was once their teacher whom they served with the four requisites [of clothing, alms, lodging and medicine]; rather they are the agents of his misery and misfortune exactly as stated. In this way confidence in the teacher in a religion that does not lead to release is not appropriate: even when it lasts for some time, it eventually comes to nothing' (Ps II 13–14).

Chapter 11

Dual Belonging and Pure Land Buddhism

Caroline Brazier

Why would a person want to be Pure Land Buddhist and Christian? In the discussion of dual belonging, the dialogue between these two faith-based traditions offers a tantalising glimpse of possibilities which are, perhaps, different from those commonly identified in the conversation between Buddhism and Christianity. In this chapter I will identify areas of commonality and differences which may challenge or complement a Christian viewpoint as well as exploring some controversies within Pure Land which mirror dilemmas between the two faiths. As a Pure Land Buddhist, descended from a family of non-conformist Christian clergy, my position is not unbiased. I do not personally pretend to dual belonging, and do not feel particularly qualified to comment on details of Christian doctrine, but nevertheless I am interested to explore what contribution to the dialogue Pure Land can offer.

The question of dual belonging itself brings questions. Why does anyone wish to inhabit the borderlands between faiths, or indeed between any belief systems or ideologies?

Let me hypothesise three possibilities:

Firstly, a person may wish to belong to two faiths in order to reconcile conflicting areas of his or her life. Often this kind of dual belonging is pragmatic. Finding common ground with a partner, or parents, or reconciling one's adoptive culture with one's past may give reason to discover commonalities and smooth over discordances. This process might well involve multiple religious participation, as described by Catherine Cornille but does not necessarily lead to the achievement of a more doctrinally consistent position. The dual-participation is nevertheless important to the person, establishing personal coherence and integration in their religious life, and giving them the opportunity to participate in spiritual community with loved ones.

Secondly, a person may want to live in the borderlands, fully committed to neither position, a maverick within each. A second affiliation, here, offers other ground from which to critique and challenge. This can be fruitful. In many ways it is the modern, or postmodern, position; a response to a world in which global communication and the resultant diversity of cultures disallows the idea that any particular way of construing things is uniquely right. At best this position produces a creative tension between worlds in which light is shone into the dark corners of each tradition and new angles emerge, but at worst it leads to a cat-and-mouse game of scepticism and a kind of circling groundlessness which never commits to anything but its own constant reinvention.

Thirdly, a person may find complementarity between the two faiths in which elements from each throw light on a greater whole. Each faith offers a perspective. These may be seen as different roads up the mountain, or different parts of the elephant, to use two well-worn metaphors. In the Buddhist-Christian arena, for example, a Christian may learn Buddhist meditation to develop inner calm so that the voice of the (Christian) God can be better heard.

As we can see from this example, the integration of two faiths need not be made on an equal footing. A person may stay broadly located within one tradition, but draw on features of another to deepen their insight. Thus in my own work as a psychotherapist, I work basically from a Buddhist model, but have no difficulty in integrating Western psychodynamic or behavioural concepts into my practice where these offer ways to expand and deepen my work. The integrating frame is provided by my core model, and other concepts are added, often stripped of their accompanying context.

Sometimes, too, despite achieving a deep understanding and appreciation of another religious framework, a person may conclude their studies feeling confirmed in their own position. For example, in encountering Pure Land, though he reached a deep appreciation of the insight of its founder, Shinran, Karl Barth[1] ultimately confirmed his own view that Christianity was the only true path.

Nor are people internally consistent. Even the most philosophically astute among us live with contradictions as the layers of personal history, unconscious process and other circumstantial influences create habits and reactions of which we are often hardly aware. Inconsistency is part of the human psyche. As humans we seem capable of living with mentalities constructed upon a huge array of unexamined assumptions. Indeed, as J.P. Williams suggests, it is often in enquiring into such anomalies that we deepen and develop our religious experience.

Considering this complexity of motivations and experiences which is brought to the question of dual belonging, it is apparent that any exploration of the subject must take into account both the subjective experience of the

---

[1]   Karl Barth, *Church Dogmatics*, trans. G.T. Thomson and Harold Knight (Edinburgh: T&T Clark), 1–2, 342.

Dual Belonging and Pure Land Buddhism

practitioner and the doctrinal boundaries of the two traditions involved. In this chapter I will explore what benefits dual belonging might bring for those interested in the interface between Pure Land Buddhism and Christianity. How can these two traditions, which both put salvific faith at their centre, together provide a framework for religious practice which is, at least for some, a better or truer prospect than practising one individually?

Context of Pure Land Buddhism

Pure Land Buddhism is not well known in the West. Although Japanese Pure Land has made some inroads in North America due to Japanese immigration to that continent, even there temples remain predominantly Japanese in ethnicity. Whilst small numbers of Caucasian converts are gradually joining these groups, many do so because they have Japanese partners, and relatively few discover this branch of Buddhism independently. In the UK the longest established temple is Three Wheels in Acton, founded by Rev Kemmyo Sato in 1994. Another longstanding group of Pure Land practitioners grew up around Rev Jack Austin (1917–93), who was closely involved with The Buddhist Society. He was active in establishing Pure Land interest in the UK since the 1950s, joined by Jim Pym, for many years editor of the newsletter, *Pure Land Notes*.

Pure Land is a devotional strand of Buddhism. Originating in India, it developed into separate schools in China and, particularly, Japan. It centres on devotion to Amida Buddha, an amalgamation of two other Buddhist figures: Amitābha, Buddha of Infinite light, and Amitayus, Buddha of infinite life. Amida literally means 'without measure', thus representing infinite time and space, or, more symbolically, the presence of Buddha in the world for all time.

Pure Land Buddhism draws inspiration from three main texts:[2] the Greater and Lesser Pure Land Sutras and the Contemplation Sutra. In the Greater Pure Land Sutra, Dharmakara, a devotee of a previous Buddha, made an aspiration to Buddhahood conditional on 48 vows. In the eighteenth of these, he vowed that he would create a Pure Land where anyone who called on his name might be reborn. There people would automatically become enlightened. After long ascetic practices, Dharmakara finally attained enlightenment and became Amida Buddha. In the process he created the Pure Land on which the traditions of that name are centred.

---

[2]   Skt. Larger *Sukhāvatīvyūha Sūtra*, Skt. Smaller *Sukhāvatīvyūha Sūtra*, *Kuan wu-liang-shou ching*.

In Pure Land Buddhism the primary practice is *nembutsu*. *Nembutsu* literally means mindfulness of Buddha. The practice usually involves reciting the phrase 'Namo Amida Bu' or 'Namu Amida Butsu'. This phrase literally means 'I call on measureless Buddha'.

Pure Land in the Context of Buddhism

Whilst in the past, scholars within Japanese Pure Land had little interest in linking the movement to other Buddhist traditions, since the mid-nineteenth century, factions within Jodo Shinshu (Shin), the largest Japanese Pure Land school, became keen to understand the roots of the tradition in its Indian and Chinese precursors. Some Jodo Shinshu scholars began studying Pali and Sanskrit, locating the Pure Land doctrines within the corpus of Buddhist teachings. Others travelled to Europe to study European philosophy and religious thought. For example, Kiyozawa Manshi played a leading role in integrating Western and Buddhist ideas within Jodo Shinshu by synthesising Hegelianism and Amidaism.[3] This contextualisation of the teachings challenges those who would link Pure Land and Christianity on the basis of superficial similarities since it embeds the tradition in Buddhist thought which is broadly non-theistic.

Recently, whilst some remain convincedly literalist in their interpretation of Pure Land,[4] others, perhaps in response to the popularity of Zen in the West, have been keen to link the tradition more firmly with Mahayana. Shigaraki,[5] Suzuki[6] and Innagaki[7] all explore the relationship between Shin and Zen, emphasising the provisional nature of its traditional teachings and ultimate emptiness which lies behind them. Meanwhile Tanaka links Pure Land teachings to tathagata-garba traditions, comparing the experience of shinjin (faith) to Mahayana concepts of Buddha-nature by recognising the intrinsic capacity for enlightenment.[8]

---

[3] Joseph Kitagawa *On Understanding Japanese Religion* (Princeton, NJ: Princeton University Press, 1966), 215.

[4] See particularly views of Adrian Cirlea and Eiken Kobai (http://amida-ji-retreat-temple-romania.blogspot.co.uk/2008/09/kobai-senseis-statement-amida-is-true.html).

[5] Takamaro Shigaraki *Heart of the Shin Buddhist Path: A Life of Awakening* (Berkeley, CA: Wisdom Publications; Tra edition 2013; original Japanese edition Hozokan, 2005).

[6] D.T. Suzuki, *Mysticism: Christian and Buddhist* (London and New York: Allen & Unwin, 1957).

[7] Zuiken Innagaki in 1971 letter to Jack Austin (http://www.nembutsu.info/horai/letters_ja1.htm).

[8] Kenneth Tannaka, *Ocean* (Berkeley, CA: Wisdom Publications, 1997).

Hirota also contextualises Shinran, founder of Jodo Shinshu, within mainstream Buddhism. Here, in discussing Shinran's view of evil, Hirota sees links to core Buddhist doctrine regarding the nature of attachment and aversion, as set out in the teaching of the Four Noble Truths: 'Evil in Shinran's sense is one's personal inability to eradicate delusional thought and perception that gives rise to the reification of self and other, the passions of self-attachment, and the pain experienced and inflicted, that characterises unenlightened existence'.[9]

Buddhism asserts the insubstantiality of the self. Its core teachings show how a state of inauthenticity or delusion is created and maintained through distorted perception and processes of mental attachment and clinging. The path to liberation is the transcendence of these falsities. One of these teachings, The Four Noble Truths, addresses this process.

The first Noble Truth is affliction (*dukkha*). Among those things listed as *dukkha* are sickness, ageing, death and disappointment. Knowing that we cannot escape from *dukkha* evokes feelings of fear and dread, which understandably people want to avoid experiencing. As a result, they tend to cling to things which give comfort, seeking stability and permanence in the familiar, even though, in fact, life is uncertain and loss inevitable. Clinging is habitual and leads to unskilful actions. These in turn create a false sense of security and an illusion that life is controllable and predictable. As part of this process, they tend to reify a sense of identity or self.

The process of 'becoming', or self-building is itself a source of *dukkha*. Driven by the senses, the mind grasps at experience, building a worldview in which objects are experienced as indicators of the self. The perceptual process exists in a mutually conditioning relationship with the identity,[10] creating a kind of psychological bubble which protects the person from seeing the anomalies in their worldview. This state of delusion, *avidyā*, is the source of human misery, not least because it is unreal and disappointing.

Enlightenment is liberation from this ordinary, conditioned relationship with phenomena. It is the state in which self, the process of conditioned thought, perception and action, is abandoned. A quality of enlightenment is non-self (*anattā*). All Buddhist schools are concerned with enlightenment, but different schools have different approaches to it.

---

[9]   Dennis Hirota, *Shinran, Barth, and Religion: Engagement With Religious Language as an Issue of Comparative Theology* (http://www.shindharmanet.com/wp-content/uploads/2012/pdf/Hirota-Barth.pdf, downloaded 1 May 2014).

[10]   Caroline Brazier, *Buddhist Psychology* (London: Constable Robinson, 2003).

Pure Land as Other-Power Buddhism

Pure Land Buddhism is considered to be an other-power school. This makes it particularly interesting to dual belongers who might equate the concept of other-power with some form of theism, however to reach a fuller understanding of the concept of other-power requires a contextualisation of the doctrine within Buddhism as a whole, and an appreciation of its relationship to the teaching of non-self.

Nagarjuna, who lived around the second century CE, is often considered to be the most significant figure in Indian Buddhist philosophy after the Buddha himself. He is listed amongst the patriarchs of many Mahayana schools of Buddhism, including Pure Land. Nagarjuna wrote the *Commentary on the Ten Bodhisattva Stages*, a text only existent in the Chinese, in which he distinguished two paths of practice: the difficult path, known as the path of sages, and the easy path.[11] The latter, which became the *nembutsu* path, was likened to travelling by boat on the ocean instead of walking on foot. Thus other-power Buddhism meant reliance upon the power of the Buddha rather than on one's own efforts. From these roots, two distinct styles of practice emerged, which came to be called self-power and other-power Buddhism, *jiriki* and *tariki* in Japanese.

Self-power practice focuses on dismantling delusion (*avidyā*) through meditation, insight and ethical living. It reveals the insubstantiality of self-structures and eradicates their foundations. Other-power practice, as found in Pure Land schools, focuses on the futility of effort and, rather, invites direct experience of Buddha. This experience, an experience of grace, is seen as the saving embrace of that which lies beyond human limits. Other-power practice can thus be conceived as direct engagement with *anattā*.

In my book, *Other Buddhism*, I explained the distinction between self-power and other-power using the analogy of a person caught in a snowdrift.[12] This person might free himself by digging away the snow. This is self-power. Alternatively, he may catch a rope thrown by somebody on the outside of the snowdrift, and be hauled out. This is other-power.

In looking at this analogy of the man in the snow drift from a perspective of dual belonging we might ask whether the conception of a rescue is valid for both religions, and if so, whether the rescuer outside the snowdrift is construed in the same way in the two traditions. At the same time, even within the religious

---

[11] Harold Stewart, *Reflections on the Dharma* (http://www.nembutsu.info/hsrnagarjuna.htm).

[12] Caroline Brazier, *Other Buddhism* (London: O-Books, 2007), 76–80.

traditions, different practitioners may have different views about what it is that rescues us from ourselves. Between traditions the problem becomes even more complex.

The Concept of Faith in Pure Land Buddhism

The faith experience of Pure Land, *shinjin*, is described as absolute and unwavering. This term, though often translated as faith, is probably better understood when translated as entrustment.[13] Pure Land Buddhism recognises the limitations of human understanding in its emphasis on the fallibility of the unenlightened person. People are enmeshed in their karma and caught by their passions, a state which is referred to as *bombu-nature.*

As limited beings, human understanding of the limitless is only partial. This kind of agnosticism can be seen as a feature of Pure Land faith. As in Buddhism generally, faith of this kind enables uncertainty. For example, in the Tannisho, Shinran says: 'I have no idea whether the nembutsu is truly the seed for my being born in the Pure Land or whether it is the karmic act for which I must fall into hell. Should I have been deceived by Master Honen and, saying the nembutsu, were to fall into hell, even then I would have no regrets'.[14] Shinran is making the point here that he is not omniscient and his faith is not founded on certainty or beliefs. He follows the teaching and his teachers, trusting that they will lead him better than he can lead himself.

This idea of faith as trust is echoed in the relationship to Amida. According to Pure Land Scholar, Alfred Bloom,[15] shinjin is a spontaneous arising of faith in response to hearing the Buddha's teachings, not achieved through the will. Monshu Koshin Ohtani[16] also emphasises the receptive nature of this process: '[Shinjin] means my heart has been transformed into a heart that entrusts. It points to a change that has come over my heart'.[17] Such discussion of entrustment leaves space for dual belonging in as much as we recognise the limited capacity of

---

[13] Dennis Hirota, *Shinran, Barth, and Religion: Engagement With Religious Language as an Issue of Comparative Theology* (http://www.shindharmanet.com/wp-content/uploads/2012/pdf/Hirota-Barth.pdf, downloaded 1 May 2014, 1).

[14] Tannisho II.

[15] Alfred Bloom, *Strategies For Modern Living; A Commentary With the Text of the Tannisho* (Berkeley, CA: Numata, 1992), 124.

[16] Koshin Ohtani, *The Buddha's Wish for the World* (New York: American Buddhist Study Centre Press, 2009).

[17] Ibid. 121.

the practitioner to conceptualise Amida, however we will return to this central matter in a later section.

Provisional Truth and the Role of Uncertainty

In his book, *Heart of the Shin Buddhist Path*,[18] Takamaro Shigaraki draws on a popular Mahayana image to discuss the role of metaphor in religious thought. Nagarjuna's doctrine of two truths is illustrated by the image of a finger pointing to the moon. If absolute truth is unknowable, the moon represents that truth, and the finger the metaphor, not the truth itself.

Shigaraki sees the figure of Amida Buddha and the stories in the Pure Land Sutras as symbolic:[19] 'The realm of awakening or enlightenment, which Gautama Buddha realised in his life, as well as ultimate truth and value, constitute the moon. The teaching of Buddhism is always expressed by the relationship between the finger and the moon, between the words of the teaching and suchness or truth itself, which is the essence of that teaching'.[20]

This understanding of metaphor and its relationship with ultimate truth is relevant to dual belonging, since it provides a frame which allows the practitioner to draw on metaphors of both traditions to point towards a common truth which is beyond words. Buddhism overtly discusses this kind of metaphor in its scriptures, for example in the parable of the raft in the Pali texts[21] or the apparitional city in the Lotus Sutra.[22]

Nagarjuna's image of provisional truth serves Buddhism well in its relationship with other faiths. All religious assertions potentially point towards the same moon. Buddhism has historically tended to incorporate indigenous religions of the countries which it spread to into itself, creating doctrinal anomalies which have always been accepted because they lie in the domain of provisional truth. With this precedent, a Buddhist might practise Christianity, believing it to offer provisional truth, conducive to the path. Within Buddhism, contradictory statements are common and not regarded as problematic. Teachings tend to be regarded as skilful means, evoking particular behaviours and perspectives, rather than absolute truth claims.

---

[18] Takamaro Shigaraki, *Heart of the Shin Buddhist Path: A Life of Awakening* (Berkeley, CA: Wisdom Publication; Tra edition 2013; original Japanese edition Hozokan, 2005).
[19] Ibid. 27–9.
[20] Ibid. 27–8.
[21] Majjhima Nikāya 22.
[22] The Lotus Sutra VII.

Three Bodies Teaching

In Mahayana Buddhism the issue of provisional and absolute truth, and the role of metaphor as a bridge between them, is addressed by the teaching known as *the three bodies*. According to this teaching, Buddhas take three forms or bodies. These bodies represent three types of spiritual encounter. They are:

- *Nirmāṇakāya*: the embodied Buddha, exemplified by the historic Buddha, Gautama.
- *Dharmakāya*: the absolute essence of Buddha-ness; the heart of the spiritual mystery.
- *Sambhogakāya*: the symbolic level which mediates the pure essence, making it accessible to people living in the world now.

In Mahayana Buddhism, celestial bodhisattvas such as Amitābha and Amitayus are considered to be *Sambhogakāya* figures. Many Mahayana practices centre on devotion to such Buddhas. A *Sambhogakāya* Buddha, like other spiritual representations, is symbolic. This does not make it less important or 'real' than the pure essence of *Dharmakāya*. All three bodies are considered to be true facets of Buddha, and each has its function. By making the religious experience perceivable, the *Sambhogakāya* creates a bridge between the *Dharmakāya* and the ordinary person. Shigaraki says:

> We are able to see the moon because of the finger. However, it is because of the light of the moon that we are able to see the finger and the finger is able to function as a finger. The finger is something connected to this earth, and yet at the same time is also an extension of the light of the moon. In other words, the teaching – as symbol – points Dharmakāya toward ultimate value and truth, which transcends the secular world. Conversely, that which transcends the secular world also draws near to this world.[23]

The *Sambhogakāya* reveals the Dharmakāya. It points towards the ultimate truth which is expressed inadequately in words. Dharma, personified in the *Dharmakāya*, is the foundational order of things, universally available, but not directly perceivable by ordinary people. In Jodo Shinshu, the three bodies are commonly viewed as aspects of a whole, as for example, we see in this explanation:

---

[23]   Takamaro Shigaraki, *Heart of the Shin Buddhist Path: A Life of Awakening* (Berkeley, CA: Wisdom Publications; Tra edition 2013; original Japanese edition Hozokan, 2005), 29.

Trikāya, meaning Three Bodies, is not three separate bodies but three aspects of the one body of Buddhahood. Buddha as Dharmakāya resides in everything. The Dharmakāya is impersonal law, principle, ultimate reality, the Truth of the Universe. It is indescribable and inexpressible. The Buddha as Sambhogakāya is personal and appears before our religious awareness as Amida Buddha of Wisdom and Compassion. Buddha as Nirmanakaya refers to the historical Buddha Sakyamuni who appeared on earth 2,500 years ago.[24]

This interpretation of the teaching has a precedent in Shinran's thought. He equated Amida with all three bodies, and particularly with Dharmakāya. Shinran wrote: 'The highest perfect enlightenment is none other than the realm of nirvana. The realm of nirvana is the ultimate Dharmakāya. To realise the ultimate Dharmakāya is to reach the ultimate end of the one vehicle [Mahayana]. There is no other Tathagata, there is no other Dharmkaya. Tathagata is itself Dharmkaya'.[25] In his understanding of the intimate relationship between the symbolic and the ultimate, Shinran often speaks of the three bodies as facets of the one. The symbolic is no less real than the absolute. Rather, it enables understanding of reality. 'According to Shinran, in a manner of speaking, this dharma-body[26] that does not have colour or form works for us continually in our world and delusion ... Amida has all three bodies but his distinctive characteristics are those of a Sambhogakāya Buddha ... Amida represents ultimate reality which is beyond time and space'.[27]

Whilst Shinran's writing explores the close relationship between symbol and reality, other Pure Land Buddhists refuse to accept that Amida might be seen as symbolic. Shigaraki critiques this view as superficial literalism, which he sees in the traditionalist views found in some Jodo Shinshu temples. 'Traditional Shin Buddhist doctrine is not clear on this point [the symbolic nature of Amida], and often confounds the finger and the moon'.[28]

Pure Land Buddhism, with its reverence for Amida Buddha, is particularly open to literalism. This is not necessarily a difficulty. Despite the doctrinal injunction to distinguish between symbol and essence, with a central emphasis on entrustment, intellectual clarity is not the foremost quality of the practitioner. Too much cleverness in doctrinal interpretation can itself be a

---

[24]   http://shinmission_sg.tripod.com/id12.html.
[25]   *Collected Works of Shinran* vol. 1, 60–61.
[26]   Dharmakāya.
[27]   *Jodo Shinshu a Guide* (Kyoto: Hongwanji), 72.
[28]   Takamaro Shigaraki, *Heart of the Shin Buddhist Path: A Life of Awakening* (Berkeley: Wisdom Publications; Tra edition 2013; original Japanese edition Hozokan, 2005), 28.

barrier to recognising bombu-nature and other-power, and the ideal-type figure of Pure Land is the person of simple faith, known as the *myokonin*, or 'shiny person'. Myokonins are often uneducated, and live ordinary working lives whilst showing absolute devotion to Amida Buddha. Shinjin, as Kemmyo Sato points out,[29] is beyond morality or intellect. Entrustment involves relinquishing intent. Accepting the gift of Other-Power 'we should let Amida Buddha work to save us just as he will'.[30]

God and Amida: Can Pure Land Buddhism be Theistic?

Westerner converts to Buddhism often have ambivalent feelings about questions of faith. They have often been attracted to the tradition because it offers spiritual practice without requiring beliefs.[31] Whilst a minority are happy to consider or even embrace dual belonging, many are wary of anything suggesting theism and so are wary of Pure Land, fearing the reintroduction of a god-figure into the otherwise tidy landscape of emptiness. In the past, and in recent times, such concerns led Buddhist writers in the West to consider Pure Land an inferior form of Buddhism.

Because Buddhism is generally practice-based rather than belief-based, Buddhists can remain agnostic regarding metaphysics. This agnosticism reflects the Buddha's own teaching which warned against preoccupation with speculative questions. The Buddhist sources include a list of 'unanswerable questions'[32] about which the Buddha declined to teach. These included questions on the origins or extent of the universe and on what happens to a Buddha after death. They were deemed unconducive to the spiritual path and likely to lead to speculative thinking. Buddhist practice focused on observing immediate experience and testing knowledge against these observations[33] rather than on exploring the practitioner's relationship to the spiritual realm.

This focus on practice has created a difference of emphasis between Buddhism and theistic religions which is felt in a different weighting given in the balance between doctrine and practice. Whilst Buddhism has spawned schools of philosophy and engaged in doctrinal argument, its main concern has

---

[29]   Kemmyo Sato, *Great Living; In the Pure Encounter Between Master And Disciple* (New York: American Buddhist Studies Centre, 2010).

[30]   Ibid., 121.

[31]   Stephen Batchelor, *Buddhism Without Beliefs* (New York: Riverhead, 1997).

[32]   This list appear in two Suttas: Majjhima Nikāya 63 and 72.

[33]   The Kalama Sutta, Anguttara Nikāya 3.63.

nearly always been with practice and direct experience. Even the most significant thinkers like Nagarjuna were practitioners first and foremost, grounding their sophisticated arguments in meditation and devotional practices. For this reason, Buddhists have often been flexible in their doctrinal interpretations, accommodating contradictions and differences of interpretation without great concern, differences being simply explained in terms of two-truth doctrine. This pre-eminence of direct experience does not, however, negate some doctrinal limits. As we will see, some points of Buddhist doctrine, common to all schools, are problematic to dual belonging and, while not insurmountable, cannot be ignored.

Pure Land Buddhism with its strong mythos of salvation can appear very different from popular secular Buddhism[34] of the West. The founders of the Japanese traditions wrote books and letters which are filled with expressions of gratitude for Amida's compassion and confidence in the power of Amida Buddha to rescue the practitioner from the pit of samsara. Similar devotional sentiments are apparent in Pure Land writings from China and India since at least the time of Nargarjuna.[35] All of these writings centre on the salvific relationship between Amida Buddha and the practitioner, which is commonly referred to as a relationship of grace. Shinjin and the consequent promise of birth in the Pure Land are described as gifts, originating without effort or intention from Amida Buddha, who offers the only hope of salvation for the ordinary person. With such a structure of ideas, can parallels be made between Pure Land and Christianity which are strong enough to support dual belonging? Can Amida Buddha be viewed as a manifestation of God?

The devotional nature of Pure Land Buddhism suggests potential for dual belonging. It is hard to believe, reading the passionate devotion of such texts, that their authors did not feel inspired by a felt connection to the ultimate which has strong similarities to that experienced by theistic practitioners. To the Pure Land practitioner, Amida is a mysterious embodiment of love and generosity, sometimes viewed so infinitely powerful as to be only partially viewed,[36] and other times as an intimate embrace.[37] In the immediacy of this experience, it

---

[34]   Stephen Bachelor, *Confession of a Buddhist Atheist* (New York: Spiegel and Grau, 2011).

[35]   *The Stanzas of Nagarjuna on the Amida Buddha and His Pure Land*, trans. from The Pure Land, vol. 1, no. 1, June, 1979, from the French, by Franny Sime, August, 1980. First published by the Buddhist Discussion Centre (Upwey) Ltd, Newsletter No. 5, September, 1981.

[36]   This view would tend to be more common in Jodoshu Schools.

[37]   An expression more typical of Jodo Shinshu.

can be tempting to simply exchange the name Amida for God and bridge the two traditions.

As we have already seen, experience is often expressed in metaphor and imagery. Metaphor can express spiritual experience which is not necessarily easily conceptualised. The common imagery can be one starting point for those who wish to practise between traditions. For example, Pure Land Buddhist and Quaker, Jim Pym, finds parallels between images of light in both religions. 'The Buddha tells us the story of Amitābha, the Buddha of Infinite Light, while the Christian Epistle of John states that, "God is Light, and in Him there is no darkness at all" ... "Can there be two Infinite Lights?"'.[38]

For Pym, the rhetorical question invokes commonalities of imagery and experience to create a comfortable synthesis of both his allegiances. To call on the infinite light to call on the absolute, whatever form it takes.

The simplicity of *nembutsu* practice, however, belies the theological depth of the writings of Shinran and Honen, and, as Pure Land scholars seek doctrinal convergence with other Buddhist schools, doctrinal differences between the tradition and Christianity become more apparent. Some writers, like Dennis Hirota, are keen to point out that simplistic assumptions of commonality may be ill-founded: 'Because Shin Buddhist statements about reality and human engagement with it had seemed so similar in some respects to some Christian doctrines, it has been assumed that the conceptions of truth are the same, and therefore such problems as the nature of religious engagement or the ontological status of a supreme being are the same'.[39]

The difference which Hirota refers to in particular is the difference in ontological status between God and Buddha. In Christianity, man does not become God. In Buddhism, the Buddha and man are the same in essence. For example, the humanity of the Buddha is central and consequential to Jodoshu priest, Sho-on Hattori.[40] He asserts: 'The difference between God and Buddha in relation to man would be as follows: God is different from man epistemologically and ontologically, whereas Buddha is different from man epistemologically but not ontologically'.[41] Hirota agrees: 'while the concept of faith stands on the duality of God (creator) and man (created), shinjin is the oneness of Buddha

---

[38] Jim Pym online article, *Buddha and God* (Contemplative Consciousness Network http://c-c-n.org/buddha-and-god-by-jim-pym/, downloaded 21 April 2014).

[39] Dennis Hirota, *Toward a Contemporary Understanding of Pure Land Buddhism* (New York: University of New York, 2000), 4.

[40] Sho-on Hattori, *A Raft from The Other Shore Honen and the Way of Pure Land Buddhism* (Tokyo: Jodo Shu Press, 2001).

[41] Ibid., quoted http://www.jodo.org/about_plb/what_plb.html.

210   *Buddhist-Christian Dual Belonging*

and man, or man's becoming a Buddha'.[42] The humanity of Buddhas applies to Amida Buddha as much as to Shakyamuni. Those arguing this position point to the fact that although Amida Buddha, and other Sambhogakāya figures may appear to be treated as gods in Buddhist devotional practices, the Pure Land sutras are clear that even Amida Buddha was once a human being, Dharmakara, who achieved enlightenment through diligence and devotion.

Ignorance and Apophatic Approaches

The pragmatic nature of the Buddhist approach creates an asymmetric attitude to dual belonging. Since Buddhism remains a religion more grounded in practice than conceptualisation, assertions about the nature of God, Buddhas and humans are less important to most Buddhists than they are to those of other faiths. They rest in religious discourse that is founded in reason. The Pure Land conception of bombu-nature undermines reliance upon the intellect conversely, resting as it does on an understanding of our basic nature as one of fallibility and ignorance. Even when wisdom (*prajñā*) is sought in Buddhism, it comes by cutting through ordinary kinds of knowing (*samjñā*).

    Enlightenment does not come about through seeking omniscience, but rather through exploring 'what is not'. The fundamental non-self nature of being, *anattā*, is realised, according to the Pali *suttas*, through recognising 'This is not mine, this I am not, this is not my self'.[43] This recognition, at the heart of Buddhist experience, expressed in Mahayana Buddhism through the concept of *śūnyatā* (emptiness), involves the elimination of the personal and a transcendence of ordinary mind and its conceptualisations. The experience of *anattā* is not simply an experience of nothingness, however. As self-factors are removed, they are replaced by experience of other-factors, described by Vietnamese Zen Master Thich Nhat Hanh as the fullness of all things.[44] The experience of this spiritual breakthrough is commonly described in terms of radiance or clarity, love or wisdom. It is the 'unborn' state,

---

    [42] Paraphrasing Yoshifumi Ueda in Dennis Hirota, *Shinran, Barth, and Religion: Engagement With Religious Language as an Issue of Comparative Theology* (http://www. shindharmanet.com/wp-content/uploads/2012/pdf/Hirota-Barth.pdf, downloaded 1 May 2014, 1).

    [43] This refrain is found in many suttas of the Pali Canon.

    [44] Nhat Hanh, *Awakening of the Heart: Essential Buddhist Sutras and Commentaries* (Berkeley, CA: Parallax Press, 2012).

referred to in the *Udāna*,[45] an unconditioned space where self-attachments are eliminated. This is the goal of the Buddhist path.

Shinran suggests that terms like nirvana, *śūnyatā*, Dharmakāya, and the unborn all refer to this being that lies beyond ordinary being. All these terms describe the same phenomenon, albeit nuanced in different ways. Mysterious and undefined, this ultimate state transcends the duality of self and other; a state more clearly defined by what it is not, than by what it is.

The focus on what is not shares ground with the apophatic approach in Christianity. In this approach, truth is explored through an interrogation of assumption and a creative pursuit of doubt. Apophatic theology addresses unknowability in particular by clarifying what is not so. The negative statements and unanswerable questions at the centre of the Buddhist thought have been located within this apophatic discourse. This apophatic path in Christianity has often focused on the direct experience of the mystical, exploring personal encounter with the unknowable, as can be seen in what is perhaps the best-known example, the medieval Christian mystical writing, *The Cloud of Unknowing*.[46] The ineffable is only experienced indirectly, interpreted through symbolic representation. If we draw parallels with Pure Land it seems possible to view the representation of Amida Buddha, the measureless light and life, as a representation of unknowability.

Under attack from both the new scientific knowledge and the complex cultural and spiritual perspectives of modern society, some religions have turned to fundamentalism and the assertion of one truth, but other traditions have embraced pluralism and a deeper appreciation of the unknowable. In this spirit, some modern thinkers, particularly within the more liberal branches of their traditions, are exploring common ground between faiths. As science has challenged the literal interpretation of the religious mythos, they have adjusted their discourse to embrace uncertainty and pluralism. John Hick, the theologian and philosopher, in his paper 'The Buddha's Undetermined Questions and the Religions'[47] discusses how both Buddhism and Christianity can find common ground in the rejection of certainty.

---

[45]   *Udāna*, Khuddaka Nikāya 3.

[46]   *The Cloud of Unknowing* is an anonymous work of Christian mysticism written in the late 14th century.

[47]   John Hick, *The Buddha's Undetermined Questions and the Religions* (http://www.johnhick.org.uk/article8.html, 2004).

Duality and Non-Duality

In Mahayana Buddhism, the ultimate state is commonly described as non-dual. When self is transcended, all is Buddha. There is one-ness. Christianity is necessarily dualistic. God and human form an irreducible dyad: Creator and created. Buddha and humanity are of one nature, God and humanity are not. Whilst similarities of faith experience might make the synthesis of Pure Land Buddhism and Christianity attractive to some, the difference in conception of the relationship with the spiritual source in the two traditions creates doctrinal distinctions which are hard to eliminate. Non-duality is therefore problematic to dual belonging.

Pure Land is ultimately non-dualistic in its understanding, but it remains dualistic in its commonly practiced form. This paradox can be perplexing. Describing the nature of shinjin, Kemmyo Sato suggests that the relationship between Buddha and practitioner is neither one nor two.[48] In the embrace of Amida, there is unity, but in the bombu humanity of the practitioner there is separation. The two coexist. At a relational level, *nembutsu* practice and the experience of shinjin bridge the psychological walls created by the ordinary grasping mind, but at absolute level, through shinjin, in Amida's embrace, the duality between person and Buddha disappears.

In this way, despite its promise to the dual belonger, Pure Land Buddhism does not represent an easy bed-fellow for Christian affiliates. Doctrinally its roots are generally now seen as firmly within the Mahayana non-dual tradition, though not all traditionalist writers agree with this emphasis. At the same time, at the level of practice and experience, the ordinary devotee may feel a close affinity with theistic traditions and this opens up the possibility of finding common ground in worship through the felt connection to the immeasurable.

The Question of Evil

Perhaps the most significant contribution which Pure Land Buddhism makes to the field of religious belonging is its view on the matter of evil. The Pure Land traditions propose a radically non-judgemental framework of religious experience which goes beyond anything found in Christianity. In this, Pure Land is more radical than other Buddhist schools, since its other-power position relies upon

---

[48] Kemmyo Sato, *Great Living; In the Pure Encounter Between Master And Disciple* (New York: American Buddhist Studies Centre, 2010).

Dual Belonging and Pure Land Buddhism

an exposition of the futility of personal effort and the bombu-nature of human beings. Shinran in particular emphasised that it was only through the recognition of one's evil nature that one could appreciate the immensity of Amida's power. He commonly lamented the immeasurable depths of his own bad karma, accumulated over lifetimes, and the hopelessness of his case. Pure Land texts are filled with references to sinfulness, to an extent which makes modern people quite uneasy.

What has to be understood, however, in reading these texts, is that in Pure Land Buddhism sinfulness is not a barrier to salvation, but, rather, the route to it. By recognising the depths of his bad karma, the practitioner sees his complete incapacity to help himself and simultaneously realises the absolute compassion of Amida. These twin realisations are the ground of Pure Land faith. Far from being a source of divine judgement, Amida is universally portrayed as a source of indiscriminate love and compassion. There is no concept of forgiveness within Pure Land because none is needed. Amida does not discriminate between good and bad, so he does not need to forgive. For the person who is mostly deeply enmeshed in bad karma, Amida's help is most needed. As Shinran's famous statement in the Tannisho states: 'Even the good person attains birth in the Pure Land, how much more so the evil person.'[49]

This view of negative karma is not substantially different from that of other Buddhist schools, though the solution proposed in Pure Land is more radical. Self-power Buddhism emphasises the route of mind training and ethical frameworks as the means to escape its influence. Pure Land emphasises reliance on what is beyond the self. Buddhism understands karma as natural forces, operating in the world, effecting consequences when people act unskilfully. This action-and-consequence model does not involve an external judge, effecting retribution. It is thus sometimes described as non-ethical. We create our own karma and suffer its consequences through our own ignorance. Karma is the main mechanism by which the structures of the conditioned mind and the self are maintained. It influences our actions and our perceptions.

Recognising the depth of bombu-nature leads to salvation. Realising total dependence on Amida's care, the practitioner sees the futility of self-rescuing and is embraced by complete faith. The self tries to find independence, but in Pure Land practice there is only dependence. Recognising one's sinfulness therefore evokes gratitude and joy, as well as regret, in the practitioner, but it does not evoke fear. As D.T. Suzuki suggests, without self, nothing need be subdued. He writes: 'as there is no self, no crucifixion is needed, no sadism is to be practised, no shocking sight is to be displayed by the roadside. According to Buddhism, the

---

[49] Tannisho 3.

214   *Buddhist-Christian Dual Belonging*

world is the network of cosmic interrelationships and there is no agent behind the net who holds it for his wilful management'.[50]

The removal of judgement from the central paradigm of the religious process is radical in its impact. Western Buddhists, steeped in habits of guilt-based thinking, often fail to recognise how ideas of judgement have infiltrated their spiritual mindset. Yet in Pure Land, Shinran's provocative language of sin and evil provides a direct challenge to such self-related patterns of thinking. The result is freeing. Without judgement, there is no need to hide aspects of behaviour or experience. Without judgement, there is no need to fabricate self-importance or an inflated personal image. Without judgement, there is no need to put oneself up and others down.

For dual belongers, the Pure Land view of evil is a provocative challenge. Those who lean towards this position in all probability draw on a liberal form of Christianity which is less concerned with judgement than with forgiveness, but either of these positions is founded on a dualistic paradigm, which in its essence seems difficult to transcend. As Kemmyo Sato suggests in the ideas quoted earlier, in the paradoxical relationship between the practitioner and Amida, it is possible to see both duality, from the bombu perspective, and non-duality, from Amida's perspective, but neither perspective has any possibility of external sources of judgement implied.

Conclusions

Pure Land Buddhism has often been hailed as offering the potential for dual belonging. In this chapter, I have set out some of its basic framework of ideas, locating these within the wider frame of Buddhist thought. As a living religious tradition, interpretation of Pure Land doctrine has evolved in modern times to accommodate both the broader arena of religious and philosophical thought, and the political position of the school in relationship to other Buddhist traditions. This process creates a richly nuanced milieu in which dialogue and exchange can happen. Whether this dialogue can extend to dual membership of Pure Land and Christianity is, however, less clear.

Core to this investigation is the location of Pure Land Buddhism within the non-dual paradigm of Mahayana Buddhism. Many modern Pure Land thinkers referred to in this chapter consider that this position is a correct understanding

---

[50]   D.T. Suzuki, *Mysticism: Christian and Buddhist* (London and New York: Allen & Unwin, 1957), 120.

of Pure Land doctrine. If this position is insisted upon, then at a doctrinal level, a true integration of the two traditions can never be achieved.

As Kemmyo Sato suggests, however, aspects of Pure Land can be seen as dualistic. The experience of the practitioner is of a separation between himself, embedded in karmic perspectives, and Amida, as the source of salvation. At this level, an experiential amalgamation of the two traditions becomes possible, but from a Pure Land perspective this would need to be provisional. Just as, for the Roman Catholic Magisterium,[51] involvement with Buddhist practice would need to lead ultimately to a fuller relationship with Christ, from a Pure Land perspective, in order to achieve doctrinal consistency, dual belonging needs to lead to the non-dual and to enlightenment and nirvana.

Despite these difficulties, however, the tantalising similarities of experience between the two traditions offer the potential for enrichment and dialogue. At the level of practice, there seems plenty of opportunity for shared direction and worship, and opportunities for learning and deepening of respective faiths through conversation. From the side of bombu-nature, our limited capacity to grasp the ultimate leaves space for uncertainty, and it is perhaps within this space of not knowing that the most effective meeting between the traditions can happen. In this process, an understanding grounded in an appreciation of metaphor and the poetic can be facilitative. This understanding with its multi-levelled capacity to hold paradox, combined with apophatic enquiry into the nature of the religious encounter can establish a solid, ever-changing alliance between the two parent religions.

---

[51] D'Costa, G. 2015. 'A Roman Catholic Approach to Buddhist-Catholic Dual Belonging', in G. D'Costa and R. Thompson (eds), *Buddhist-Christian Dual Belonging: Affirmations, Objections, Explorations* (Farnham: Ashgate).

Chapter 12

Going Beyond the Creator God: An Apophatic Approach to Buddhist-Christian Dual Religious Belonging

J.P. Williams

The question posed by the organisers of our symposium was whether dual belonging is 'possible when one faith is centred on a Creator God while the other rejects creation and regards belief in God as irrelevant or inimical'. There appear to be three main strategies available to those who wish to defend the possibility of dual belonging from a Christian perspective. One addresses the specific doctrinal issue, developing an understanding of the Creator that is more nuanced than the simple assertion that 'a Creator exists, and is the centre of our faith', and by the same token therefore has some immunity to the Buddhist critique.[1] The second attempts to defuse the apparent contradiction, in relation not simply to this doctrine but more generally, by arguing that it is not as it appears: that these are incommensurable systems of thought and practice, as incapable of contradicting one another as a game of golf is of 'contradicting' a game of tennis. The approaches to dual belonging offered or addressed by other contributors to this symposium seem to belong very broadly to one or other of these first two types. The third approach accepts the premises of the question and argues that a spiritual life that embraces opposites of faith and practice is not only possible, but has the capacity to be richly rewarding, and indeed a mode of belonging which is an authentic expression of elements intrinsic to the tradition.[2] I offer a contribution to the debate from some resources of the

---

[1] This strategy of course leaves open the possibility that an insuperable obstacle to dual belonging might be found in another area of doctrine – such as eschatology, or soteriology.

[2] In her contribution to this book, Cornille asserts that 'on a ... basic level, the two traditions hold certain mutually exclusive or incompatible beliefs, so that adhering to one logically precludes simultaneous adherence to the other'. The first approach identified here challenges the first part of Cornille's statement by demonstrating that any religious tradition's set of beliefs is broader and more varied than is generally acknowledged, and that there is both more mutual incompatibility among beliefs within particular traditions, and less

Christian apophatic tradition, drawing to some extent on the first approach and seeking to develop the third. I will first explore what an apophatic theology of the Creator might look like, and then argue that *even if* Christian faith is centred on a Creator God, and *even if* Buddhism rejects just the sort of Creator that the Christian faith posits, *even so* one might from a Christian apophatic perspective validly claim to practise and belong in both traditions.

Apophasis in Brief

Apophasis, *unsaying*, is the discipline of recanting whatever we have been impelled to say. Developed in the early centuries by Fathers of the Church who built upon resources inherited from Jewish and Greco-Roman philosophical spiritualities to articulate their own experience of a life surrendered to the divine and to encourage the communities they served, the apophatic discipline has inspired mystics and teachers of the faith throughout the centuries, but in the Protestant West has not hitherto been widely known in popular circles.

Apophatic method is predicated upon a process of spiritual development and maturation. At each stage, we struggle to put into words what we have so far encountered of the divine: we make assertions – *God is thus and so*. Wisdom and shame drive us sooner or later to admit that we have not caught it: divine reality has eluded our formulations, God is more and other than we have said. Therefore we must unsay them; we negate our assertions – *God is not thus and so*. Both our assertions and our negations are true: true in the sense that there is something in them that expresses what we have experienced, true in the sense that they have a kind of calorific value – they energise us. For example: we say that God is good, because the divine as we experience it is bright, gracious, life-giving, redemptive and death-defeating; because there is in the divine a blazing purity which convicts us of our own impurity (Isaiah 6.5) and requires that we refrain from sin; because God is good to us – merciful, kind and loving. We go on to deny God's goodness when we realise that the good we can grasp is not Godself; when we realise that there are depths of divinity transcending all our knowledge of the good; when our desire for intimacy with the divine shatters our complacent categories of 'good and evil', showing them up for the self-referential constructs they necessarily are.

---

between them, than often claimed. My third approach contests Cornille's inference that mutually exclusive beliefs render dual belonging theoretically illegitimate.

Just as our affirmations concerning God require unsaying, the same also applies to our negations. These are as inadequate as our affirmations, though their inadequacies are complementary: they have fewer calories, and by leaving us hungry are more likely to spur us on to the next stage of our development. Neither adequately captures what needs saying: to assert *only* that 'God is good' invites complacency at the least, and tends towards an idolatrous identification of the divine with *what is good for us*, good as we see and know it – and it leads to the terrible, familiar sin of identifying as evil all that is alien and other. To assert *only* that 'God is not good', on the other hand, gives too inadequate a basis for worship, for formation in discipleship, and for appreciation of the biblical witness. What is omitted by both our affirmations and negations seems, in moments of encounter at least, more important than what they contain. So we grow through affirmation and negation, and through the denial of both, always driven by desire and experience further on and further in to divine reality.

Apophasis is thus one of the Christian tradition's primary defences against idolatry: it systematically dethrones the idols we create when we try to fit the divine within the terms of our language or the conceptual frameworks of our culture.[3] Its Latin name is the *via negativa*, but this tends to mislead: negations are denied, as consistently as assertions of the divine, and it proceeds as much by recognition of the superfluity of divine meaning, the superabundance of divine reality, as by removal of word and concept.[4] One might say that apophasis is an experiment in taking what is propositionally irreconcilable, and existentially reconciling it through an integrated spiritual ascesis; in other words that we do not need to demonstrate that our dual belonging contains no propositional contradictions,

---

[3]   Those Christians who practise within other faith traditions are sometimes accused of idolatry. Framing our apologetics within the terms of the Christian apophatic tradition should give us grounds for confidence that this accusation is unwarranted.

[4]   Hence Dionysius the Areopagite's foundational works are peppered with neologisms formed by adding the prefix 'hyper'- to Divine action and attribute; for example, *The Divine Names* 593C 'the thearchic hyper-beingness, which is the hyper-existence of the hyper-goodness ... ' (my translation). The inadequacy of the Latin term '*via negativa*', in my view, is of a piece with the lesser status given to apophasis in the Latin West following Aquinas: here negation tends to be limited to a provisional role, before affirmation and denial are both subsumed under a transcendent affirmation. I offer a more developed argument against this and other construals of apophasis in my *Denying Divinity* (Oxford University Press: 2000). In the work of the Greek Fathers such as Gregory of Nyssa, Dionysius the Areopagite and Maximus the Confessor, apophasis is more robustly developed, and indeed has arguably more in common with the tetralemma ascribed to Nagarjuna the Buddhist philosopher. By this tetralemma, all four of the following modes of speech are rejected as inadequate to ultimate truth: *affirmation, negation, both affirmation and negation, neither affirmation nor negation*.

220   *Buddhist-Christian Dual Belonging*

so much as that one healthy integrated human life might – in Ross Thompson's words – 'roam between' the two. In this instance, the self-contradiction involved in fidelity, both to faith in a Creator God and to faith in the non-theistic Dharma, might be sharpened into a tool for the contradiction of the self that clings to one or another view – a contradiction of the self which is required both by the practice of Buddhist *anatman*, and by Jesus' demand that we 'die to self'.[5]

What Might an Apophatic Doctrine of God the Creator Look Like?

The Christian doctrine of creation, as a distinct and organised body of teaching, emerged not merely out of a developing tradition of biblical exegesis and spiritual-philosophical reflection within the churches, but in particular out of the Christological debates of the early centuries. Following the Nicene settlement, Christians understood Christ as begotten, *not made*. To be created is to be made, as in the great Biblical image of the potter's vessel.[6] That which is created is not the same stuff as its creator: God's creatures are not divine. Utterly dependent on their creator for form and existence, they are *made by*, not *made of* divinity. Nicene orthodoxy here insists on an ontological gulf between heaven and earth; a gulf which is bridged when divinity takes on humanity in the person of Christ – but that is redemption or *new creation*, a doctrine at least theoretically distinguishable from original creation.[7] Creation itself is *ex nihilo*: God does not spin the world out spider-like from the divine guts, God's own essence; nor do divine hands shape pre-existing matter, but where nothing was, God's creativity brings substance itself into being, endowing it with form and life.

    This is the classical view posited in the terms of this debate: God is prior, separate, knowable only in part, by a sort of analogical reasoning which supposes

---

[5]   Such readiness to undergo existential self-contradiction seems to me to set serious dual or multiple belonging, such as that advocated by Velez, Thompson, Knitter and Drew in this volume, apart from the kind of voluntaristic eclecticism that features in Cornille's arguments here and elsewhere.

[6]   See Jeremiah 19; Isaiah 29:16, 45:9,64:8; Job 10:8–12; and Romans 9:20–24.

[7]   Those discussions which take the Christian doctrine of a Creator God as a flat contradictory to the Buddhist denial of a Creator tend not only to fail in recognition of the complexity of each tradition, and the many nuanced philosophical, theological and soteriological positions developed within them, but further tend to separate out this Christian teaching about a Creator from its cognate doctrines, with their moderating influence on how it is to be construed. These include not just Christology, soteriology, eschatology and theological anthropology, but also specific teachings such as the Orthodox *theosis* or 'divinisation'.

Going Beyond the Creator God

that the creator must value the qualities that seem to be exemplified in the creation. It is the view of a transcendent Creator which seems most clearly exposed to the Buddhist critique. However, even here, there are seeds of an apophatic understanding. First, there is an epistemic humility built in to such a doctrine of the Creator: we do not know God because we are not God. We must await an encounter in which we are known by God, and by grace receive some revelation proportional to our own mental capacities. A transcendent Creator by definition transcends not only our world but also our minds and our languages, which are conditioned by our experiences in the world, and thus transcends our capacity to give an accurate account of 'him': this is the substance of the biblical challenge repeatedly made by psalmist and prophet, such as Isaiah 55.8–9: 'For my thoughts are not your thoughts, nor are your ways my ways, says the Lord. For as the heavens are higher than the earth, so are my ways higher than your ways and my thoughts than your thoughts'. Therefore all human accounts of our Creator, recognising their incompleteness and inadequacy, must be provisional and subject to denial.

Second, the classical accounts of the Creator's work bear the tell-tale stains of apophatic superfluity. Biblical writers and editors move on from the first to the second chapter of Genesis where transcendence gives way to immanence, and the height of God's power is met by the depth of divine intimacy; and thence on again to the other variants on creation in the Torah – including the recreation of order following the flood, and the creation of tribe and nation. They move on from the opening of Genesis to the Prologue of John's Gospel, and on again to the great Hymn of the Cosmic Christ in Colossians Chapter One – where the creative speech of God becomes the Logos who indwells, forms and enlivens the entire cosmos.[8]

The style of our doctrine of the Creator is thus intrinsically akin to apophasis: how we speak as Christian theologians about our Creator is by a continual performance of hesitation and of unsaying, by retraction, by falling silent, by saying something at least partially contradictory. This being so, the question arises, why we make any affirmations at all? Not only because they express the truth as seen by a particular person from a particular vantage point at a particular time; but also because they contain within them the resources for the next step

---

[8]   Both Knitter and Thompson have acknowledged that the complexity of the Christian understanding of creation is largely unknown to popular Christianity, which relies almost exclusively on a dualistic understanding of divine transcendence. See Knitter, *Without Buddha I Could not Be a Christian* (London: OneWorld, 2009), 8; Thompson, *Buddhist Christianity: A Passionate Openness* (New Alresford: O-Books, 2010), 239.

on the journey. In every great teaching, the seeds of its own contradiction are buried, ready to spring up when exposed to the moist warmth of our attention.[9]

Turning from style to content, we find within the range of Christian theologies some which, while not drawing explicitly upon apophatic concepts and vocabulary, are highly amenable to them by virtue of the place they give to difference, polysemy and kenotic openness. Both Joseph O'Leary and Peter Phan, for example, offer intriguing points of departure from classical Trinitarian theology. O'Leary, seeking a Christian theology of God which is not hostage to Greek metaphysics, suggests 'the dynamic Johannine and Pauline conception of God as an event of Spirit, light, agape' which is arguably closer to Buddhist intuitions than to classical metaphysics.[10] Phan affirms a Triune Creator whose unity is not 'deadly uniformity' but the mutual indwelling of difference; and that creation consists in 'bringing into existence a genuine other ... which reflects and embodies divine plurality in the variety and multiplicity of creation'.[11] More generally, an apophatic approach is likely to draw on accounts of the Creator which begin with verb and adverb rather than noun and adjective – which are process-based rather than substance-based; which explore the radical and sacrificial self-emptying which creates, enables and loves emerging difference; which seek to articulate what a Creator who is personal but not 'a Person' might be like; where theism shades more towards panentheism than deism.[12]

Further, some particular accounts of creation and Creator within the Christian mystical tradition are thoroughgoingly apophatic in character, and have caught the attention of scholars working in the field of interfaith dialogue and encounter. To name just two examples, Brian Pierce and Beverley Lanzetta have both drawn extensively on Meister Eckhart: Pierce to consider the resonances between Eckhart's *'bullitio'* and *'ebullitio'* and Buddhist

---

[9] Diane Butler Bass argues, similarly, that the notion of *doctrine* should be understood not simply as authoritative teaching but as '*healing teaching*', drawing on the same etymological root as *Doctor – Christianity After Religion*, 134, cited in Brian McLaren, *Why did Jesus, Moses, the Buddha and Mohammed Cross the Road?* (London: Hodder & Stoughton, 2012), 93.

[10] Joseph O'Leary, 'Toward a Buddhist Interpretation of Christian Truth', in *Many Mansions? Multiple Religious Belonging and Christian Identity*, ed. Catherine Cornille (Eugene, OR: Wipf and Stock, 2002), 32.

[11] Peter Phan, *Being Religious Interreligiously* (New York: Orbis Books, 2004), xxi, xxv.

[12] Drew's 'pioneers' of Buddhist-Christian dual belonging appeal to several of these approaches to the doctrine of creation: *Buddhist and Christian? An Exploration of Dual Belonging* (Oxford: Routledge, 2011), 75–7.

Going Beyond the Creator God 223

'*Tathagata*' and '*Tathātā*',[13] and Lanzetta to work through an account of the Creator as Nothingness, pure potentiality, as the creative ground from which all creation emerges.[14]

An apophatic theology of the Creator will thus be marked by epistemic humility and superabundance of meaning; it will be recursive, returning over and over to its starting point to begin again. The account of a transcendent Creator of literally unimaginable power and glory (the account so apparently inimical to the teaching of Gautama the Buddha) will be offered, enjoyed, and its calories turned into energy. And then another account may be offered, where the Creator dwells within and among us as living breath. And another, where Christ is our form and deepest identity creatively unfolding within the entire cosmos. And more: God as nothingness beyond all concepts of Godhead; God as creative process; God as Being Itself; God as 'supersubstantial', beyond-being and the source of all being. Our apophatic 'doctrine' of the Creator will be complex, exploratory, welcoming towards new insights, resilient in the face of challenge. Both in style and in content, our talk of the Creator will overflow all ordered and settled boundaries; it is, after all, an account of energy and life. The one thing it will *never* be is complete.

What is the Apophatic Understanding of the Process and Goal of Spiritual Development, and in Particular the Role Within it of Difference and Contradiction?

Apophatic traditions envisage the process of personal spiritual formation working in the same way as the development of theology. We never progress as our *whole* selves: in order to move forward, we need to leave behind not only the place where we have been standing, but the perspectives peculiar to that place, and traces at the very least of our own selves – the skin we shed there, the elements we excrete there, the air we exhale there. The information conveyed in our theologies of the Creator therefore concerns not so much the nature of our being's source, as the state of our development and spiritual apprehension.

On the apophatic way the suffering of contradiction is not incidental but deliberately methodical, not contingent but integral to the spiritual path. Challenges to our existing understanding of God are welcomed, because they

---

[13] Brian Pierce, *We Walk the Path Together: Learning from Thich Nhat Hanh and Meister Eckhart* (Maryknoll, NY: Orbis Books, 2005), 81.

[14] Beverley Lanzetta, *The Other Side of Nothingness* (Albany: SUNY, 2001), 114 et passim.

will lead us further on.[15] The apophatic theologian, then, far from constructing a dual religious identity in the manner identified by Marianne Moyaert in this volume, avoiding the pinch-points of difference by 'spiritualising' and prioritising bloodless abstractions over the particularities and materialities of lived religion, instead tends to value the latter over the former: their tangible inconsistencies are potent aides on the way. Thus dual practitioners of my acquaintance are likely to construct a prayer space in which the crucified one and the enlightened one, side by side and together, confront the one who kneels before them – compassionately, interrogatively. Thus the familiar words and gestures of a Mass celebrated in the midst of a Zen Sesshin (meditation retreat) are heard afresh, yielding significance that was always there but is only now apprehended.[16]

We who belong to both the Buddhist and Christian traditions do not have to choose *either* to affirm our faith in a Creator God *or* to echo the Buddha's denial of 'his' existence; nor do we have to accept either of the alternative options of a lazy agnosticism or a passive appeal to mystery.[17] We can choose the active path of unsaying, the positive discipline of unknowing. We can choose to study deeply and existentially the Buddhist denial of a Creator God in order to inform and nourish our own apophatic practice. We can choose to affirm and deny each element of our traditions in whatever order they arise for us, and then deny our denials too. As we affirm each concept, we take our time, waiting as it matures within us, exploring the savour of its echoes, and finding the places within ourselves where their antiphonal voices create new harmonies. This may sound strange, but arguably it is merely an application to doctrinal theology of a move that is increasingly recognised and valued within applied theology and

---

[15] In the work of Dionysius the Areopagite, the scriptural 'unlike likenesses' of God have a privileged position, as pointers to and guarantors of this method of seeking the divine through the use of language which demands denial. *The Celestial Hierarchy 141A*: 'So it is that scriptural writings, far from demeaning the ranks of heaven, actually pay them honor by describing them with dissimilar shapes so completely at variance with what they really are ...' Luibheid's translation, in *Pseudo-Dionysius the Complete Works* (London: SPCK, 1987), 150.

[16] The same point is made by Sallie King among Drew's interviewees, and quoted in Drew's contribution to this volume: King finds the concrete structures and practices of both Buddhism and Christianity helpful.

[17] I do not mean by this to belittle or deny the place of proper agnosticism or of appreciation of mystery, both of which are displayed by many of the dual practitioners interviewed by Drew and/or referred to here. But unsaying is not the same as agnosticism, unknowing is not ignorance in its usual sense; appreciation of mystery is not not-being-bothered to try finding out; and self-contradiction may be performed anywhere along a spectrum from a demanding intellectual/existential practice, to simple carelessness.

ecclesial poetics: the *indaba*-style practice of deep listening.[18] It is the practical skill of reconciliation which our communities are being encouraged to develop: of refraining from seeking too early a closure or resolution of difference, of not declaring one side right and the other wrong, but finding the wisdom, the friendly affirmation and challenge which each has to offer the other. It would be odd to recognise this as a practical virtue but deny its application to faith and belief.[19]

We are beginning, in Geffré's phrase, 'to understand that religious truth is not necessarily under the sign of the principle of noncontradiction'.[20] This ancient law of logic, that a proposition and its contradictory cannot both be true – that something cannot be both p and not-p at the same time – is valid in regard to everything that is a *something*: it applies to everything in the world, to all finite beings; and if we disregard it, the price we pay is to render our speech nonsensical. But when we begin to speak of the divine, we are no longer speaking of *something*, or of *a being*: we speak of that which is 'beyond being' or 'the source of being' or 'Being itself'. It is admittedly a contestable claim, but one which I wish to make nonetheless, that the principle of noncontradiction cannot be applied to the source of being or to our experience of passing from one partial perspective on it to another.[21] If Christian faith and identity is not an institution or a set of doctrines, but a mystery into which we penetrate ever more deeply, then we cannot know in advance what will or will not be compatible with our practice, nor should we expect our practice to remain unchanged through time.

---

[18] The process of Indaba originates from South Africa, where it is a gathering of Zulu or Xhosa elders. It was adopted at the Lambeth Conference in 2008, as a process of communal wrestling to come to a common mind or story, rather than the more traditional processes of adversarial debate, and used from time to time since by the Church of England General Synod and the Scottish Episcopal Church among others.

[19] Thompson responds by arguing that these two positions are not so much alternative views of reality, as ways of describing and responding to it (ibid., pp 252 ff.). This is an easier argument to accept, as he recognises, if one's theology of creation eschews the popular dualist version of it.

[20] Claud Geffré, 'Double Belonging and the Originality of Christianity as a Religion', in Cornille, op. cit., 101.

[21] Jeannine Hill Fletcher, in 'Feminisms: Syncretism, Symbiosis, Synergetic Dance', acknowledges the important general role that the principle of non-contradiction plays in arguments against pluralism, and indicates the practical discipline of promoting the well-being of women – and, more generally, all that is 'othered' – as the criterion which saves those of us who contest its application to the divine from a careless 'anything goes'. In Alan Race and Paul Hedges, *Christian Approaches to Other Faiths* (London: SCM, 2008), 142.

While all this needs to be said and often resaid, it applies – so far – only to our experience on the path of dual belonging. More demanding still is what the apophatic tradition may have to say about the goal and end of the spiritual life.

Many commentators are prepared to see contradictions, such as that between Christian faith in a Creator God and Buddhist dismissal of such a Creator, as creative and developmental; but, they insist, these must in the end be resolved. The goal of the spiritual life is presence or union, an immediate encounter with the absolutely real – and at that point, surely, dualities are united, opposites reconciled, difference resolved? Contradictory truths are only relatively true, and in the end must recede before Absolute Truth, which can only be one.

Rose Drew, for example, quoting Keenan, argues that *at some level* there must be a 'compatibility of truths', a level at which 'the truth of each tradition can be integrated with the truth of the other'.[22] We appear to have different views on just where this level is reached.

All that I have said so far about the value of contradictory propositions, of affirmations and negations on the way, should be enough to warn us against pre-empting this level. Nonetheless, it is a trap into which many fall. It is a criticism often made of pluralist approaches to religions, that they seek too cheap a unity by privileging similarity over difference; and of inclusivist approaches, that by discovering adumbrations of their *own* truth in other faiths they are really masked exclusivism. Moving from the world of theory to that of practice, Ama Samy speaks of many Christian-Zen practitioners who cheapen Zen by finding facile consensus and 'false convergences'.[23]

In fact, if we seek an approach which offers a reconciliation of apparently conflicting or even contradictory claims, but neither too early nor too easily, then the Christian apophatic tradition might seem to offer exactly what we need, for it can be taken – I would say, is usually taken – as suggesting that this integrative level is reached when we attain our goal. In the classic patristic presentations of apophasis, the end is union with God, achieved in intimate silence where no more words are heard, and symbolised in the Hebrew Scriptures' two great images of mystical union: the dark cloud atop Sinai where Moses dwelt alone with God (Exodus 20.21; 24.15–18), and the mystery of love's consummation in the Song of Songs. By prayer and contemplation, by ascending the way of negation in mind and heart, thought and deed, we are led to a non-dual consciousness of pure presence. Later writers such as Nicholas of Cusa speak of the 'coincidence of opposites', where what would be flat contradictions if applied to the finite – such

---

22 Drew, op. cit., 8.
23 Ama Samy, 'Zen and Christians', *The Way* 46:2 (2007), 90–96.

Going Beyond the Creator God   227

as 'good' and 'not-good' – are seen as non-antagonistic visions of the infinite. In Christian theological terms, the unity and simplicity [24] of God both guarantee that 'he' will at the end be 'all in all', binding up all that once was broken or divided. Thus, it is argued, we can affirm that there is an ultimate reconciliation between all contradictions, including the affirmation and the denial of the existence of a Creator God, while at the same time acknowledging that so long as words persist, our contradictions will remain unresolved.

For example, Ruben Habito, in his commentary on Master Hakuin's *Song of Zazen*, presents meditation as a lure towards the presence where we find ourselves whole, and all conflicts, including those between faith-propositions, cease:

> As we deepen our awareness in the silence of seated meditation, we can sense our whole lives as permeated with this wholeness, whereby every moment we are totally and completely in this moment. ... We are able to experience our lives in completion, in every here and now. It is toward this wholeness that we are moving as we make every step.[25]

In this state of consciousness duality is transcended, the discriminative mind and all its claims are left behind; we enter a state of pure presence where we apprehend both that 'all sentient beings are originally Buddhas' and that 'all things in the universe manifest Divine Presence'.[26]

Dupuis too distinguishes between the present 'incomplete mutual complementarity and convergence' of all religious traditions, and their complete eschatological convergence. As a good inclusivist, he envisages this final convergence in terms of de Chardin's 'mysticism of unification', and the 'recapitulation in Christ of all things'. [27] With rather more apophatic hesitation, Phan argues that dual fidelity is 'a lived drama of tension, never fully resolved on the theoretical level but affirmed at the existential plane, a continuing quest for harmony and dissonance, ever elusive, provisional, and unfinished, to be heard fully only on the "other shore"'.[28]

---

[24]   'Simple' in the philosophical sense of not being divisible into parts with different characters.

[25]   Ruben Habito, *Living Zen, Loving God* (Boston, MA: Wisdom Publications, 2004), location 1316 Kindle edition.

[26]   Ibid.

[27]   Jacques Dupuis, 'Christianity and Religions: Complementarity and Convergence', in Cornille, op. cit., 68.

[28]   Phan, *Being Religious Interreligiously*, 74–5.

228   *Buddhist-Christian Dual Belonging*

Writing about the final goal of the spiritual life is an exercise in almost comical temerity, of course, and the point is that we have no way of knowing for sure.[29] Yet we do have indications, and on their basis some are moved to suggest that the kind of reconciliation available even on that 'other shore' is not a simple resolution of all differences, not a settled unity. I appeal to four witnesses to make this case. The first is St Gregory of Nyssa, that great father of the apophatic spiritual tradition, whose understanding of the infinity of God leads him to challenge the notion of any rested end to the ascent through negations.[30] The second is Abe Masao, that great champion of the Christian apophatic tradition's potential as a ground for Buddhist-Christian dialogue: Abe argues that the logic of non-dualism is that opposites must achieve a non-dualistically non-dual resolution. In other words, ultimate resolution of differences cannot rest on a type of union which is the dualistic antithesis of difference.[31] The third witness is the Jesuit Ama Samy, who cites Master Dogen's teaching that 'opposites of dualities are not obliterated or even blurred; they are not so much transcended as realised. The absolute freedom in question here is that freedom which realises itself in duality not apart from it'.[32]

My fourth and final witness is Beverley Lanzetta, who appeals to a view she finds '[h]idden in apophatic discourse ... but obscured by the politics of theology', namely that 'linguistic uncertainty and ontological ambiguity are not only a function of the limitations of mind and text, but are *qualities* of God's most indistinct nature'.[33] Lanzetta's point about the politics of theology is well made. Here the content of our theology of Creator-and-creation matters: if creation is the establishment of order by unitary power, then order will probably have to be guaranteed in the end by the obliteration of all difference. If on the other hand creation is divine self-abandonment in order to release difference into being, then the goal and end of it all might be better seen as the full non-dualistic realisation of difference.

Against those theologies of religions which blunt the edges of difference and contradiction either by identifying common ground, or by the

---

[29]   Drew, in her contribution to our discussion, takes this point from Hick (*Death and Eternal Life*, London: Collins, 1985, 427–8) and attests that her interviewees 'concur' with it.

[30]   Gregory's teaching of '*epectasis*', never-ending ascent into the immensity of divine truth, is explored in my *Denying Divinity*, 31–4.

[31]   Masao Abe, 'Zen is not a Philosophy, but ... ', in *Zen and Western Thought* (Basingstoke: Macmillan, 1985), 3–24.

[32]   Samy, op. cit. 92, citing Hee-Jin Kim, *Dogen Kigen: Mystical Realist* (Tucson, AZ: University of Arizona Press, 1987), 52–3.

[33]   Op. cit., 10.

Going Beyond the Creator God

incommensurability thesis or by positing an eschatological resolution, the apophatic tradition offers us the means to explore the option of taking difference all the way to the end, finding difference in the divine nature and purpose. It allows us to imagine the attainment of non-dual awareness without supposing everyone will in the end think the same. It allows us to aim for union rather than uniformity.

That being said, we might now be able to hear with new ears Henry Smith's suggestion that freedom from confusion is indeed achievable, but only provisionally:

> the multireligious pilgrimage allows us to achieve provisional syntheses between solutions that are normally taken as alternative and contradictory. Temporary 'stops' on the journey towards the open horizon satisfy the human thirst for unity. On the other hand, they avoid the dictatorship of unitary visions and monolithic systems.[34]

Buddhists and Christians, for example, while remaining entirely agnostic about any future consensus, might agree that in particular times and places they are entirely of one mind in regard, for example, to the need for action to protect our environment, or to the benefit of contemplating together their utter contingency and dependence on a reality beyond them.[35]

Conclusion

The question of the Creator God is a substantial nettle to grasp: it is suggested that the Buddhist-Christian dialogue has been reluctant to address this issue because it might turn out to be 'an unbridgeable gulf' that would wreck the entire eirenic interfaith enterprise.[36] Is Buddhist-Christian dual belonging possible when one faith is centred on a Creator God while the other rejects creation and

---

[34] Henry Smith, 'Beyond Dual Religious Belonging: Roger Corless and Explorations in Buddhist-Christian Identity', *Buddhist-Christian Studies* 17 (1997), 171.

[35] Drew's interviewees make the same point, as she shows in her contribution to this symposium, in her careful distinction between their sense of shared Buddhist and Christian orientation and their agnosticism as to whether there is a single unified end. In this I think she is more accurate than Cornille, who claims that dual belongers choose apophatic language because 'the apophatic language of different religions actually reflects a same understanding of the ultimate reality'.

[36] Perry Schmidt-Leukel, cited in Drew op. cit., 75.

regards belief in God as irrelevant or inimical? From the perspective of Christian apophatic theology, Yes. Yes, because all our speech about the Creator God needs to be denied. As Dionysius the Areopagite said many centuries ago:

> The Cause of all is above all ... It is neither one nor oneness, divinity nor goodness. Nor is it a spirit, in the sense in which we understand that term. It is not sonship or fatherhood and it is nothing known to us or to any other being. It falls neither within the predicate of nonbeing nor of being. Existing beings do not know it as it actually is and it does not know them as they are. There is no speaking of it, nor name nor knowledge of it.[37]

Or as Meister Eckhart said,

> I say that man should be so poor that he should not be or have any place in which God could work. When man clings to place, he clings to distinction. Therefore I pray to God that he may make me free of 'God', for my real being is above God if we take 'God' to be the beginning of created things.[38]

The apophatic theologian affirms the existence of a Creator God and denies it, both centres her faith on it, and empties her faith of it, in order to penetrate to a deeper realisation. Furthermore, the Bible presents 'theology' in its primary sense of 'God's own speech' as creation itself: God does not speak in words, as we do, but in beings – from his mouth flows a stream of existence, worlds and seas and fish and fowl ... all brought to summation in the Logos who is the living Word made known in the life and work of a Galilean peasant. If divine words are beings first and teachings only derivatively, then the role of doctrine within Christian faith and life must be subordinate to flourishing, to abundant existence.[39]

From an apophatic standpoint, therefore, we would benefit from adopting an aesthetic or ethical perspective as we approach the task of speaking about God the Creator. Rather than seeking to find a unified and settled account which would do justice both to our theological commitments and to our lived

---

[37] *The Mystical Theology* (1040D–1048A) – Luibheid's translation, op. cit., 141.

[38] From 'Sermon 52', in Edmund Colledge and Bernard McGinn's translation, *Meister Eckhart: The Essential Sermons, Commentaries, Treatises, and Defense* (New York: Paulist, 1981), 202.

[39] Knitter, in the context of his discussion of creation in *Without Buddha ...* (15) derives a version of this insight from both the Buddha and Karl Rahner: '"God", he asserts, 'must be an experience before "God" can be a word'. Another version of the same insight might arguably be found in the ancient maxim '*lex orandi, lex credendi*'.

Going Beyond the Creator God   231

experience, let alone – God forbid! – seeking to establish a consensus among Buddhist non-theists and Christian theists, we might instead adopt the practice of the *via interrogativa*, the skill of enquiry: 'what beauty at this time does this teaching illumine for you?' and 'in what way at this time does this teaching support your growth in the arts of peace, compassion and generosity?' And of course, 'on deeper inspection, what hints do you find in this teaching now that encourage you to move beyond it?'

Both the ancient apophatic tradition and contemporary theologies marked by liberation movements tend to demand of the affirmation of a divine Creator not simply 'is it true?' but more importantly 'why do *you* say this?' and 'why say this *now*?' In dialogue between Christians and Buddhists, and in the internal dialogue – the 'dialectical interplay of love and wisdom'[40] – of the dual practitioner, a loving interrogation may take place, gently unmasking the cravings and compulsions, the ghosts of past experience and the spectres of desire that bind us to particular insights and blind us to others, and patiently repeating the invitation to travel on to newer and deeper wisdom.

Sometimes the affirmation of a Creator is a claim to power: an absolute Author and Authority exists, which demands that you declare yourself for or against it, insists that you acknowledge your profound ontological and existential dependence upon it and that you obey its constituted authorities in the human realm, whether they are the interpreters of Holy Scripture or the officers of the institution. Other times the affirmation of a Creator is – in Lanzetta's lovely phrase– an intuition of 'profound and utter claimlessness'[41] which releases us into being and offers us the invitation of desire: 'come to me ... '

In so far as apophasis is a theology of withdrawal, of iterative self-emptying in order to be filled with the new wine of divine presence, then it is the authentic voice of a certain theology of creation. An apophatic theology of the Creator will be its own enemy, forging alliance against itself with accounts which differ. It is increasingly recognised, not only by Christian theologians but also by scholars and practitioners of other faiths, that the Christian mystics have created a treasury of apophatic insights and resources that not only have traction in our encounters with other faiths, but in our increasingly plural religious world even celebrate the 'unlike likenesses' offered by other faiths, and require that we accept their gracious hospitality on the journey. A full appreciation of apophasis leads one to encounter with other religions, and for Christians particularly to that

---

[40] Drew's quotation from Pieris, *Love Meets Wisdom* (New Delhi: Intercultural Publications, 1988), 9–10.

[41] Op. cit., 40.

232   *Buddhist-Christian Dual Belonging*

most 'other' tradition, Buddhism.[42] It may be, as Bruno Barnhart argues, that the implication runs in the other direction too: our encounter with Buddhism is likely to draw us Christians into a deeper encounter with our own apophatic traditions.[43] Both apophasis and interfaith encounter are processes of genuine unlearning, movements from closed to open systems of thought and hearts, from preconceptions to personal transformation.

Those who are drawn to practice dual belonging will recognise and negotiate the tensions between the Christian and Buddhist narratives about a Creator God. These tensions may often be painful, as they were for Roger Corless. They also have the capacity to be nourishing and creative. While some may hope for an eschatological resolution of differences, others will celebrate the possibility that the differences between our traditions will be perfectly realised.

Ultimately, the doctrine of God as Creator and its denial by the Buddha cannot legitimately be used as a theological bogeyman to frighten the children of Christian-Buddhist dual belonging into going obediently to bed. To put it simply and bluntly: over the long term, a contradiction-free faith, if such a thing were ever achievable, would be neither fully Christian nor fully Buddhist, but idolatrous, for it would reduce the scope of ultimate reality to something less than 'the All'. For the Christian wrestling with the task of living in fidelity towards the Giver of life, the Buddha's teaching may be heard as a voice of a true friend reminding us how much bigger our hopes and dreams of God are, than we have yet realised. Apophatic saints and teachers encourage us to continue to take the risk of contradiction. They know that the mystery is not dissipated when it is encountered.

---

[42] 'A theology of radical openness is irretrievably and inexorably connected to the kenotic generosity of faith' (Lanzetta, op. cit., x).

[43] Bruno Barnhart and Joseph Wong, *Purity of Heart and Contemplation: A Monastic Dialogue Between Christian and Asian Traditions* (New York: Continuum, 2001), 294. Werner Jeanrond similarly attributes the contemporary revival of interest in Christian apophasis at least in part to the post-war encounter with Japanese Zen: 'Belonging or Identity: Christian Faith in a Multi-Religious Word', in Cornille, op. cit., 117.

Conclusion

Ross Thompson and Gavin D'Costa

Our articles and conversations have resulted in no dramatic conversions. The Buddhists among us have remained Buddhists, the Christians Christian and the dual belongers remain dual belongers. However, the contributors bear witness to how fruitful the discussion can be, and how complex and many sided the issues involved. This conclusion therefore draws no conclusion regarding the appropriateness or otherwise of Buddhist-Christian dual belonging, but attempts to map out some of the issues involved, and the different kinds of reason people have both for affirming and for challenging it.

It would be tempting to think of the contributors as lying on a one-dimensional line with, at one end, exclusively committed Christians like Strange who altogether reject dual belonging, through Christians like Drew who affirm the possibility of dual belonging, then entirely even-handed dual belongers such as Knitter and Vélez de Cea, then Buddhists like Gethin who are sympathetic to dual belonging and then finally Buddhists like Tilakaratne who exclude it. However it is evident from the discussions that many more dimensions are involved.

Firstly, there are different reasons for affirming dual belonging – such that our four main advocates, Drew, Knitter, Thompson and Vélez de Cea would not agree among themselves about all the issues.

Secondly, there are different reasons for challenging dual belonging. As noted in the introduction, some reasons are confessional, and these objections obviously rule out each other as well as dual belonging. For Strange, dual belonging is wrong because Buddhism is idolatrous and wrong. For Tilakaratne, dual belonging is wrong because Christianity, for all its virtues, rests on a mistaken theistic understanding. Other arguments begin from the nature rather than the content of faith. Cornille and Moyaert argue that something vital to faith is lost when belonging is dual.

Thirdly there are different understandings of what it means to be Buddhist or Christian, or to *belong* to the Buddhist and Christian faiths or faith communities. Different kinds of Buddhism – Theravāda, Mahayana, Vajrayana and Pure

234 *Buddhist-Christian Dual Belonging*

Land – are represented, and also different understandings of Christianity – Reformed, Catholic and Anglican. These vary not only in the content of faith but in the degree of stringency they apply to the question of whether a given person belongs to their faith. Our discussions often returned to noting how for many strands of Buddhism it is no big deal for a Christian to practice as a Buddhist, whereas most Christian denominations (with notable exceptions such as the Quakers) apply more exclusive criteria. That may be one factor making dual belonging more of an issue for most Christians than for many Buddhists.

Ways of Affirming Dual Belonging

The three chapters in the first section all affirm dual belonging, though among the authors only Knitter now describes himself unreservedly as a dual belonger; Drew remains a Roman Catholic regarding her own commitment, while Thompson would (in the light of the discussions) argue that he is a dual belonger on some definitions but not others. And they affirm dual belonging in significantly different ways. In her challenge to dual belonging Cornille distinguishes four strategies for dual belonging, and these authors can be read, with qualifications, as illustrating three of them. They all to a degree also illustrate the fourth strategy, based on combined practice and participation, but this strategy does not constitute the core of their arguments.

Drew, then, might be regarded as an exemplar of Cornille's second strategy based on the transcendent unity of the goal, the ultimate reality which Buddhism and Christianity, among other religions are argued to point to and lead to. This could be named 'convergent' dual belonging. Elsewhere Drew describes this understanding as 'monocentric pluralism', as argued for, pre-eminently, by John Hick. This strategy accounts for differences between Buddhist and Christian (and other religious) understandings 'not by positing the existence of different "ultimates", but rather by interpreting these differences as relating to differences between the Buddhist's and the Christian's respective *experiences* of *one* ultimate reality, and how those experiences are *expressed*.[1]

This approach represents a sophisticated version of the widely made assertions such as 'we all believe in the same God'. It has the advantage of allowing for Buddhism and Christianity to be seen as complete and viable ways of relating to the ultimate, so that dual belonging is not seen as an advance on straightforward Buddhism or Christianity. Nor does this approach apply only to Buddhism

---

[1] *Buddhist and Christian*, 53.

Conclusion 235

and Christianity; it might be advanced to justify Muslim-Jewish or Hindu-Confucian dual belonging, or multiple religious belonging (though it does not necessarily entail that all belief systems and ideologies are valid expressions of the ultimate). The approach is based on the ineffability of the goal, as transcending all concepts, and on a clear distinction between the ultimate religious goal or object, on the one hand, and experiences and expressions of it, on the other. Among the contributors, Tilakaratne was a specially sharp critic of ineffability as applied to the Buddhist nirvana, while Moyaert vehemently rejected the 'spiritualisation' of religion that presupposes a sharp distinction between its goal or inner meaning and practical expressions and experiences.

By the same token Knitter's chapter relies heavily (though not exclusively) on Cornille's fourth strategy: the development of a 'personal synthesis' based on the complementarity of the religions in question. We could call this 'complementary' dual belonging. For Knitter, Buddhism and Christianity have '1) a common starting point in their quest for truth and liberation, 2) a shared diagnosis of the fundamental human problem, 3) differing remedies for this problem, and 4) a complementary liberative praxis' (p. 33). Complementary liberative praxis is seen primarily in terms of the Christian emphasis on social justice complementing the Buddhist stress on personal transformation, which Knitter regards as interdependent.

This approach differs from the previous (numbered 1–3 in the paragraph above) in being less global. The transcendental unity of all faiths is not a requirement, and may or may not be believed – though in the case of Knitter it probably is. The approach is more specific, both to the faiths in question and their relation to the believer. It is Buddhism and Christianity specifically that are believed to be complementary, for Knitter specifically; in that sense it is a case of 'personal synthesis'. On the other hand many of the arguments legislate with universal intent, such that a Buddhist-Christian dual belonging is advanced as a very positive and liberating faith, and (in that each offers something the other lacks) an advance on straightforward Christianity and Buddhism. 'Both traditions can foster a dual-identity and a dual liberative praxis that is, through their duality, *more effective* in realising the goals of both Buddha and Christ: to liberate people and all sentient beings from suffering'.[2] What we might term the 'complementary' dual belonging of Knitter is therefore both humbler and prouder than what might be termed the 'convergent' dual belonging of Drew. Humbler in that there is less of a meta-story about the nature of ultimate reality, transcending both faiths, but prouder in that an individual is proposing some kind of advance on both faiths. There

---

[2]   41, our emphasis.

are quite clearly points of difference here between Drew and Knitter that might be further explored. On the other hand the contrast should not be exaggerated: complementarity implies a unifying whole into which the parts fit, while (as Drew notes) there would be no point in being a Buddhist-Christian if each faith on its own represented an unsurpassable approach to the ultimate.

The third chapter illustrates something of what Cornille calls the 'interpretation of one religion in the light of another' – an approach which might be dubbed 'hermeneutical dual belonging'. In the most common case, Buddhist philosophy is advanced as a set of concepts for interpreting the Gospel of Christ: an alternative to the neo-Platonic and Aristotelian Greek metaphysics which provided the framework for the initial development of Christian doctrine, and remains the norm especially in Catholic and Orthodox, but arguably also Protestant Christianity. Thompson's approach is more complex, in that each faith is offered as an interpretation of the other, creating a kind of 'inter-illumination'. Neither religion alone represents the metaphysical form or the faith content. Moreover contemporary science is advanced as providing a third source of interpretation. The result is a mutual questioning between all three belief systems, resulting not in a single set of concepts but distinct ways of seeing. There is something of 'convergence' here, in that the different ways of seeing converge on a reality that cannot be stated outside the different approaches; and also something of 'complementarity', in that the flipping between the different perspectives is seen not just as disconcerting but also balancing and healthy. In this sense Thompson's chapter also suggests something more forcefully expressed in Williams's: an embracing of paradox and even seeming contradiction as providing a healthy apophasis in one's faith.

The kind of dual belonging envisaged here might be advanced as enabling interfaith dialogue to be fiercer, less polite and perhaps more creative than it sometimes is. Because in the dual belonger the Christian and the Buddhist is criticising herself, she may feel entitled to be more ruthless than if she were criticising another, whose faith she did not at all embrace. Whether that potential for creative sharpness outweighs the possibility which concerns Cornille and Moyaert, that the clarity, sincerity and embodiment of both Buddhism and Christianity might be blunted by the dual belonging, is a matter the reader must evaluate.

Conclusion 237

The Confessional Challenges to Dual Belonging

The challenges to dual belonging fall, as noted, into two categories: those that challenge it as not doing justice to the claims of one of the religions believed in, and those that challenge it as not doing justice to the nature of belief itself. For the first group, the dual belonger cannot be (according to Tilakaratne) a true Theravāda Buddhist, or (according to Strange) a true Reformed Evangelical Christian or (according to D'Costa) only in extreme and strange circumstances, a true Roman Catholic. For the second group, the dual belonger is (according to Moyaert) relying on a false dualism between the faith-embedded practice of religion and a 'spiritualising' theory of what it is all really about; or else (according to Cornille) committed in the articulation of her belief to strategies that do not, on the face of them, seem to work.

The chapters by Strange and Tilakaratne show interesting likenesses as well as contrasts. Both are based strongly on a canon of infallible scripture which is believed to convey authentically and exclusively the teaching of the founder. Both are clear and simple in the way they start from this well-defined starting point and, though by no means dismissive of other faiths, make no concessions regarding positions that contradict their own tradition. Both make reference to the postmodern understanding of faith traditions as self-contained and incommensurable worldviews. On the other hand the moral rhetoric in Strange's chapter contrasts with the intellectual detachment of Tilakaratne's, in a manner that perhaps reflects the former's Protestant Christianity, where passion and faith are given a constitutive role, and the latter's Buddhism – a faith which from the founder onward has relied heavily on rational and philosophical argument. In their strong adherence to a specific tradition, combined with a postmodern rationale, both chapters could be described as offering a neo-traditional approach in which not only dual belonging, but the faith of the other, is opposed.

D'Costa's contribution is different again. It resembles the Tilakaratne chapter more than the Strange in its cool use of rational argument and the absence of rhetoric. D'Costa is, like the other two, arguing on the basis of a clearly defined authority, but this authority includes, as well as the canon of scriptures, the magisterial teaching authority of a faith community, as expressed in the declarations of its popes and councils. It also differs in that – strikingly in view of this basis – it allows dual belonging as a theoretical possibility. If a Roman Catholic missionary working to convert Tibetan Buddhists, say, to a Buddhist-inculturated form of Roman Catholicism could be accepted by the Buddhist community as, in the fullest sense, a Buddhist, then D'Costa finds to his surprise that in view of the Vatican pronouncements this person could be deemed a dual belonger in the full sense. It is a big 'if'. The chapter ends tantalisingly suspended between theoretical openness to dual belonging and what is probably in practice closure.

However another kind of opening is suggested by D'Costa's very useful distinction between different dimensions of belonging: dimensions that appear independently under other names in Vélez de Cea's chapter. One dimension concerns the degree to which one is accepted by each faith community and fulfils its requirements regarding belonging. This opens up the possibility of a single-community dual belonger, who is Buddhist and Christian in beliefs but only Buddhist or only Christian in terms of community belonging. The other dimension runs from point A, which represents a totally eclectic choice of the Buddhist and Christian beliefs that seem evident or acceptable to the believer, to point Z, where the dual belonger attempts to embrace all the beliefs of both systems. Drew ascribed 'authentic dual belonging' only to the double-community dual belonger who is at or very close to point Z, and this is the position most of D'Costa's chapter is largely dealing with. But his nomenclature raises the possibility of positions around the middle of the alphabet that rely neither on totally autonomous choice, nor on totally heteronomous abjection before the authority of the religious systems, but a careful and respectful exercise of discernment that does justice both to one's own experience of reality and attentiveness to the voice of the traditions. Though not 'authentic' in Drew's sense, could authentic Buddhist-Christian positions be developed along such lines?

At first sight it would seem that dual belongers need not be at all troubled by any of these three confessionally based critiques. Would it not be obvious at the outset that the confessional positions outlined here, conservatively doctrinally based as they are, would rule out departures as radical as Buddhist-Christianity, since they also rule out many other variants of their own religion? Since Calvinism and Catholicism are incompatible with each other, it might be questioned, is it surprising that both are incompatible with Buddhist-Christianity? The Buddhist-Christian might then argue that his Buddhism is simply not of the Theravāda kind represented by Tilakaratne, and his Christianity is based neither on the infallible scripture of the Calvinists nor on the magisterial authority of traditional Catholicism. It is hardly surprising that Theravāda Calvinists are few, if any in number. But the combination of a liberal Catholicism or Anglicanism, or Quakerism, with Zen or a (liberally understood) Vajrayana, or maybe Pure Land, may well prove more viable.

However, the questions these writers raise are not so easily laid aside. Mahayana and Vajrayana Buddhism see themselves not as overturning Theravāda

Buddhism, but as adding to and enriching it, building on its foundations. It follows that a position that conflicts with Theravāda fundamentals is likely to conflict with those other forms of Buddhism too. Likewise, Calvinism and Catholicism see themselves as carrying forward and explicating a revelation given in Christ. The question needing to be asked, therefore, is whether, when these authors put forward an argument from their traditions, they are representing merely a variant of the Buddhist or Christian faith that has no consequence for Buddhists, Christians or dual belongers in general, or whether they are witnessing to something of essential importance to their faith to which all Buddhists and Christians, and *a fortiori* Buddhist-Christian dual belongers, must attend. The question cannot be answered in general, but requires evaluation of each argument piecemeal.

The General Challenges to Dual Belonging

The two other challenges are very different, in that they build not on the content of Buddhist and Christian religious beliefs but on the nature of religious belief itself. Their evaluation therefore does not require any piecemeal examination of Buddhist and Christian beliefs, but rather a heart-searching on the part of the would-be dual belonger as to whether in trying to believe both she really believes either, or believes anything in the sense demanded by either of those traditions, or can really be said to belong, in the full sense, to either religious community.

For Moyaert, dual belonging rests on a false dichotomy – characteristic of our 'detraditonalised' times – separating religious belief from religious practice and ritual. The dual belonger embraces Buddhism and Christianity as abstract belief systems, but not as religions in all their embodied richness as soul-forming practices. She sees dual belonging as an aspect of the more general postmodern turn to the subject, with its consumerist emphasis on personal choice. Behind this lurks a weak understanding of symbols and rituals as conventional expressions of meanings that might otherwise be expressed, rather than being constitutive of the religious meanings. It is this that enables the dual belonger to sit light to the very different practices of the religions and focus on an ultimate reality 'behind' the symbolism that is believed to be the same.

It is here that a query suggests itself. Is it really the case that symbols and practices are harder to amalgamate than the ideas and beliefs of the religions? There seems to be no inherent difficulty in combining the practice of, say, insight meditation with that of participation in Christian prayer and the Eucharist. Many people clearly do combine them. It is arguably much more difficult to combine Christian and Buddhist *ideas* of God or the soul (or their absence), or the nature of the ultimate goal. However, Moyaert might point out that such combinations of practices and rituals typically involve detaching them from their original context of meaning and grafting them onto the context of your own beliefs. So when Christians practice insight meditation they detach it from Buddhists' understandings of insight into transience and soul-lessness, and use it as a kind of purification on the pathway to union with God.[3] Conversely, though less frequently, Buddhists may attend the Eucharist interpreting it in terms of Tibetan Buddhist *puja* with its visualisation and dissolving.[4] Moyaert may then be right to see these cases as relying on a typically postmodern understanding of symbols bearing a merely contingent, readily dissolvable relation to spiritual meaning. But yet again, dual belonging may arise when a Christian practicing, say, insight meditation refuses to dissolve the intrinsic link such practice has with Buddhist insight. The practice then resists a simple assimilation to his Christian context and begins to shift him in a Buddhist direction without his necessarily relinquishing his Christianity. It may then be taking the embodiment of meaning in symbols seriously that necessitates dual belonging, as opposed to being satisfied with just dual practice.[5]

Cornille's chapter shares much of the same perspective as Moyaert's, but while Moyaert's challenge is focused very powerfully on one front, Cornille argues on a broader front, tackling in turn the main strategies for dual belonging which she has encountered, three of which we have already noted. At the heart of her argument is her conviction that religious demands are heteronomous and total. On the one hand, in the Christian understanding, a less than total response fails to do justice to God who is the unsurpassable ground of everything; while in the Buddhist understanding, a qualified response will fail to do justice to the urgent need of our situation as depicted by the Buddha. (It is here that the chapters by Strange and Tilakaratne lend support to Cornille's case.) And on the other hand a qualified response will disable the believer as he seeks to follow Jesus Christ or the Buddha, both of whom emphasise that only by giving ourselves wholly to their pathway can we attain the goal they set before us. The attempt to serve both is then analogous (as Strange also argues) to infidelity or adultery, in which in attempting to honour two partners we fail to do justice to either.

---

[3] Cf. Thomas Merton's descriptions of meditation as purgation, and the practice of 'Christian insight meditation' advocated by Mary Jo Meadows and others.

[4] Cf. John Makransky in 'Buddha and Christ as Mediators of the Transcendent', in Perry Schmidt-Leukel, ed., *Buddhism and Christianity in Dialogue* (London: SCM, 2005), 178–89.

[5] At this point Ross Thompson is being autobiographical.

Conclusion

241

Explorations

The four chapters in the 'explorations' form a more diffuse group, but all in their different ways address the issues raised in the preceding two parts, and in particular the question of the nature of religious belief and practice, as raised by Moyaert and Cornille.

Vélez de Cea's chapter is the most direct response, being addressed directly to Cornille's (but also Strange's) arguments for the heteronomous and total demands of faith. He argues strongly that a double-belonging need not represent a qualified faith in which half of one's commitment is given to each faith. The dual belonger's faith is not more eclectic, more a matter of personal choice, than the single belonger's. In both cases, as we might put it, we are usually more chosen – more grasped by the faith we find ourselves following, for all sorts of external and internal reasons – than choosing. Vélez de Cea discerns two dimensions in one's commitment to a faith, which he terms 'affiliative' and 'incremental'. As with D'Costa's two dimensions, one is either/or, and determined by the fulfilment of requirements for affiliation to a faith, while the other admits of degrees of intensity. Vélez de Cea rejects the analogy of monogamy for religious commitment, proposing instead that one's religious allegiance is more like one's love for two or more different children; each is loved totally, not half and half (or at third if there are more children, or if one loves one's wife too).

A very significant point is made here, regarding the way our personal loves are not divided, such that one allots competing percentages of a finite quantity to each of those we love, and perhaps another quantity to God and/or the Buddha. To this, Cornille, along with the other challengers, would perhaps retort that religious love is different, being an unconditional and total allegiance that underwrites (rather than competing with) all other loves. But then the question becomes: Can Christianity and Buddhism be such total allegiances, underwriting each other? This would be the case if, for example, though both are termed religions, they are not actually the same kind of thing, and do not compete for the same ground. For example, Buddhism might be given total allegiance as a practical philosophy, underwriting one's personal devotion to Jesus Christ better than the alternative Platonic and Aristotelian philosophies traditionally adopted by the Church. Admittedly, that is not quite the way Vélez de Cea works things out.

Gethin's contribution raises, from a Theravāda Buddhist point of view, the possibility of implicit as well as explicit faith. His close analysis of the Pali texts shows that Buddhism can envisage the presence of faith, leading to a wholesome state of mind, in non-Buddhists such as Christians and animals. In these texts faith is not necessarily a conscious state of mind, or explicit doctrinal affirmation, for we may not always be conscious of what we do and do not believe.[6] What we believe is rather shown by what we do, such that a Christian's acts may exhibit an underlying Buddhist faith while a professing Buddhist may by his bad actions and mind-state exhibit a lack of real Buddhist faith.

If this is right, it might be appropriate, as Gethin notes, to reverse Karl Rahner and refer to good Christians as 'anonymous Buddhists'. If good Buddhists are also, following Rahner, anonymous Christians, then it might even be possible to see all Buddhists and Christians as dual belongers, for whom one religion denotes the explicit and conscious, and the other the implicit or unconscious aspect of their faith. This of course could be offensive to some and a compliment to others. Gethin would agree with Moyaert about the primacy of practice over professed doctrinal belief, but this leads Gethin in the opposite direction from Moyaert, towards sympathy with dual belonging.[7]

Brazier's comments affirm a similar possibility from a different Pure Land perspective, where saving faith is understood in terms of trust in the saving Other, rather than doctrinal belief. She uses the famous Mahayana distinction between the moon and the finger pointing at it, as well as the three bodies doctrine which distinguishes the ultimate reality of the dharma from the realm of imagination and devotion, and that again from embodied physical practice. Though specific Pure Land doctrines are not easy to square with Christian ones, both may relate us to the same saving mystery.

Williams's apophatic emphasis, which sees it as symbolically important both to affirm and negate the doctrines, symbols and practices of our faith, opens up the possibility that it is not any easy harmony of Buddhist and Christian doctrines that makes dual belonging viable. On the contrary it may be the very way each faith challenges and calls into question what is believed in the context of the other that enables the dual belonger to engage with the ultimate. Each faith would then be, as just suggested, not only the unconscious faith represented consciously by the other, but the apophatic other of the other. On the other hand, many of the authors represented in the volume, on both sides of the argument about dual belonging, would wish for a more positive affirmation of the search for clarity and consistency in the expression of faith.

---

[6]   **Page ref in text**.

[7]   At least as a valid *penultimate* pathway. Complete realisation requires, in Buddhist terms, detachment from such 'views'. See Gethin's conclusion.

Conclusion

Key Emerging Questions Regarding Dual Belonging

From the discussions in this book there emerge, we suggest, a series of questions to which dual belongers need to respond if their position is to be acknowledged and attended to by the wider Buddhist and Christian communities. Otherwise dual belonging remains, at best, an eccentric personal option. The questions are independent, but interrelated, in the sense that it is possible to have affirmative answers to some of the questions and negative answers to others, but as the order of the questions reflects, answers to many of the questions have implications for answers to others.

1. *Is it real belonging?* The issue Vélez de Cea distinguishes as 'affiliative' belonging: are the faith communities themselves likely to accept one as an authentic member if one retains commitment to the other faith? There are probably variations here between different traditions in both faiths. In many Christian traditions baptism includes an act of renunciation of other faith commitments, and Tibetan Buddhism can involve exclusive adherence to a specific lineage. And as noted above, on the whole, Christian traditions are historically more hostile to double-belonging than Buddhist ones.

2. *Is it practically possible?* Even if the faith community accepts one, can one fulfil the ethical and ritual requirements of both religions to one's own satisfaction, or the satisfaction of that religion? For Moyaert, down-to-earth and embodied ritual requirements are all important markers of one's true belonging. Gethin offers Buddhist reasons for regarding ethical practice as decisive in the same way. For other contributors one's explicitly declared allegiance is central.

3. *Is it psychologically feasible?* It may seem relatively easy to fulfil the practical requirements of both Buddhism and Christianity. It is not practically difficult, for example, to attend the Eucharist on Sundays and holy days, to pray and to meditate daily and to attend the Buddhist Temple on full moon days.[8] But such dual practice, as well as the shifts in religious perspective required, might have a psychological cost. Might dual belonging divide one against oneself, leading to inner confusion or even religious schizophrenia? Or is an integration of perspectives in mind and soul possible? Or thirdly, can dual belonging involve a spiritually healthy

---

[8] Sunday full moon days, which occur on average once every seven months, would seem to present the most obvious example of divided loyalty.

244   *Buddhist-Christian Dual Belonging*

and wisdom-inducing flipping between equally valid perspectives, as Thompson argues?

4. *Is it ethical?* If it is totally impracticable, or psychologically or spiritually confusing, dual belonging cannot be ethical. But even if it is none of these things, does it not involve serving two masters, or 'chasing two rabbits'? In Buddhist terms might it involve an attachment that needs to be relinquished in the interests of a full engagement with the eightfold way? Or in Christian terms, as with different degrees of vehemence Cornille and Strange both argue, does it not involve the spiritual equivalent of polygamy or adultery? Or is it, as Vélez de Cea suggests, more like honouring both father and mother, or each of your children, each being loved with a total but distinctive love?

5. The fundamental issue on which contributors are divided here is between autonomy and heteronomy. Cornille and Strange present faith as resting on a total surrender to the Other as the sole source of one's salvation; and Pure Land Buddhism works in the same way. Theravāda Buddhism as presented by Tilakaratne, on the other hand, rests on an autonomous decision predicated on the absence of a saving Other. Moyaert sharply criticises the postmodern tendency to pick one's own spiritual mix on a consumerist basis, which represents an extreme form of autonomy, being accountable to no reality outside oneself. But most dual belongers insist they did not choose to be such, and do not simply pick ideas they like from each faith. In D'Costa's terms, 'A' represents the position where a believer chooses beliefs autonomously by his own criteria, while 'Z' represents total heteronomous surrender to the authority of a faith tradition (though paradoxically, in these multicultural days such a surrender may be autonomously chosen.) Where then does the ideal lie – is it in total autonomy or heteronomy, or somewhere in between, at D'Costa's 'M' or 'S', for example?

6. Simone Weil maintained that religious authorities have a right to command our attention, but not our belief.[9] And indeed – as the dual belongers seem to be clearest about – believing is not normally something that we can choose or will ourselves into, but something that arises from a complex interactive mix of attention to experience, argument and persuasion, trust in authority, interpretation and evaluation. A modern could not choose to believe in a flat earth, for example, but a complex

---

[9]   See 'Forms of the Implicit Love of God' in *Waiting for God* (London: HarperCollins, 2009), 83ff.

mix of the above elements might in principle force such a belief on that person. Might it be possible, then, to offer each faith system one's attention, entering deeply, trustfully and imaginatively into the ritual and conceptual world of the faith, in a way that allows it to challenge one's own preconceptions and to transform one, without necessarily giving the religion the last word regarding the truth, or accepting without question everything its scriptures or authorities say?

7. *Is it coherent?* Even if it is practicable, psychologically viable and ethical to seek to combine the beliefs and practices of the two faiths, it may not be intellectually possible because of the contradictions between the affirmations of the faiths Thompson and D'Costa were both very concerned with this, while for some others, notably Williams, seeming inconsistency, confusion and paradox could actually make a positive contribution to the journey of faith. It was also noted in the discussions that not all versions of each faith are consistent with one another. So it may be possible to render consistent the affirmations of some Buddhist and Christian traditions, but not others. Some contributors had a strong idea of what constituted Buddhist or Christian orthodoxy, while others were happier to be – in the recently coined expression – effectively polydox.[10] One significant question is whether a Buddhist-Christian has to be polydox regarding both faiths.

Some Big Issues: Ineffability, Incommensurability, Realism and Inclusion

The question of coherence (and perhaps the other questions too) lead us into another set of questions about the nature of faith and its object or objective, which kept recurring in our discussions because of the effect they have on how dual belonging is regarded. Perhaps the most significant of these questions concerns the ineffability of the ultimate. Such ineffability enables statements in each faith that contradict one another to be taken symbolically or metaphorically as pointers to the ultimate, rather than literally as descriptions of it. The metaphors are then seen as being in creative tension rather than straightforward contradiction. The advocates of dual belonging in this volume all affirm the ineffability of the ultimate, while challengers like Tilakaratne and Strange

---

[10] Cf. Catherine Keller and Laurel Schneider, eds, *Polydoxy: Theology of Multiplicity and Relation* (London and New York, Routledge, 2011). Polydoxy is here distinguished from sheer heresy or heterodoxy. See also the follow-up collection of essays, 'Polydox Reflections', *Modern Theology* 30:3 (July 2014).

rejected or qualified it. A distinctive strategy of the challengers was that of Moyaert, who accepts the irreducibly symbolic nature of religious language and practice but criticises the dual belongers for a weak understanding of symbolism, which allows them to detach an ineffable reality from the symbols that merely 'express' it in different ways.

An issue underlying this one is whether there is a real ultimate goal to which the religions relate, or whether each religion constructs its own 'world' in ways that are incommensurable with the others. And what implications does the answer have for dual belonging?

In principle, incommensurability and constructivism can work both ways. Incommensurability can be taken to mean that contradictions between the faiths cannot be established, since for example what Christians mean when they talk about God cannot be measured against what Buddhists mean when they deny or defer God's existence. To be a Buddhist-Christian is not then to contradict oneself, but to shift back and forth between different religious paradigms. On the other hand, incommensurability can equally be taken to mean that one can only make and understand religious sense by participating in the conceptual and ritual framework of a particular religion, so that one has to choose and participate in one paradigm alone. This is Moyaert's central point, which has been central to thinkers like George Lindbeck.[11] On this account, the dual belonger will not contradict him/herself, but s/he will fail to make sense to his/her co-religionists and ultimately to him/herself. Many of the challengers to dual belonging alluded in some way to this postmodern, postliberal, constructivist understanding, though they were not in the main committed to a wholly constructivist understanding, being realists on matters like God's reality or otherwise.

That evidences the fact that dual belonging can also be opposed on realist grounds. As Strange and Tilakaratne show, if our religion shows us fully what really is the case, other religions, when they contradict our own, can only be wrong. On the other hand we have just seen that a realism that affirms that the ultimate really exists, beyond the constructs of our language and religion, can serve the claims of dual belonging. Indeed all the advocates of dual belonging in this volume are realists in this respect. In this connection we need to note that it is not only ultimate reality that realists believe to be beyond language. For realists, tables and quarks and colours exist when unperceived and undescribed. They are even ineffable, in that it is impossible to convey in words to a person

---

[11]   George Lindbeck *The Nature of Doctrine: Religion and Theology in a Postliberal Age* (Louisville, KY: Westminster John Knox, 1984).

Conclusion 247

blind from birth what green looks like, and if you describe a table to a person who is not seeing it, they are unlikely to be able to reproduce it with complete accuracy. All the more so with the realities described by the religions.

We noted how Moyaert accused the dual belongers of an indefensible dualism between symbols and their underlying meaning, such that dual or multiple expressions are possible for a single alleged religious meaning. This may be something of which dual belongers as well as pluralists generally are sometimes guilty. Sometimes the reality that religions are alleged to symbolise in their different ways are identified and described with a suspicious degree of ease. This reality can turn out to be simply the ethic of liberal Western modernity, that is, the real belief system of the dual belonger, onto which the 'symbols' of the two faiths are grafted.[12]

That said, the real duality dual belongers are relying on is often a different one, namely that between symbolic *and* literal language on the one hand, and reality on the other. This distinction is essential for any realist, and arguably for any Christian or Buddhist. Simply to identify the symbolism and language of a religion with the reality it depicts amounts, in Christian terms, to idolatry, and in Buddhist terms, to delusive attachment. Thus what Drew, for example, argues for in her chapter is not some clear liberal description of ultimate reality, or reality centeredness (such that John Hick might offer), which the symbols of Buddhism and Christianity are then shown to be referring to. Rather she argues very clearly that there can be only one reality that is the ultimate referent and goal of life (for if there are more, neither is ultimate). Therefore *if* Buddhism and Christianity are describing some valid ultimate goal, they must be describing, in their different ways, one and the same thing, though there may be no way of describing what that something is apart from Christianity and Buddhism (or perhaps some other religion). And if that is the case, then though there may be many penultimate differences, there can be no ultimate divide between the two religions, and dual belonging cannot involve an ultimate and insurmountable divide in the believer.

This affirmation of dual belonging can be rejected if the premises are rejected. Maybe either Buddhism or Christianity, or both, fail to relate us to ultimate reality, in which case dual belonging would be partially and perhaps totally misguided. Maybe there is no ultimate reality, but a plurality of different

---

[12]   Cf. John Milbank 'The End of Dialogue', in Gavin D'Costa ed. *Christian Uniqueness Reconsidered* (London: SCM, 1990), 174–91; and *The Meeting of Religions and the Trinity* (Maryknoll, NY: Orbis Books, 2000), 19–53.

possible goals which different religions enable one to pursue,[13] in which case one would have to choose between the Buddhist goal and the Christian goal. Finally, the unity in the ultimate goal or object may not be sufficient to make dual belonging acceptable to the religious communities, practical, psychologically viable, ethical or intellectually coherent. The subtlety of Drew's chapter lies in the way it moves from the affirmation of ultimate unity to consequences for what we might call penultimate unity: namely the viability of pursuing both paths in one's life, which need not be negated by the manifest differences between the paths, provided one is prepared to leave unresolved those big divergences that cannot be resolved within the perspective of this life. But Drew's argument will not convince everyone.

Alternatively, it may be that one of the religions tells us how reality really is, and in the light of that religion the other religion makes more sense than on its own terms. That position, generally called inclusivism, might make it possible to be both Buddhist and Christian, but the two faiths would not then be embraced on the equal terms which all the advocates in this volume are committed to. However if a *mutual* inclusivism were shown to be possible, whereby *both* Christianity tells us how reality is, and makes sense of Buddhism better than Buddhism does on its own terms; *and* Buddhism tells us how reality is, and makes sense of Christianity better than Christianity does on its own terms, then once again a balanced dual belonging, of a rather paradoxical kind, would be possible. A dual belonger would in this case be the Buddhist-inculturated Catholic missionary among Buddhists accepted by Buddhists as a Buddhist, which D'Costa affirms as the one kind of full dual belonger the Catholic magisterium could accept. But s/he would also be a Christian-inculturated Buddhist missionary among Christians accepted by Christians as Christian. That is a tall order, but those of us who call ourselves dual belongers may be doing so because we wish both to evangelise Buddhists and convert Christians to the dharma. This seems to be Thompson's position.

There is much more to be said, but this much is clear. As a phenomenon that is at this stage in history counterintuitive to the majority of Christians and Buddhists, the burden of proof lies on those who advocate it. All of the questions need to be answered affirmatively for the case for dual belonging to be made. The jury will surely be out for a long time to come, but we hope that this book has gone some way at least to clarify the issues at stake.

---

[13]   Mark Heim argues the subtler point that though there is an ultimate reality, it is complex enough to allow for a diversity of ends (*Salvations: Truth and Difference in Religions* (Maryknoll, NY: Orbis Books, 1995)).

Index

Abhidamma, Abhidharma 179–95
adultery
  contested 164–5
  dual belonging as 74, 145, 240, 244
Amida Buddha, Pure Land Buddhism
    199–200, 203–4, 211–15, 242, 244
  and God 207–10
  and trikāya 206–7
anattā, no-self 35, 41, 67, 81, 202
  in Pure Land perspective 210–11
apophatic, negative way
  as basis of dual belonging 24, 44,
    149–52, 217–32, 242
  and Pure Land Buddhism 210–12
  see also transcendence
Aquinas, St Thomas 66
  creation 51, 53, 55, 58
  negation 219n4
  salvation 113
atheism in Buddhism 49–50, 99–101
atonement, crucifixion 16–17, 214
avidyā, ignorance, illusion 18–20, 201,
    202, *see also* three poisons

Barth, Karl 36, 75, 198
bodhisattva 37–9, 97, 205
  vow 27

children, love of one's
  as model for dual belonging 7, 145,
    161, 165–7, 241, 244
communion with God 14, 15, 22–3
  Holy –, Eucharist 120, 129, 130, 148,
    239–40
compassion
  Amida Buddha 206, 208, 213
  in both 39–41, 42–8

in Buddhism 22, 37–8,
in Christianity 38–9
consciousness
  in relation to matter and universe
    57–66
  false, deluded 18, 20, 44, 93, 181
  moral, skilful, enlightened 182–3,
    187–92, 226–7
  see also mind
conversion 83, 121–2, 138, 180
Cornille, Catherine 32n1, 84n51, 86,
    102–3, 109n5, 110n6, 114, 126,
    132, 162, 164, 167, 170–75, 197,
    217n2, 220n5, 229n34, 234–6,
    240, 241, 244
Corless, Roger 13, 27–8, 149, 155, 232
cosmos, cosmology 59, 60–61, 221, 223
creation
  Buddhist rejection of 49–50, 76, 100,
    217
  and causality 51–6, 61, 63–7
  in Christian understanding 65, 72,
    74–5, 77–80, 82–4, 220–23, 228,
    230, 231
  see also cosmology, dependent
    origination
cross, *see* atonement

Dalai Lama 27, 76
D'Costa, Gavin 85, 104, 237–8, 241, 244,
    248
delusion, *see avidyā*, three poisons
dependent arising, co-arising, *pratītya
    samutpāda* 50, 52–3, 58–9, 63–4,
    67, *see also* interbeing
detraditionalisation 131–2, 134, 135

250   *Buddhist-Christian Dual Belonging*

dharma, dhamma 99n21, 181, 183, 184,
    194, 220, 242, *see also* triple refuge
dharmakāya 19, 22, 205–6, 211
    dual belonging passim
    criteria for authenticity 13–14, 17, 28,
        155, 237–8, 243
    types 104, 108n4, 109–12, 116–18,
        121–2, 168–72, 175, 177–9, 243
dialogue, interreligious, interfaith 1, 97, 99,
    144, 152–3
    as basis of dual belonging 67, 163–4
Drew, Rose 67, 77, 102, 108n4, 123, 134,
    136–40, 144n3, 146n8, 150, 171,
    224 notes 16, 17, 226, 234, 235–6,
    238, 247, 248
dualism, duality, non– 47, 228
    God and world 23–4, 44, 96, 210, 211,
        212–13, 214, 227
    mind and object 20–21, 59, 62, 64, 66
    symbol and reality 27, 237, 247
dukkha 18, 21, 34, 80, 201
Dupuis, Jacques 76–7, 109, 115n23, 118,
    227

Eckhart 222–3, 230
emptiness, *see śūnyatā*
enlightenment
    Buddhist goal 41, 190, 194, 299–301,
        204, 206, 210,
    'The Enlightenment' 32, 62, 98, 131–2
eternal life 25, 78, 93–4
ethics 76, 80, 101, 180–82, 213–14
    of dual belonging 74, 243–4
Eucharist, *see* Communion
evolution 19–20, 56–65
exclusivism 102–3, 130, 145–6, 179,
    181–3, 226, 237, 243
    exclusive Christian claims 74, 84–7,
        135, 233–4

feminism, feminist 41, 107
four noble truths 33–4, 90, 100, 167n7,
    186, 201
freedom 19, 22, 34, 91–4, 136, 194, 228–9,
    see also liberation

glory 49, 74, 77–86, 223
grace 17, 21–3, 82, 83, 86, 164, 166
    in non-Christian faiths 115–17, 191
    and works 44, 101, 202, 208
Griffiths, Paul 149, 173, 175

Habito, Ruben 13, 17–18, 21, 25–6, 30,
    137, 227,
Heim, Mark 15, 23, 26, 29n69, 247n13
Hick, John 4, 16–17, 25, 29, 36–7, 97–8,
    105, 138, 212, 234
Holy Spirit 75
    present in non-Christians 119–20

idolatry
    failure to glorify God 80–85, 86
    identifying symbol with reality 130,
        131–2, 133–4, 219, 247
illusion, delusion 20, 35, 47, 89–92,
    181, 189–90, 192, 201, 202,
    206; *see also avidyā*, three poisons
incarnation
    in Christ 135
    of meaning 124, 129–30, 133–4, 138
inclusivism 118, 180, 226–7, 248
incommensurability 32, 74, 217, 228–9,
    237, 245–7
ineffability of the ultimate 51, 93–4, 97–9,
    139–40, 149–50, 157, 211, 235,
    245–7
interbeing 59, 95, 153n22,
    see also dependent arising

justice 34, 39, 41–3, 46–8, 75, 106, 235

Keenan, John 13, 153, 226
King, Sallie 13, 26, 27, 135, 153, 224n16
Knitter, Paul 76, 84–5, 95–102, 104, 106,
    111, 115, 116, 135–6, 140, 149,
    150, 153, 157–8, 178, 220–21,
    230n38, 234, 235–6

liberation
    in Buddhism 16, 18–25, 26, 29, 34, 86,
        90, 96–7, 101, 104, 181, 192–4,
        201

political 41–3, 45, 231
theology 32, 39, 47–8, 49
love 28–9, 211
in Pure Land Buddhism 209, 213
of God 16–19, 22–3, 84, 121, 226
God's 38, 46, 65, 75, 78, 83
of oppressor 47–8, 86
v. wisdom 105, 231
see also children, compassion

Madhyamaka (Madhyamika) school 59, 64,
96, 153–4, 157
magisterium 108–11, 112–20, 176, 215,
248
Mahayana
contrast with Theravāda 95, 97, 99,
152, 238–9
discriminative v. non-dual
consciousness 15, 16, 18–25, 204,
212, 215
on nirvana and samsara 27,
see also bodhisattva, Madhyamaka,
śūnyatā, trikāya, śūnyatā, Yogācāra
Makransky, John 15, 18–25, 326, 28, 45,
47–8, 240n4
material(ism)
concreteness 124, 141
philosophical 61, 63–4; 186
meditation 24, 39, 62, 64, 115, 120–21,
144, 148–9, 153, 187, 189, 208,
224, 227, see also mindfulness,
prayer and meditation
Mind Alone, Mind-Only, see Yogācāra
mindfulness 40, 42–3, 46, 148, 149,
181–2, 200, see also meditation

Nagarjuna 95–7, 154, 202, 204, 219n4
negative theology, see apophatic
New Age 110, 144, 156 1S
Nhat Hanh, Thich 47, 59–, 211

orthodox(y) 17, 72, 116, 158, 220, 245
Eastern 220n7, 236
Panikkar, Raimon 99, 153, 163–4, 167,
174

Pieris, Aloysius 29, 39, 94, 105, 115,
pluralism 115–16, 118, 138–40, 150–51,
211–12, 225–6, 234, 247,
see also relativism
politics 38–48, 119, 215, 228,
see also liberation, political
pratītya samutpāda, see dependent
origination
prayer 22, 236
and mediation 131, 136–7, 139, 149,
198, 224, 239–40
praxis, 33, 40–48, 73, 147–9, 235
Protestant(ism) 87, 95, 130, 218, 236, 237
Pure Land (Buddhism), see Amida Buddha

quantum physics 50, 61–2

Rahner, Karl 230n38; 'anonymous
Christian' 191, 242
Reis Habito, Maria 13, 18, 24–5, 27, 41,
139–40, 153,
relativism 114, 115–16, 119–20, 152,
see also pluralism
resurrection 16–17, 146
ritual 243, 245–6
neglected in dual belonging 123–34,
137–41, 152, 239
possible basis of dual belonging 147–9,
156
see also symbol

samsara 18, 53, 104, 185, 188, 208
identity with nirvana? 16, 21, 27, 95–7
Schmidt-Leukel, Perry 23–4, 30, 49–50,
51–3, 140
Shin Buddhism 200, 204, 206–7, 209,
see also Amida Buddha
sin 18–21, 75, 90–81, 86, 169, 214, 218;
original 19–21, 36
suchness, see tathatā
suffering, see dukkha
śūnyatā, emptiness 21–4, 28, 37, 61, 64, 95,
96–7, 153n22, 200, 207, 211
and form 39, 44, 46–7
symbol(ism)

practice, ritual 102–3, 123–33
theory of 133–44, 138–41, 239–40
and (ultimate) reality 33, 152, 154,
156–7, 193–4, 204, 205–7, 211,
245–7
syncretism 85, 120–21

taṇhā, grasping 90, 93, 97, 188
tathatā, suchness 64, 98, 223
theism 49, 79, 130–31, 201, 207, 222
Theravāda 59, 98, 144, 238–9, 244
contrast with Mahayana 16, 95, 97, 99
see also Abhidamma
Thompson, Ross 67n51, 80n32, 84n44, 87,
220, 221n8, 225n19, 236, 248
three poisons (greed, hatred and delusion)
35, 89–91, 181, 189–90, 192
Tibetan Buddhism, *see* Vajrayana
transcendence
of God 74–5, 78–9, 100, 220–23
ultimate 50, 51, 58, 97–8, 105, 128,
130–31, 146, 149–52, 155, 156,
234–5
of self 16, 22, 201, 211, 212, 227–8
qualities 189–90
see also apophatic
trikāya, three bodies of Buddha 67, 205–7
and Amida 206
Trinity 65n47, 67
analogy for dual belonging 174–5;
ontological 74, 77, 78, 80
triple refuge (Buddha, dharma, sangha) 13,
137–8, 167, 170, 179, 180–85, 193
trust 244–5

in Buddhism, saddhā 105, 180, 182,
184–5, 193 203–4, 207, 242,

ultimate reality, the ultimate
as basis of religions' unity? 15, 16,
19, 22–4, 76, 136, 138, 149–52,
232, 234–5, 239, 242
personal? 50, 74, 80, 96
see also symbolism and ultimate reality
uniqueness of God or Christ 78–9, 83

Vajrayana, Tibetan Buddhism 13, 32, 44,
95, 173, 238, 243
Vatican II 17, 108, 112–15, 118–19, 237–8

Williams, Paul 50–54, 57, 59, 81n36,
101n28
wisdom
Buddhist 22–4, 28–9, 92, 181–2, 185,
189–90
and compassion 37–48, 105, 206,
210–11, 231
of God 78

Yogācāra, Mind-Only 20n29, 59–60, 62,
64

Zen 59, 144, 200, 211, 226, 227, 238
meditation 13, 24, 137, 139, 149, 224